A JOURNEY TO EVERY COUNTRY ON EARTH

MICHAEL DAVID

Dedication

To my mentors, Mrs. Lillian Brown, Mr. Joaquin Archie Archilla, and Mr. James Mitchell, who always believed in me and encouraged me to follow my dreams. I am deeply grateful for your guidance, wisdom, and strength. You have made a profound difference in my life, and I am forever grateful.

I want to express my deep appreciation to my family and friends from all around the world for their love, care, and incredible support, which made this book possible. Your belief in me and your encouragement mean the world to me.

Copyright © 2023 by Michael David

All rights reserved. No part of this book may be reproduced or transmitted in any form or by any means, electronic or mechanical, including photocopying, recording, or by any information and retrieval systems, without the written permission of the Author.

TABLE OF CONTENTS

1 Asia
Bhutan 🌐 Jordan 🌐 Israel 🌐 Kyrgyzstan 🌐 Mongolia 🌐 Syria 🌐 Turkey
Page 4

2 Africa
Kenya 🌐 Madagascar 🌐 Morocco 🌐 Rwanda 🌐 The Seychelles
Page 52

3 North America
Canada 🌐 Haiti 🌐 Honduras 🌐 Mexico 🌐 The United States of America
Page 86

4 South America
Argentina 🌐 Brazil 🌐 Ecuador
Page 116

5 Antarctica
Antarctica Journey
Page 136

6 Europe
Croatia 🌐 France 🌐 Greece 🌐 The Netherlands 🌐 Portugal 🌐 Ukraine
Page 146

7 Oceania
Australia 🌐 New Zealand 🌐 Papua New Guinea 🌐 Tonga
Page 186

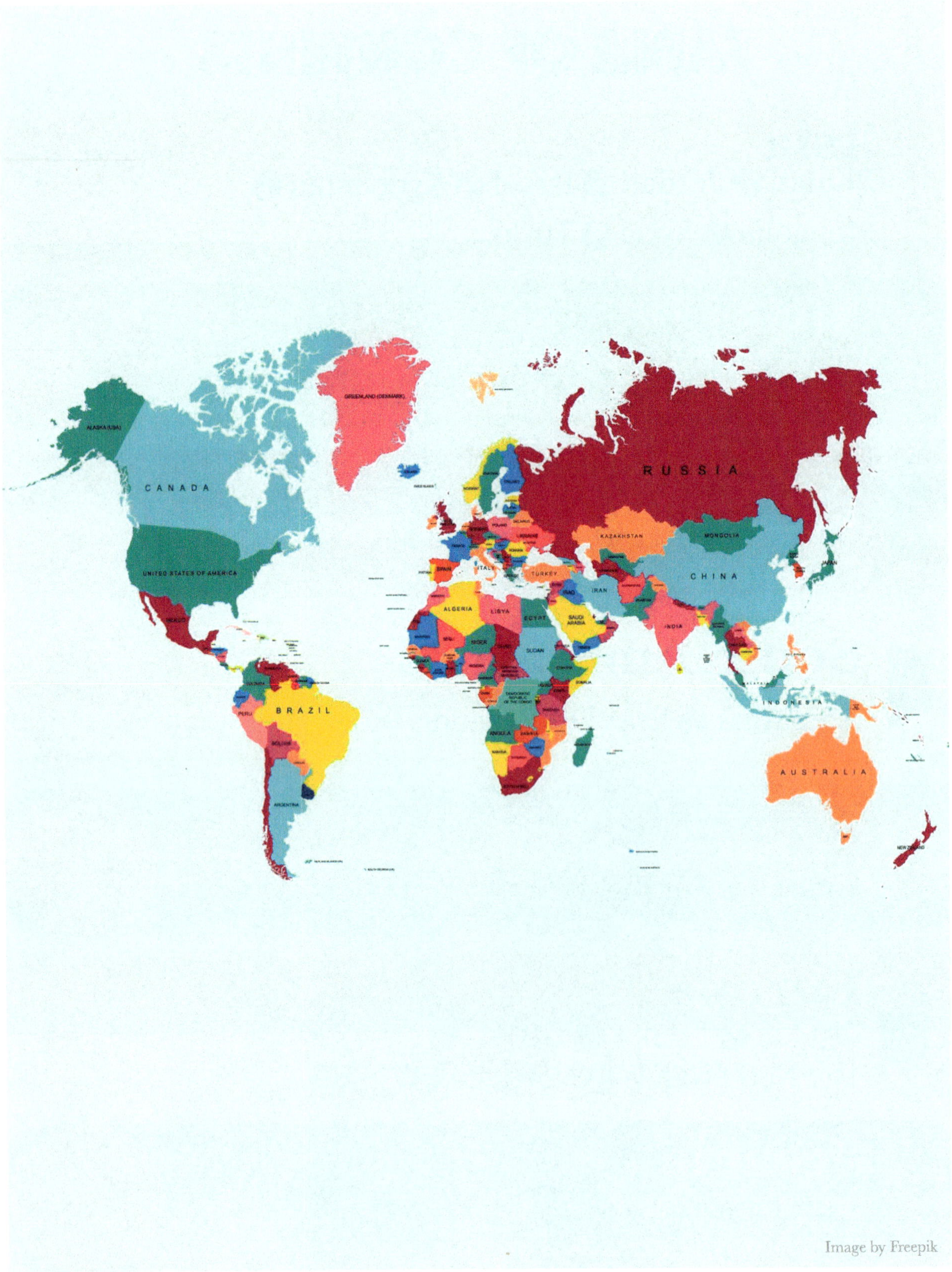

Image by Freepik

THE JOY OF TRAVEL, MY STORY

The transformative experience of traveling the world has exceeded my wildest imagination, offering an exhilarating adventure filled with boundless excitement, unbridled joy, and profound gratitude. My insatiable curiosity for exploring the world was sparked at a young age and truly ignited when Morgan Freeman and Jack Nicholson posed profound questions in the film **"The Bucket List"**: **"Have you found joy in your life? Has your life brought joy to others?"** These questions stirred my soul, propelling me on a lifelong mission to seek joy and happiness and share them with others in every facet of my existence.

My professional journey as an engineer in the fields of technology and aviation provided extraordinary opportunities to traverse international frontiers. Collaborating with international organizations, forging meaningful connections with individuals from diverse backgrounds, and immersing myself in the kaleidoscope of cultures our world offers were privileges. However, I hungered for **a grander quest—the audacious goal of visiting every country on Earth**.

I was blessed with the extraordinary privilege of witnessing Antarctica's breathtaking landscapes and awe-inspiring wildlife. I marveled at New Zealand's stunning vistas, delved into the essence of happiness in Bhutan, immersed myself in the rich tapestries of Spain and Italy, savored the finest wines in France, unwound on Australia's pristine beaches, reveled in the delectable cuisine and affordable living in Thailand, and basked in the warmth and hospitality of the people in Goroka, Papua New Guinea.

Each locale, a unique gem in our global tapestry, left an indelible mark on my heart. I consider myself immensely fortunate to have experienced them all. Yet, my journey wasn't merely about personal gratification; it was also about giving back. From volunteering at orphanages in Haiti and South Africa to teaching English in Guatemala and Thailand, I found immeasurable happiness and fulfillment in sharing my love of travel and making a positive impact on the lives of others.

After over a decade marked by unyielding determination, relentless hard work, and numerous unpaid leave days, **I finally achieved my monumental ambition in December 2019 when I set foot in Syria, marking my 193rd country visited**. Words cannot encapsulate the overwhelming sense of joy and gratitude that surged within me at that pivotal moment. Among the 8 billion inhabitants of our planet, only around 250 individuals have accomplished this awe-inspiring feat, making it a staggering 1 in 32 million achievement. I remain profoundly grateful for this unparalleled opportunity to savor the world's splendors and to learn so much from this unique experience.

My wish is to excite you into traveling and experiencing the world and all of its diverse and enchanting nuances for yourself and discovering how much more your life will be enriched with these new experiences. So come along with me and see the world through my eyes, and hopefully, it will inspire you on your own personal journey.

And now, I'm thrilled to share my personal odyssey and joy of travel with you through the pages of this book. I will be your guide across **all seven continents, recounting the highlights of my adventures and tales**, and unveiling the captivating photographs I've captured along the way. But this journey doesn't stop at mere storytelling. I'll also provide you with invaluable recommendations on the optimal times to visit these enchanting destinations, ensuring that you not only maximize your enjoyment but also contribute to the preservation of our magnificent planet.

I am acutely aware of the profound blessings and privileges that have bestowed these experiences upon me, and my deepest desire is to share them with you, nurturing a deeper appreciation for the beauty that envelops our world. Today, I can confidently affirm that "**I have found joy in my life and my life has brought joy to others**." For this, I am eternally grateful. It is my fervent hope that this book serves as an inspiration for you to embark on your adventures, seek your joys, and, in doing so, become a beacon of joy and happiness for others. Together, we can revel in the boundless wonders of our planet and make our world a brighter, more joyful place for all. It is my hope that your travels will be a transformative experience that enriching your life like it has done for me.

Peace & Love.
Michael

ASIA CONTINENT: 46 COUNTRIES

Flag	Country	Flag	Country	Flag	Country
	Afghanistan		Japan		Philippines
	Armenia		Jordan		Qatar
	Azerbaijan		Kazakhstan		Saudi Arabia
	Bahrain		North Korea		Singapore
	Bangladesh		South Korea		Sri Lanka
	Bhutan		Kuwait		Syria
	Brunei		Kyrgyzstan		Tajikistan
	Cambodia		Laos		Thailand
	China		Lebanon		Timor-Leste
	Cyprus		Malaysia		Turkmenistan
	Georgia		The Maldives		United Arab Emirates
	India		Mongolia		Uzbekistan
	Indonesia		Myanmar		Vietnam
	Iran		Nepal		Yemen
	Iraq		Oman		
	Israel		Pakistan		

ASIA CONTINENT

Welcome to Asia, the largest and most populous continent in the World. It is home to some of the oldest civilizations and some of the most diverse cultures, languages and religions. It is a continent of great economic and cultural importance. It is a land of great extremes and contrasts with some of the highest mountains and most of the longest rivers on earth, it is land of fascinating beauty and a continent ripe with adventure and is one of the sparkplugs of the 21st century economy.

Asia, an extensive and remarkably diverse continent, brims with wonder and adventure at every corner. Its rich history, stunning landscapes, and unique cultures make it no surprise that Asia has become a magnet for adventurers and explorers from around the world. From the dynamic Far East to the captivating Middle East, our journey through Asia promises an exhilarating odyssey overflowing with excitement and boundless joy. As we embark on this extraordinary adventure, let's delve into the essence of Asia's allure, tracing its origins and celebrating the astonishing diversity that makes it a true marvel.

But first, let's uncover the origins of the name "Asia," a term steeped in history. This term can be traced back to its ancient Greek usage, where "Ἀσία" originally referred to a region in western Anatolia, now part of modern-day Turkey. Over time, this appellation expanded to encompass the vast eastern landmass we know today. While the precise etymology of "Asia" remains intriguing, some theories suggest it may have originated from the Akkadian word "asu," meaning "to go out" or "to rise." This connection could be linked to the radiant sunrise in the east, as Asia lay to the east of the ancient Greek world.

The people of Asia, diverse and warm-hearted, exude a deep reverence for tradition and a zest for celebration that is nothing short of infectious. When it comes to cuisine, Asia is a kaleidoscope of flavors and spices, offering a gastronomic journey that varies dramatically from region to region. The music and art of Asia are vibrant and rich, bearing witness to a captivating history that continues to thrive in the present day. Now, **let's take a look at Asia's most extraordinary destinations**, each offering a unique blend of wonder and awe that will leave you breathless with excitement.

Our journey takes us to the "land of the Rising Sun" and to its ancient feudal capital **Kyoto, Japan**, an ancient capital filled with rich culture and ancient architecture and beautiful Zen gardens. It is a city that effortlessly weaves tradition and modernity into an enchanting tapestry of timelessness. Here, you can wander through the mesmerizing Arashiyama Bamboo Grove, where towering bamboo shoots create a spellbinding pathway. Temples like Kinkaku-ji, adorned with layers of glistening gold leaf, and the iconic

Fushimi Inari Shrine, renowned for its vermillion torii gates, beckon you to explore their serene depths. Don't forget to partake in a traditional tea ceremony, a tranquil art that embodies the essence of Japanese aesthetics. During cherry blossom season, Kyoto transforms into a dreamscape of delicate pink petals, filling your heart with unbridled joy and reverence for the breathtaking beauty of nature.

Next on our journey is **Bali, Indonesia**, a tropical haven where bliss knows no bounds. Bali enchants with its lush landscapes and a serene ambiance that invites you to unwind and let go. Explore the vibrant green rice terraces of Ubud, an artistic marvel created through harmonious agriculture. Bask in the golden rays on sun-kissed beaches in Seminyak and Jimbaran, where crystal-clear waters beckon you to dive into adventures of swimming, surfing, and snorkeling. Discover the island's spiritual side by visiting the majestic Tanah Lot Temple, perched dramatically on a rocky outcrop, or the awe-inspiring Uluwatu Temple, where traditional Kecak dance performances come alive against the backdrop of a fiery sunset. Bali's people, steeped in reverence for nature, its vibrant culture, and tranquil shores, create an atmosphere of blissful wonder that will leave you brimming with excitement.

Our journey then leads us to **Bagan, Myanmar**, a surreal landscape where ancient temples and dreams converge. In the heart of Myanmar, over 2,000 temples and pagodas rise from the plains, crafting a surreal and awe-inspiring panorama. Capture the sunrise from a hot air balloon as it bathes this ethereal landscape in golden light, an experience that will elevate your spirit and leave you with a profound sense of joy.

But we don't stop here! Our adventure takes us to the **Great Wall of China**, a monumental feat of human endeavor that stands as an awe-inspiring testament to tenacity. The Great Wall is an extensive bulwark erected in ancient China and one of the largest building-construction projects ever undertaken by humans and stretches over 4000 kilometers. Traverse its undulating path as it winds through vast landscapes and dramatic mountains, whether in the bustling sections near Beijing or the quieter stretches further afield. The sheer immensity of this historic structure will ignite a sense of adventure and triumph that will resonate deeply within you.

Seoul, South Korea, our next destination, seamlessly merges the old with the new in a vibrant metropolis pulsating with energy. Explore the bustling markets of Myeongdong, where the tantalizing aromas of street food stalls will entice your taste buds. Step back in time in Bukchon Hanok Village, a preserved enclave of traditional Korean homes nestled amidst the city's skyscrapers. Dive into the K-Pop phenomenon by visiting entertainment districts like Gangnam, where music, fashion, and culture intersect in a whirlwind of excitement. After a day of exploration, unwind in a traditional jjimjilbang, a Korean bathhouse, or savor the joy of a barbecue feast with local tasty kimchee at a local restaurant.

Now, we venture to the Middle East, to **Petra, Jordan**, one of the modern day seven wonders of the world and remains one of the most visited places in Jordan. Petra a UNESCO World Heritage site is a rose-red city that unveils its secrets amidst imposing rock formations. Hidden in this mystical landscape, the Treasury's façade emerges as an architectural masterpiece from a forgotten era. Lost for centuries, the city was rediscovered in 1812, prompting historians to call it the "Lost City of Petra". As you wander through the narrow Siq, a breathtaking canyon that leads to this ancient wonder, you'll be swept away by a sense of wonder and amazement that transcends time itself.

Then the journey continues to **Dubai, United Arab Emirates**, a gem of modern opulence where the future meets the present in an exhilarating fusion of technology and tradition. As you step into Dubai's futuristic landscape, you'll be greeted by a skyline that defies imagination. The Burj Khalifa pierces the heavens, a symbol of mankind's audacious ambition. Dive into an extravagant shopping experience at the Dubai Mall, home to an indoor ice rink and the captivating Dubai Fountain show, a breathtaking synchrony of music, water, and light. For a taste of tradition, visit the bustling Gold and Spice Souks, where fragrant spices and glimmering jewelry will dazzle your senses. Dubai's architectural opulence, bustling markets, Arabic architecture and rich cultural tapestry create an exhilarating atmosphere that guarantees memories of boundless joy. Dubai is famous for its ultramodern architecture, luxury hotels, most famous shopping centers and vibrant night scene. Lastly, it is a new international travel hub with flights to more than 85 locations globally.

THE BEST TIME TO VISIT ASIA CONTINENT

Asia, the world's largest continent, is a treasure trove of diverse cultures, breathtaking landscapes, and extraordinary experiences, each uniquely flavored by its four distinct seasons. Embarking on a journey across Asia throughout the year promises not only a wealth of adventures but also a deeper understanding of the region's rich heritage.

Spring (March - May): As winter's chill recedes, Japan's enchanting city of Kyoto undergoes a mesmerizing transformation. Cherry blossoms, or Sakura, adorn the streets, parks, and temples, creating an otherworldly atmosphere for visitors. Amid this ethereal backdrop, ancient temples like Kinkaku-ji (the Golden Pavilion) and Fushimi Inari Shrine come alive with the colors of spring. While in Japan, a visit to the serene countryside of Hokkaido is a must during spring. The island's rolling hills and flowering fields, combined with pleasant weather, make it an ideal season for outdoor enthusiasts.

Summer (June - August): Across Asia, the summer months herald different experiences. The lush region of Kerala in India comes alive with the monsoon rains, transforming the landscapes into vibrant green vistas. This season provides the perfect opportunity to embark on rejuvenating Ayurvedic treatments and explore the tranquil backwaters on traditional houseboats. In contrast, northern Japan's Hokkaido region offers respite from the heat. Here, you can lose yourself in the pristine beauty of national parks, crystal-clear lakes, and scenic hiking trails. Summer in Bali, Indonesia, reveals the island's natural beauty and cultural vibrancy. From its iconic rice terraces in Ubud to the vibrant ceremonies and festivals, Bali invites travelers to immerse themselves in its rich tapestry of traditions and natural wonders.

Fall (September - November): As summer transitions into fall, Istanbul, Turkey, presents itself in all its glory. The city's historic sites, bustling bazaars, and delectable Turkish cuisine are best enjoyed under the mild and pleasant fall weather. Wander through the grand halls of the Hagia Sophia, delve into the labyrinthine streets of the Grand Bazaar, and savor mouthwatering kebabs while taking in the sights and sounds of this mesmerizing city. In Nepal, the capital city of Kathmandu and the picturesque town of Pokhara come alive with trekkers and adventurers during the autumn months. Crisp air, clear skies, and breathtaking mountain vistas create the perfect setting for hiking and trekking in the Himalayas. Meanwhile, China's capital, Beijing, basks in the crisp days of fall, offering an ideal opportunity to explore its rich history and culture. From the awe-inspiring Great Wall of China to the Forbidden City, the city's historical treasures are yours to discover.

Winter (December - February): As winter descends, Goa, India, awakens with its warm beaches, vibrant nightlife, and distinctive blend of Indian and Portuguese influences. It's the season for relaxation, water sports, and savoring the fusion of flavors in dishes like vindaloo and xacuti. Tokyo, Japan, takes on a magical quality during winter, with festive lights illuminating the city's streets and parks. Visitors can indulge in therapeutic hot springs, or onsens, and savor seasonal cuisine, including steaming bowls of ramen and fresh sushi. For a contrast in experiences, Dubai in the United Arab Emirates offers mild winter weather, perfect for outdoor activities. Desert safaris, architectural marvels like the Burj Khalifa, and luxurious shopping experiences await visitors in this modern metropolis.

Each season in Asia and the Middle East paints a unique and unforgettable canvas, from the awakening of nature in spring to the vibrant festivities of summer, the kaleidoscope of fall colors, and the cultural and natural charms of winter. By aligning your travel plans with the rhythms of these destinations, you'll unlock a deeper understanding of their beauty, history, and culture. Every moment spent exploring these regions during their prime seasons becomes a chapter in an incredible journey of discovery.

So, get ready for an exhilarating odyssey as I unveil the extraordinary stories and breathtaking photographs that encapsulate my epic expedition across the sprawling continent of Asia. Each moment of this incredible journey has been a treasure trove of experiences that have not only filled my soul with immeasurable joy but have also left an indelible mark on the very essence of my existence. The profound encounters with the diverse cultures, mesmerizing landscapes, and the incredible people I had the privilege of meeting along the way have woven a tapestry of memories that are nothing short of life-altering. The vibrant tapestry of experiences, from exploring ancient temples steeped in history to indulging in the delectable flavors of street food markets, has left me awestruck at every turn. I am bursting with boundless excitement and deep-seated gratitude for the opportunity to set foot on this captivating continent, where every moment has been an amazing discovery and a testament to the unparalleled beauty of Asia.

> "TRAVEL IS THE ONLY THING YOU CAN BUY THAT MAKES YOU RICHER."
> -Unknown

TIGER NEST

BHUTAN

Bhutan, a small landlocked country in the eastern Himalayas, is often called the "Land of the Thunder Dragon." Bhutan is known for its pristine natural beauty, rich cultural heritage, and its unique philosophy of **Gross National Happiness (GNH)**. Bhutan is a fascinating and inspiring country that offers a different perspective on what it means to live a happy and fulfilling life. Its philosophy of Gross National Happiness serves as a reminder that there are other ways to measure progress and development beyond just economic growth, and that happiness and well-being should be at the forefront of any society's priorities. Bhutan is a land with breath taking views of the Himalaya mountains, glacial rivers running through steep mountain gorges, Buddhist temples perched on the side of mountains, along side virgin forests inspired with a deep spiritual love and respect for nature. The people of Bhutan strive to be one with natural surroundings and the beauty of the land resonates with their happy and harmonious culture. Bhutan is not called "one of the happiest places on earth" for nothing. The resilient and highly spiritual people of Bhutan respect and protect their natural environs with a spirit that borders on being religious.

Bhutan's philosophy of Gross National Happiness is a holistic development philosophy that emphasizes sustainable development, environmental conservation, cultural preservation, and good governance. It measures progress in terms of the happiness and well-being of its citizens, rather than solely relying on economic growth as a measure of development. Bhutan was the first country in the world to adopt GNH as its official development policy in the 1970s. The visionary Bhutanese leaders believe that economic growth alone does not necessarily lead to well-being and happiness, and that other factors such as cultural preservation, environmental conservation, and good governance are equally important.

The GNH Index measures the country's progress in terms of 33 indicators, including physical and mental health, education, cultural diversity and resilience, environmental sustainability, good governance, and time use. Bhutan uses the GNH Index to guide its policy decisions and prioritize the well-being of its citizens. Bhutan's commitment to GNH has garnered international attention and praise, and the country has become a model for sustainable development and environmental conservation. It has also attracted tourists who are interested in experiencing the country's unique culture, natural beauty, and philosophy of happiness.

During my visit to Bhutan, I had the opportunity to explore some of the country's most beautiful and culturally significant sites. My adventure started with a drive to **Punakha**, a town known for its breathtaking scenery and historical significance. As I explored the old capital of Bhutan, I couldn't help but feel amazed by the resilience of the people who built this fortress. **The Punakha Dzong** is a remarkable fortress perched precariously on the side of a steep, snow-covered mountain, that has stood the test of time, and it was an honor to be able to explore it.

The next morning, we drove to **Gangtey** and visited the Phobjika valley. It was a beautiful valley with stunning views of the eastern Himalayan ranges, including the highest mountain in Bhutan, Mt.Gangar Punsum at 7520 meters. This beautiful valley is also home to the rare Black Necked Cranes migrating from the Tibetan plateau to escape the harsh winter. Currently, there are 200 to 300 cranes residing in this valley, and the Royal Society for Protection of Nature is taking every measure to ensure the safety of the cranes.

One of the highlights of my trip was hiking to **Takshang monastery**, also known as **"Tiger Nest"**. The hike was all the way uphill through pine forests and took about 3 to 4 hours through pine forests. The monastery clings to a huge granite cliff 800 meters from the Paro valley, and the view was simply breathtaking. It was believed that the great saint Padmasambhava came in the 7th century on a flying tigress and meditated in a cave for 3 months, converting the Paro valley into Buddhism. Visiting the Tiger Nest monastery was a pilgrimage site for every Bhutanese to visit once in their lifetime. The view was simply breathtaking, and I felt a sense of peace and serenity that is hard to describe. A great place to just stop and take in the beauty all around you. A great place to meditate and be one with nature.

During my trip, I also had the opportunity to **visit a school** in Bhutan and interact with the children. The kids, who were between 6 to 8 years old, were wearing traditional Bhutanese uniforms and were just adorable. I brought a bag of smiling face balloons and asked the kids about their dreams and put them on the balloons. Some kids wanted to be engineers, doctors, teachers, police persons, and one kid wanted to be a taxi driver. Then I talked to them about how to achieve their dreams and asked them if their happiness is 10 on the scale of 1 to 10, to stand up. All 45 kids stood up, and it was an amazing moment to see these happy kids. It was heartwarming to see how happy and content they were with simple things and how committed they were to their education.

Another aspect of Bhutan that left a lasting impression on me was the country's commitment to environmental conservation. Bhutan is one of the few countries in the world that is **carbon negative**, meaning that it absorbs more carbon dioxide than it emits. The country has implemented policies to protect its forests, which cover over 70% of the country's land area, and to promote sustainable tourism. The government has also set aside over 50% of the country's land area as protected areas for wildlife, including rare and endangered species such as the black-necked crane and the snow leopard.

During our travels in Bhutan, we were able to experience the amazing Bhutanese warmth and hospitality. We happened to be there during the **American Thanksgiving holiday** and I was wondering how to celebrate it in this peaceful mountain kingdom. With great excitement, I approached our hotel owner and asked him how do the Bhutanese celebrate a big holiday. He asked me what was the holiday and I explained the details of our Thanksgiving day celebration of consuming turkey like the early Pilgrims. He smiled and said he didn't have turkey, but instead he prepared a sumptuous Bhutanese-style chicken and fresh vegetables that was simple delicious. To add to the occasion, the kind hotel owner gifted us a delightful bottle of French wine, which we gratefully accepted. With the dinner plans all set, we invited our guide, driver, the hotel owner and his family, and the hotel staff to join us for the Thanksgiving feast. We were overjoyed to have such wonderful company to share this special moment with us. As we sat down to eat, the delicious aroma of the food filled the room, and we raised a toast to our newfound friends and to the blessings of life. It was a beautiful moment of sharing and bonding over a meal, despite being in a foreign land.

The next day was filled with even more joy and celebration as we attended the closing ceremony of the **Paro Tsechu festival** at Ringpung Dzong. The vibrant colors, traditional dance performances, and the energy in the air were simply electrifying. It was truly an unforgettable experience to witness such a beautiful display of Bhutanese culture and tradition. The unique Bhutanese architecture, colorful Bhutanese costumes and savoring Bhutanese dishes simply overwhelm the five senses.

Visiting Bhutan is a once-in-a-lifetime opportunity to be fully immersed in a culture that values happiness, spirituality, and harmony with nature. The country's breathtaking views of the Himalayan mountains are just the beginning of what makes this place so special. The vibrant festivals, colorful traditions, and unique customs all offer a glimpse into the soul of Bhutan. As I traveled through this small yet mighty country, I felt like I was on a journey of self-discovery. The people I met along the way, from the adorable school children to the friendly locals, all shared a genuine warmth and hospitality that made me feel at home. And the rare Black Necked Cranes that I encountered were a true symbol of the country's commitment to preserving nature and the environment. But what stood out the most to me was the country's commitment to happiness. It wasn't just a slogan or a marketing gimmick; it was a way of life. I was struck by how content and fulfilled the Bhutanese people were with their simple and minimalist lifestyle. This experience inspired me to simplify my own life and focus on what truly matters. Visiting Bhutan changed my life for the better and I am grateful for the opportunity to have experienced the magic of Bhutan and will cherish the memories forever.

Bhutan Archery

Sign post along the route to Tiger Nest

Paro Tsechu festival

The King of Bhutan,
His Majesty Jigme Khesar Namgyel Wangchuck

Tiger Nest

Young Monks at a Temple

Thanksgiving Dinner in Bhutan

Adorable Children of Bhutan

JORDAN

Traveling to Jordan is like stepping back into history and seeing this history come alive before your eyes. My journey to Jordan proved to be an incredibly rewarding experience as I immersed myself in the country's rich history, vibrant culture, and breathtaking natural beauty. Nestled in the heart of the Middle East, Jordan is a small nation bordered by Syria to the north, Saudi Arabia to the east and south, Iraq to the northeast, and Israel and Palestine to the west. Despite its compact size, Jordan boasts a wealth of historical significance and a diverse landscape that encompasses the arid deserts of Wadi Rum and the lush greenery of the northern forests.

Our first stop was "**Jerash**", a UNESCO World Heritage site that dates back to the 2nd century, showcasing extraordinary Greco-Roman architecture. As an enthusiast of architectural marvels, I was utterly captivated. The sprawling ruins beckoned us to explore every nook and cranny, allowing us to absorb the fascinating history and beauty that enveloped the place. We even found ourselves perched on a massive rock, basking in the sheer magnificence of it all. Every second spent in Jerash was truly remarkable, and I cherished the experience to its fullest.

However, this was only the beginning of our thrilling expedition. From there, we ventured to **the Dead Sea**, where the ethereal sensation of floating in its magical waters transported us to another realm. Known as the lowest point on Earth and renowned for its therapeutic properties, the Dead Sea provided an unmatched experience. Even though it was my second visit, I relished every moment. The weightlessness I felt while immersed in the buoyant saltwater was indescribable, bringing a perpetual smile to my face. I indulged in a unique spa treatment, smearing myself with mineral-rich mud, and then surrendered to relaxation as I floated effortlessly in the sea. To complete the day, we enjoyed the bar near the beach, catching Happy Hour while witnessing the mesmerizing sunset. The spa facilities at the hotel were impeccable, featuring a pool filled with Dead Sea water, a steam room, sauna, two Jacuzzis, and a large swimming pool. The rejuvenating spa services left me feeling elated and appreciative of such a distinctive and unforgettable adventure.

After a few blissful days at the Dead Sea, we embarked on a two-hour drive to "Petra". **Petra** was sealed off to the world until the early 20th century and was exposed by a Swiss explorer only after a severe earthquake.

Along the way, we marveled at the countless olive tree farms, and although the drive up the mountains presented some rough patches with twists and turns, the scenic vistas were absolutely breathtaking. We couldn't resist stopping at various points to capture the beauty in photographs and fully absorb the surroundings. Upon reaching Petra, anticipation and excitement surged through me. Known as the "Rose City" and recognized as a UNESCO World Heritage site and one of the New Seven Wonders of the World, Petra astounded with its awe-inspiring sandstone architecture and intricate carvings. Petra is the home of several Hollywood movies as well as Indiana Jones and the "Temple of Doom" were all filmed there.

The following morning, I eagerly explored the city's labyrinth of temples, tombs, and structures, including the iconic **Treasury**, a breathtaking carving directly hewn into the rock face. We embarked on a hike to reach the tombs and amphitheater, traversing the ancient city on foot. The experience was every bit as astonishing as I remembered from my previous visit. The hike up to the Monastery proved challenging but ultimately rewarding. Along the way, the landscape dazzled with vibrant blooming trees and the occasional sight of goats dotting the scenery. Finally reaching the summit, we indulged in two full hours of relaxation, taking in the awe-inspiring panorama. Afterward, we embarked on a hike down the Place of High Sacrifice trail, a new route for me. Though undoubtedly arduous, the vistas that unfolded were simply breathtaking.

One standout moment was exploring the Red Rock path in Petra during the day, but experiencing **Petra by night** took the adventure to another level. The Petra by night show commenced at 8:30 pm, and we joined the waiting line at 8 pm. As we walked through the siq, we were surrounded by a mesmerizing glow from hundreds of candle lights. The candles illuminated the path, creating a truly magical atmosphere that filled us with anticipation. Approaching the Treasury, we were greeted by the flickering glow of countless candles, offering an awe-inspiring sight. We found a seat on the only bench at the back of the courtyard, relishing the serene ambiance. The weather was perfect, with a comfortable temperature and no wind. Traditional Jordanian music played on flutes, accompanied by a star-studded night sky, enhancing the enchantment. Throughout the night, the host shared captivating stories about Petra's history, transporting us to ancient times. Towards the end, the host invited everyone to close their eyes and savor the profound memories being created. The experience was truly unforgettable, with the backdrop of Bedouin music, captivating stories, and a starlit sky creating pure magic. After the show, we waited for everyone to leave and savored the serene night surrounded by the glow of hundreds of candle lights. Colored spotlights added to the beauty of the Treasury. We remained until the lights were extinguished, knowing we had just witnessed something truly extraordinary. Petra is a place that is very special and was a major trading hub for the Nabataean's and was once their capital. The Nabataeans once rivaled the Roman Empire in influence and political power and challenged the Romans in the early years after the Common Era or after B.C.

The next morning, our journey continued to **Wadi Rum**, and the adventure filled me with joy and excitement. Arriving at the desert, I was instantly struck by the sheer beauty of the expansive golden sands stretching as far as the eye could see. As we delved deeper into the desert, we made a stop at a shaded area where our guide treated us to a delightful lunch. I still vividly recall the mouth-watering aroma of the tomato and onion stew he prepared, perfectly seasoned and accompanied by soft pita bread and a crisp salad. It was a moment of pure bliss, relishing a delicious meal amidst the desert's stunning backdrop.

As the sun began to set, we arrived at our campsite nestled between towering rocks over 80 feet high. Our guide set up a comfortable area with bamboo mats and cushions while preparing a delectable dinner. I wandered around, soaking in the captivating sunset and marveling at the desert's incredible beauty. The guide prepared a hearty stew with beans and tomatoes, complemented by a fresh salad. As darkness descended and stars glittered above, I was filled with awe and wonder.

Gathered around the warm, crackling bonfire, we engaged in conversations with our guide, delving into his life, family, culture, and traditions. It was a remarkable opportunity to connect with someone from a completely different world, leaving me grateful for the diversity of our planet. When it was time to rest, I settled onto a comfortable mattress, wrapped in two warm blankets and a soft pillow, feeling at home in the heart of the desert. Sleeping under the stars in such tranquil surroundings provided a sense of peace and tranquility that will forever be etched in my memory.

The following morning, I woke up early, eager to witness the stunning sunrise over the desert. As I walked from the cave to the open expanse of the desert, anticipation filled the air. The first rays of light breaking through the horizon were a breathtaking sight, leaving me in awe and wonder. After a delightful breakfast of bread, cheese, and hummus, we were greeted by a friendly camel, and we shared breakfast bread with it, creating a unique bond.

Following the unforgettable night in the desert, we embarked on a drive to Bernice Beach Resort, a stunning location on the **Red Sea** featuring three pools and beach chairs. Relaxing under a straw umbrella, I basked in the beauty of the crystal-clear waters and the warm sun. Renting snorkel gear, we ventured into the Red Sea, and I was amazed by the vibrant corals and diverse marine life that surrounded us. The water varied in temperature, providing both refreshing and warm pockets, but it was an immensely enjoyable experience that I will forever cherish.

Overall, my trip to Jordan was an unforgettable journey that I will always hold precious in my memory. I had the opportunity to explore breathtaking historical sites, immerse myself in the culture and hospitality of the Jordanian people, and be surrounded by stunning beauty. From the ancient city of Jaresh to the magical Petra by night, every moment filled me with joy and excitement. Sleeping under the stars in Wadi Rum and snorkeling in the Red Sea were indescribable experiences that will remain etched in my heart. Lastly, Amman the capital of Jordan is filled with ancient ruins and vestiges of its rich and long history and impressive museums. I am immensely grateful for the chance to have created these cherished memories in a place as inspiring and joyful as Jordan.

Savoring
PETRA BY NIGHT

Jerash

Wadi Rum

The Monastery, Petra

Selling rocks at Petra

The Dead Sea

The Red Sea

ISRAEL

Israel is a place where you can come face to face with your spiritual roots! Furthermore, Israel is a small country and easy to move around; literally just about everyone speaks English to a certain degree and the magnificent beaches and seaside restaurants will have you asking for more. Want to understand scripture better there is no better place than Israel and the ancient city of Jerusalem. But that is just the start as there is Masada, the Dead Sea and Tel Aviv just to name a few.

Traveling to Israel offered a profound and enriching experience, forging a deep spiritual connection to our faith. Israel is universally recognized as a holy land for Jews, Christians, and Muslims, boasting an extensive and diverse history spanning thousands of years. Among the essential destinations was the Old City of Jerusalem, a must-visit. This ancient city harbored some of the world's holiest sites, including the Western Wall, the Church of the Holy Sepulcher, and the Dome of the Rock. Roaming through the narrow streets of the Old City and exploring these sites evoked a powerful and poignant experience, transporting us back in time to witness the birthplace of our faith. The best time to visit Jerusalem is during Autumn, between September and November. It is really mind-blowing how many things are there to see and do in Jerusalem, with its complex history, beautiful architecture and religious significance, the old city of Jerusalem is a must see!

During my visit to Israel, I embarked on a profoundly private and profound spiritual journey. Opting to stay at a convent within the Old City, I had the opportunity to delve deeper into my spiritual quest. I visited numerous significant locations, such as the Holy Sepulcher, the Western Wall, the Mount of Olives, Via Dolorosa, Yad Vashem Museum, Bethlehem, the King David Tower, and even ventured to the Sea of Galilee.

Visiting **the Church of the Holy Sepulcher** proved to be an awe-inspiring encounter with spirituality. Nestled in the heart of the Old City, this church stood as one of Christianity's most sacred sites, believed to house the very spot where Jesus Christ was crucified, buried, and resurrected. The Church of the Holy Sepulcher comprised various chapels, each carrying its unique history and significance. I explored the multitude of rooms within the church, including the Chapel of St. Helena, where the True Cross was said to have been discovered, and the Chapel of Adam, believed to be the resting place of the first man. However, the most remarkable site within the church was the Holy Sepulcher itself, housing the Tomb of Jesus. This hallowed ground marked the place where Jesus was laid to rest after his crucifixion and where he triumphantly rose from the dead three days later. The grandeur and opulence of the church's architecture were striking, blending various architectural styles from different periods and cultures such as Byzantine, Crusader, and Ottoman. The adornment of beautiful mosaics, paintings, and ornate sculptures further enhanced the church's magnificence. Additionally, the church attracted Christian pilgrims worldwide, offering them a site of profound pilgrimage. Throughout the day, I had the privilege of witnessing several religious ceremonies and rituals, such as processions, masses, and prayer services, which moved and uplifted me. Definitely, explore the church fully as there are chapels on the roof and a deep cistern that goes back to the days of King David who founded the city. It is a trip that you will never forget.

Another immensely significant spiritual experience awaited me at **the Western Wall**, often referred to as the Wailing Wall. This ancient stone structure, the sole remnant of the Second Temple in Jerusalem, stood as the most revered site in Judaism. Situated within the Old City, the Western Wall drew Jewish pilgrims from every corner of the globe. My emotions swelled as I approached the wall and reverently touched its weathered stones, offering my prayers and leaving written notes carrying my hopes and wishes for humanity and the world. Divided into sections for men and women, the wall demanded modest attire and head coverings as a mark of respect. Beyond its religious sanctity, the Western Wall held immense historical significance, having stood steadfast for over two millennia and witnessed countless pivotal events in Jewish history, including the Romans' destruction of the Second Temple in 70 CE. The Western Wall Plaza, adjacent to the wall, served as a gathering place for momentous events and celebrations, such as Bar Mitzvahs and military ceremonies.

To fully immerse myself in the spiritual journey, I made a decision **to reside in a convent within the Old City**. The experience of staying in a convent in Jerusalem was unparalleled, offering a unique and enriching opportunity to be enveloped in the city's rich history and culture. The convent provided a serene and spiritual haven amidst the bustling streets of the Old City, allowing me to detach from the external clamor and distractions. The atmosphere within the convent emanated tranquility and contemplation, enabling me to seek solace and deep reflection. One of the most remarkable aspects of staying in a Jerusalem convent was the chance to engage with the local community. The resident nuns possessed profound knowledge of the city's history and culture, generously sharing valuable insights into the multitude of religious sites and traditions found within Jerusalem.

The next day, I visited **Yad Vashem**. Yad Vashem, the World Holocaust Remembrance Center, was an incredibly impactful and emotional experience that left an indelible mark on me. Situated in Jerusalem, Yad Vashem was dedicated to preserving the memory of the six million Jews who tragically lost their lives during the Holocaust. Upon entering the complex, the starkness of the architecture and the solemn atmosphere immediately struck me. The museum's exhibits were thoughtfully arranged in chronological order, guiding us through the events leading up to the Holocaust, the atrocities committed during that dark period, and the aftermath that followed. My emotions ran the gamut, encompassing deep sadness, profound grief, anger, and an overwhelming sense of disbelief. The exhibits themselves were immensely powerful and moving, featuring photographs, artifacts, and personal accounts from survivors and victims' that vividly brought the reality of the Holocaust to life.

One of the most emotionally charged exhibits at Yad Vashem was the Hall of Names. Housed within a circular chamber, this poignant display showcased the names and testimonies of four million Jewish victims, each represented by a page of testimony lovingly submitted by their family members and loved ones. Another profoundly moving exhibit was the Children's Memorial, a solemn and dark space that pays tribute to the one-and-a-half million Jewish children whose lives were tragically cut short during the Holocaust. The exhibit utilized mirrors that reflect thousands of points of light, symbolizing the countless lives lost. Despite the heavy emotional weight that permeated Yad Vashem, I departed with a glimmer of hope and a resolute determination. The museum also highlighted the stories of individuals who risked their own lives to save Jews during the Holocaust, serving as a powerful reminder that even in the darkest of times, acts of kindness and bravery prevailed.

One evening, I had the privilege of attending the awe-inspiring **light show at the King David Tower** in Jerusalem. This dazzling spectacle vividly brought to life the city's rich history and vibrant culture. As we gathered in the courtyard surrounding the King David Tower, we were met with a breathtaking display of lights and sounds. Using cutting-edge technology, the show projected captivating images and animations onto the tower's walls, creating an immersive and visually stunning experience. The performance eloquently narrated the tale of Jerusalem, tracing its ancient roots to its present-day vibrancy. Among the show's highlights was the depiction of King David himself, the legendary figure who established Jerusalem as the capital of Israel. Accompanied by stirring music and narration, the projection of King David truly brought his story to life in a profoundly impactful manner. The light show also showcased the modern aspects of Jerusalem, featuring its bustling streets, vibrant culture, and diverse communities. Through contemporary images and captivating music, I gained a sense of the city's dynamic energy and indomitable spirit, emphasizing its ongoing evolution.

Opting to stay within the walls of the Old City, I embarked on a poignant and emotional journey by walking **the Via Dolorosa** in Jerusalem. Also known as the "Way of Sorrows," this winding path traversed the heart of the Old City. From the moment I set foot on the Via Dolorosa, I was struck by the ancient stone walls and narrow alleyways that lined the route. The atmosphere exuded a sense of quiet reflection, occasionally punctuated by the resonant tolling of church bells or the soft murmurs of prayers emanating from nearby chapels. With each step, I encountered the 14 stations, each signifying a different event in Jesus Christ's final hours before his crucifixion. These stations included the site of his trial, the place of his flogging, and the spot of his crucifixion. One particularly poignant moment on the Via Dolorosa was the Chapel of the Flagellation, which marked the exact location where Jesus was mercilessly scourged. The chapel, with its dim lighting and intimate ambiance, emitted a haunting aura, reminding me of the immense pain and suffering endured by Jesus. Finally, at the conclusion of the Via Dolorosa, I arrived at the Church of the Holy Sepulcher, the sacred site of Jesus' crucifixion, burial, and resurrection. Stepping foot inside the church, I was immediately enveloped by a powerful and reverential atmosphere that evoked a profound sense of awe and humility.

The following morning, I embarked on a bus journey to the **Mount of Olives**, an immensely significant site in Jerusalem from both religious and historical perspectives. Located east of the Old City, this mountain has held spiritual significance for Jews, Christians, and Muslims for thousands of years. Venturing to the Mount of Olives granted me a unique outlook on Jerusalem, allowing me to delve into its captivating history and culture. Ascending the slopes, I was greeted by awe-inspiring panoramic vistas of Jerusalem sprawled out before me. From this elevated vantage point, I beheld the city's iconic landmarks, including the Temple Mount, the Dome of the Rock, and the ancient walls encircling the Old City.

The Garden of Gethsemane stood as one of the most momentous sites on the Mount of Olives, believed to be where Jesus prayed with his disciples on the eve of his crucifixion. Within this sacred garden thrived a grove of ancient olive trees, some of which were over two millennia old. Another notable attraction on the mount was the Jewish cemetery, an active burial ground spanning over 3,000 years. Esteemed figures from Jewish history, such as prophets, scholars, and rabbis, were believed to find their eternal rest in this revered cemetery. Additionally, I explored the Church of All Nations, which neighbored the Garden of Gethsemane. This modern architectural marvel captivated me with its intricate mosaics and exquisite façade, serving as a testament to the profound beauty of religious structures.

The subsequent day led me to **Bethlehem**, the birthplace of Jesus Christ, embarking on a pilgrimage of immense spiritual significance for Christians worldwide. This historic town, located a few miles south of Jerusalem, harbored the Nativity Church—an enduring testament to Christianity and a designated UNESCO World Heritage Site. This ancient church stood on the hallowed ground believed to be the very site of Jesus' birth, captivating me with its impressive architecture and storied past. Within its sacred halls, I was immersed in the ambiance of the Nativity Church, transported back in time to the miraculous birth of Jesus. The atmosphere exuded tranquility and introspection, prompting me to pause, offer prayers, and light candles in remembrance of loved ones. Venturing beyond the church, I navigated the narrow streets of Bethlehem, absorbing the town's rich history and culture. Bethlehem's vibrant Palestinian community welcomed me with open arms, and I savored local cuisine, perused handicrafts, and experienced the warm hospitality deeply rooted in Palestinian traditions.

 Continuing on my spiritual journey, I embarked on a bus journey to **the Sea of Galilee**, a breathtaking natural wonder nestled in northern Israel. Known by alternative names such as Lake Kinneret or the Kinneret, it hold profound spiritual significance for Christians. As the bus drew closer to the Sea of Galilee, I was immediately captivated by its serene beauty and tranquil waters. Surrounded by rolling hills and lush greenery, the lake exuded an aura of calmness, its crystal-clear waters shimmering under the warm sunlight. Fed by the Jordan River, this freshwater lake hold the distinction of being the lowest on Earth, situated approximately 200 meters below sea level. The Sea of Galilee, the largest freshwater lake in Israel, not only served as a vital water source for irrigation and recreation but also remained a site of immense spiritual importance. It was believed to be the location where Jesus performed numerous miracles, including calling his disciples, walking on water, and calming tumultuous storms. On the coast line of Lake Kinneret is the small fishing town of Magdala, where Mary Magdalene was born, there you can take a boat ride across the Lake and visit other cities where Jesus once visited as well.

Reflecting on my profound journey, I came to realize that this trip surpassed even my initial visit to Israel. Jerusalem, with its revered sites such as the Holy Sepulcher, the Dome of the Rock, the Western Wall, and the Mount of Olives, left an indelible mark on my spirit. A sojourn to Israel possessed the potential to be an exceptionally meaningful and spiritually enlightening experience for those seeking to connect with their faith and explored the nation's intricate tapestry of history and culture. It offered an opportunity to deepen one's understanding of the roots of their beliefs while simultaneously enjoying modern comforts and breathtaking natural landscapes. All in all, this transformative journey evoked profound emotions and left me with a profound sense of spiritual fulfillment.

"TRAVEL IS FATAL TO PREJUDICE, BIGOTRY, AND NARROW-MINDEDNESS." - Mark Twain

A Spiritual Moment at the
WESTERN WALL

Along Via Dolorosa

Christian Pilgrims

The Holy Sepulcher

The Holy Sepulcher

The Holy Sepulcher

The Star of Bethlehem

View from Mount of Olives

The Western Wall

The Convent inside the Old City

The Western Wall

Yad Vashem, the World Holocaust Remembrance Center

Sea of Galilee

KYRGYZSTAN

Kyrgyzstan, officially known as the Kyrgyz Republic, is a small landlocked country located in Central Asia. It boasts a rich and diverse cultural heritage that is deeply rooted in its history and geography. This nation is renowned for its extraordinary natural beauty, characterized by majestic mountains, pristine lakes, and vast open steppes. Furthermore, the people of Kyrgyzstan are celebrated for their genuine hospitality, warmth, and kindness.

Bishkek is the capital of Kyrgyzstan, and it borders Central Asia's Tian Shan mountain range and is the gateway to Ala Archa National Park with its breathtaking glaciers and wildlife trails. One captivating destination within Kyrgyzstan is "Chong Kemin", a village situated in the Issyk-Kul region near the picturesque Issyk-Kul Lake. This particular region is renowned for its stunning natural landscapes, making it a favored tourist spot for both locals and foreigners alike. Chong Kemin is home to numerous local families whose livelihoods are sustained through farming and animal husbandry. These families are famous for their welcoming and amiable nature, exemplifying the traditional values of the region.

During my visit to **Chong Kemin**, I was awestruck by the incredible beauty of the surroundings and deeply touched by the warmth and generosity of the local people. I had the privilege of staying at a local hotel, which was owned and operated by a kind and hospitable family. This afforded me a firsthand experience of the authentic way of life embraced by the local residents. One of the most cherished memories from my trip was attending a dinner hosted by a local family inside a traditional yurt—a Kyrgyz dwelling constructed with felt and canvas. I was fortunate enough to be invited to join them as they **celebrated a family reunion**. Inside the yurt, a total of seven families and approximately 25 individuals gathered to share food, drinks, and engaging conversations, reveling in each other's company and creating cherished moments.

The meal was a delightful feast, featuring an array of flavorsome dishes such as freshly baked bread, grilled meat, nuts, fruits, and a selection of beverages including vodka and mare's milk. Mare's milk, though possessing a distinct taste, proved to be surprisingly palatable. The locals explained that horse milk is known to be beneficial for one's stomach and digestion, and I felt honored to partake in this traditional drink. Additionally, there was an abundance of vodka, which served as a catalyst for laughter, bonding, and camaraderie. I seized the opportunity to express my heartfelt gratitude to the hosting family and the hotel owners, raising a toast that was met with joyous laughter and shared appreciation. The evening continued with the men engaging

THE FAMILY REUNION DINNER

The Family Reunion Dinner

A local Singer

The Milkman and the Villagers

in card games, the women engrossed in animated conversations, and a local singer gracing us with beautiful melodies. Furthermore, we ventured outside to witness the milkman diligently collecting milk from the local villagers, providing us with a fascinating glimpse into the traditional way of life and offering insights into the local economy and culture.

The following morning, I awoke early to witness the breathtaking sunrise over the mountains before embarking on a leisurely stroll to explore the neighboring village. The scenery was nothing short of awe-inspiring, with majestic mountains and fields adorned with vibrant purple flowers. Horses grazed peacefully in the hills, while the local villagers commenced their day's activities. It was a serene and picturesque morning, and I felt an overwhelming sense of gratitude for the opportunity to immerse myself in this extraordinary way of life. During breakfast with the families, I seized the chance to offer a heartfelt toast to the host family, the hotel owners, and the local people, expressing my deepest appreciation for their unwavering hospitality and kindness. Their response was filled with equal warmth and kindness, leaving me feeling truly blessed to have shared this remarkable experience with them.

As I bid farewell to Chong Kemin, I carried within me a profound sense of gratitude and respect for the people of Kyrgyzstan, as well as a deep appreciation for the country's rich cultural heritage and awe-inspiring natural beauty. The warm hospitality and genuine kindness exhibited by the locals will forever remain etched in my memory. I eagerly anticipate the opportunity to return to this captivating region in the future, longing to once again immerse myself in its unparalleled charm.

"The Journey of a thousand miles begins with one step"
-Lao Tzu

MONGOLIA

Beautiful and historic Mongolia, the home of the mighty Mongols and home of Genghis Khan. In Ulaanbaatar, the capital city, we can view the historic remnants of the infamous Mongol hordes, that once made all of Europe lose sleep at night, worrying about their velocity and speed on the battlefield. Historians say that the Mongols were the fastest military of their time, capable of covering 80 miles in a single day. The rich Mongol culture permeates just about everything in the Mongol national identity. I had an amazing adventure in Mongolia! This incredible country, located in Central Asia, is a treasure trove of stunning landscapes, rich culture, and a nomadic way of life that is truly unique. I was fortunate enough to visit during the Naadam festival, and it was an unforgettable experience.

The Naadam festival is a celebration of Mongolian culture, history, and national identity. Held every year from July 11th to July 13th, it is one of the most important events in the Mongolian calendar. This festival has been around since ancient times when it was held to celebrate military victories. Nowadays, it is a chance for both city dwellers and nomads to come together and enjoy traditional sports and cultural activities.

The three main sports of the Naadam Festival are wrestling, horse racing, and archery, each with a rich and fascinating history in Mongolian culture. The wrestling competition, which is the most popular event, features hundreds of wrestlers, each wearing a traditional costume and displaying their strength and skill in a series of matches. The winner is awarded the highly respected honor of "Nachin." Horse racing is another important sport at the festival, featuring long-distance races for horses of all ages. And finally, archery is a test of skill and accuracy that features both men and women. The history of horses and the Mongolian people go back centuries. The horse is a highly respected animal in Mongol tradition and history.

The Naadam Festival is not only an important cultural event for the Mongolian people, but it's also a celebration of unity and national pride. During the festival, I even saw the President of the country and his cabinet in attendance. It was truly an unforgettable experience to witness the passion and enthusiasm of the Mongolian people as they came together to celebrate their rich heritage.

After the festival, I headed to **the Gobi Desert**, one of the largest deserts in the world, stretching across northern and northwestern China and southern Mongolia. The desert is a fascinating landscape that is rich in history, culture, and natural beauty. The sand dunes are one of the most stunning features, with the Khongoryn Els sand dunes being particularly famous for the "singing sand dune", the eerie sound they make as the wind blows over them. The mountains in the Gobi Desert are also incredible, rising up sharply from the desert floor and home to a wide range of wildlife, including rare species such as the Gobi bear and the Bactrian camel. It was truly an awe-inspiring experience to explore the rugged and barren mountains and take in the breathtaking views of this stunning landscape.

I had an unforgettable journey hiking up the Gobi Desert! As I trekked along, I stumbled upon a group of scientists from the university who were **digging up fossils**. I couldn't believe my luck when asked them to let me join them and they accepted! With chisels, hammers, and brushes in hand, I began to dig alongside them. The Gobi Desert is famous for its abundant dinosaur fossils, and it was a dream come true to be a part of the excavation process. I learned that excavating dinosaur bones in the Gobi Desert requires a great deal of skill, patience, and precision, and I was honored to be a part of it. The Gobi Desert has been a rich source of dinosaur fossils since the 1920s, and it has yielded some of the most significant discoveries in recent years, including the first fossilized dinosaur egg! Incredibly after hours of digging, we found a dinosaur skull, and I was overjoyed to be a part of such a historic discovery. The work that these scientists do is simply incredible, and it has revolutionized our understanding of the history of life on Earth.

However, that was not the only incredible experience I had on this journey. On the way back to our campsite, our driver stopped to **visit a nomad family** who lived in a yurt. The Mongolian people being largely nomad live in a tent like structure with a wooden base. It is convenient as it can be moved anywhere in Mongolia. Despite having very little, they generously offered us mare's milk tea, rice, cheese, and dried meat. We spent time sharing stories and learning about each other, and their hospitality was truly touching. It was a reminder of the incredible kindness and connection that humans are capable of, even in the most challenging circumstances.

Part of my journey also involved **staying in a yurt in the Gobi Desert**. The yurt, a traditional circular tent made of felt and canvas, was surprisingly comfortable and spacious. The round shape of the yurt gave it a sense of warmth and intimacy, and the skylight at the top allowed natural light to filter in during the day. I was greeted by friendly Mongolian nomads who welcomed us with traditional Mongolian tea and snacks. They prepared delicious meals using fresh ingredients, including vegetables grown in their own gardens and meat from their own animals. One night, they even prepared a traditional Mongolian barbecue, which was an absolute delight!

But the highlight of my stay in the yurt was the sound of the desert at night. As the wind began to pick up, it created an eerie howling sound that was unlike anything I had ever heard before. It was an experience that left me feeling completely immersed in the natural world. During the day, we went on camel rides through the desert, hiked to nearby sand dunes, and even tried our hand at archery. The nomads invited us to watch them herd their animals, giving us a firsthand look at the nomadic way of life. The stars at night were also a sight to behold, with no light pollution in the middle of the desert, the sky was filled with an incredible number of stars, more than I had ever seen before. It was a breathtaking sight that left me feeling humbled by the vastness of the universe.

Overall, Mongolia offers a truly unique travel experience that combines local culture and tradition, stunning landscapes, and fascinating history. The Gobi Desert is a testament to the incredible scientific potential of this region, and the nomadic way of life is a reminder of the importance of connection to our natural world. Staying in a yurt was an experience of a lifetime, and meeting the local family was an absolute joy. I will cherish these memories forever and highly recommend visiting Mongolia to anyone seeking a truly unforgettable adventure!

NAADAM FESTIVAL IN ULAANBAATAR

Yurts in Gobi Desert

Wrestling Match at Naadam Festival

Gobi Desert

Exploring the Singing Dunes of the Gobi

A Scientist digging up fossils

Fossil found in Gobi Desert

Festival in Mongolia

SYRIA

Visiting every country in the world is an extraordinary achievement that has filled my heart with overwhelming emotions of joy and fulfillment. It is a remarkable feat that allowed me to immerse myself in a vast tapestry of cultures, landscapes, and experiences. This grand endeavor goes beyond the realms of ordinary travel; it represents a profound journey of self-discovery, cultural immersion, and an unyielding passion and labor of love.

Syria, the last country on my list of 193 countries, held a special place in my heart. The incredible feeling that accompanied such a monumental accomplishment is hard to put into words. It was a deeply emotional experience, like a crescendo of emotions that swelled within me, ranging from exhilaration to awe, gratitude to humility, and everything in between. With each country explored, a profound sense of connection to the world and its people became increasingly palpable, as the tapestry of global cultures weaved itself into the very fabric of my being.

For the journey to Damascus, Syria, I made meticulous arrangements, ensuring every detail was in place. First, I flew from Madrid, Spain to Beirut, Lebanon, then I arranged for a driver to pick me up in Beirut, and embarked on a road trip that would be etched in my memory forever. The anticipation built up as we left the bustling city behind and hit the open road, setting the stage for a thrilling adventure.

The road from Beirut to Damascus is a scenic marvel that took me through captivating landscapes, immersed me in the beauty of the region and evoked a range of emotions. As we left Beirut behind, I found myself traversing the mesmerizing Lebanese countryside. Rolling hills adorned with vibrant greenery, picturesque valleys blanketed with flowers, and charming villages nestled amidst the verdant landscape painted a picture of natural splendor. The road meandered through the magnificent Mount Lebanon range, revealing breathtaking vistas of rugged mountains and lush forests. Every twist and turn brought a new revelation, showcasing the diversity and majesty of the Lebanese terrain. The fresh mountain air invigorated my senses, and the panoramic views inspired a sense of serenity and freedom, making the journey an invigorating experience.

Approaching **the border between Lebanon and Syria**, a mix of excitement and anticipation coursed through my veins. Obtaining a visa for Syria had been a challenging and a time-consuming process, as it took nearly two years and several rejections before finally receiving approval. The perseverance and determination required to overcome these hurdles only heightened my joy and gratitude as we crossed the border into the realm of Syria, the final destination of my epic quest to visit every country on earth.

The anticipation and excitement that had built up over the course of my ambitious journey reached its pinnacle as I stood on the threshold of the last country, **ready to complete my quest of visiting all 193 United Nations countries**. It was a moment that defied words, as the magnitude of what I had accomplished washed over me in a surge of exhilaration. The elation I felt was immeasurable, for I had traversed continents, delved into the depths of diverse cultures, and absorbed the collective wisdom of countless nations. In that moment, I became a citizen of the world, with a broader perspective and a deep appreciation for the interconnectedness of our global community.

Crossing into Syria, I felt an immediate transition, a shift into a different country with its own distinct culture, traditions, and landscapes. The change in scenery became evident as we entered the Syrian countryside. Vast plains stretched as far as the eye could see, adorned with golden wheat fields swaying in the gentle breeze and scattered olive groves casting dappled shadows on the land. The journey took us through small Syrian towns and villages, each with its own unique charm and character. The warm smiles and friendly faces of the locals made me feel instantly welcome, embraced by the authentic hospitality that Syria is renowned for. It was during these moments that I truly witnessed the beauty of human connection and the power of cultural exchange. The road trip allowed me to observe the daily lives of the Syrian people, as we passed by bustling markets teeming with vibrant colors and enticing aromas, roadside stalls offering a variety of delectable treats, and traditional houses that stood as a testament to centuries of history. The simplicity and authenticity of rural Syrian life added a touch of nostalgia and forged a deeper connection to the region.

As we neared Damascus, the capital city unveiled its splendor, captivating my senses and igniting a sense of wonder within me. The bustling streets pulsated with life, adorned with ancient architecture and vibrant markets. The Umayyad Mosque, with its majestic minarets, served as a beacon, signaling my arrival in this ancient city. Navigating through the maze-like streets, I found myself immersed in a harmonious blend of modernity and history. The bustling markets enticed me with their vivid displays of spices, textiles, and handicrafts, and the aroma of freshly brewed coffee and exotic flavors lingered in the air. Every step I took was an invitation to uncover the secrets of Damascus, to witness the intertwining of cultures and the preservation of traditions that have withstood the test of time. The city's rich heritage and cultural tapestry enveloped me completely, creating an overwhelming sense of awe and wonder.

One of the standout destinations in Damascus was **the Hanania Church**, an ancient sanctuary that holds immense religious significance. Stepping into its hallowed halls, I could sense the weight of history surrounding me. Tradition claims that this sacred church stands upon the very spot where St. Paul, a pivotal figure in early Christianity, was baptized. The interior was a mesmerizing fusion of architectural styles, featuring intricate mosaics, delicate carvings, and breathtaking frescoes that depicted profound biblical stories. The serenity and reverence within the Hanania Church created a tranquil atmosphere, allowing pilgrims and visitors to connect with their spirituality and reflect on the profound impact of Christianity in this sacred space.

My next stop was the **Al-Bzuriyya Market**, affectionately known as the Spice Market, situated in the heart of Damascus's enchanting Old City. Stepping into this bustling marketplace was like entering a vibrant tapestry of colors, scents, and sounds. The narrow alleys were teeming with life as merchants proudly displayed their wares. The air was filled with the intoxicating aroma of exotic spices, beckoning me to explore and experience the tantalizing flavors of Syrian cuisine. Amidst the vibrant array of spices, I discovered an abundance of dried fruits, nuts, local sweets, and traditional crafts, making the Al-Bzuriyya Market a sensory haven for culinary enthusiasts and avid shoppers alike.

Continuing my journey, I discovered the architectural masterpiece that is **Khan Asaad Pasha**. This splendid caravanserai, dating back to the 18th century, transported me back to a bygone era of bustling trade and cultural exchange along the Silk Road. The meticulously restored Khan now serves as a vibrant cultural center, where the echoes of the past, intertwine with contemporary creativity. As I wandered through its magnificent courtyard adorned with elegant arches and stone columns, I encountered captivating art exhibitions, lively craft workshops, and talented local artisans showcasing their traditional skills. Khan Asaad Pasha became a living testament to the rich heritage of Syrian craftsmanship and a place where tradition seamlessly blends with modern artistic expression.

No visit to Damascus would be complete without experiencing the grandeur of the **Umayyad Mosque**. This architectural marvel, situated at the heart of the city, stood as a testament to the long and storied history of Syria. The imposing entrance, known as Bab al-Barqiyya, greeted me with its intricate stone carvings and towering wooden doors, hinting at the splendor that awaited within. As I stepped into the vast courtyard, I was enveloped by a sense of tranquility and awe. The central dome, adorned with intricate detailing, soared above me, while smaller domes and minarets punctuated the skyline. Exploring the prayer halls, I marveled at the exquisite calligraphy, delicate tile work, and ornate mihrabs that adorned the sacred space. The Umayyad Mosque also housed the shrine of John the Baptist, a revered figure in both Islamic and Christian traditions, adding an additional layer of historical and cultural significance to this extraordinary site.

Immersing myself further into the charms of Damascus, I ventured to the Anbar Office, also known as **Beit al-**

Anbar. This beautifully restored house, nestled in the heart of the city's old quarter, showcased the opulent lifestyle of affluent Damascene families of the past. The Anbar Office mesmerized me with its stunning courtyards, adorned with intricate mosaics, exquisite wooden carvings, and vibrant tiles that painted a picture of grandeur. Roaming through its rooms, I encountered fascinating displays of traditional furniture, textiles, and artifacts, which offered a glimpse into the rich tapestry of Syrian craftsmanship. The Anbar Office was a living testament to the elegance and artistic prowess of Damascene architecture, transporting me back in time and allowing me to appreciate the magnificence of a bygone era.

Adjacent to the Anbar Office, I discovered a culinary gem that added to the excitement and joy of my journey—**the Great Damascene House**, transformed into **the Grandmother House Restaurant**. Stepping through its doors, my senses were immediately tantalized by the enticing aroma of spices and the promise of authentic Syrian cuisine. The restaurant's cozy ambiance and warm hospitality enveloped me as I settled into a seat. The menu offered a delightful array of traditional Syrian dishes, each prepared with care and bursting with flavor. From succulent kebabs to a colorful variety of mezzes, every bite was a journey into the heart of Syrian culinary tradition. The Grandmother House Restaurant not only satisfied my cravings but also offered a genuine connection to the local culture, as the staff treated me like an honored guest, ensuring that my dining experience was truly unforgettable.

Continuing my exploration of Damascus, I encountered **the Al-Azem Palace**, an architectural masterpiece that exemplified the grandeur of the Ottoman era. This opulent residence was once the cherished home of the Al-Azem family, renowned nobles of Damascus. As I ventured through its ornate corridors and picturesque courtyards, I marveled at the intricate woodwork, adorned ceilings, and walls adorned with colorful frescoes and marble accents. Each room revealed a different aspect of the lavish lifestyle enjoyed by the elite, transporting me to a bygone era of aristocratic elegance. Additionally, the palace's museum provided a captivating insight into the cultural heritage of Damascus, with exhibits showcasing artifacts that illuminated the city's rich history and traditions. Exploring the Al-Azem Palace was like stepping into a living time capsule, where the legacy of Damascene nobility unfolded before my eyes.

My final stop was a visit to **the National Museum**, a treasure trove of archaeological wonders spanning millennia. The museum's halls held a mesmerizing collection of artifacts, each one telling a story of ancient civilizations that once thrived in the region. From prehistoric relics to Roman artifacts, Byzantine treasures, and Islamic masterpieces, the exhibits showcased the diverse and storied past of Syria. Furthermore, Syrian sculptures captured the beauty and grace of bygone eras, intricate jewelry dazzled with its craftsmanship, and well-preserved mosaics depicted scenes of daily life in astonishing detail. Ancient manuscripts whispered tales of wisdom and knowledge passed down through the ages. The National Museum offered a captivating journey through time, allowing me to grasp the depth and richness of Syria's archaeological heritage.

Every step of my Damascus adventure filled my heart with excitement and joy. All five senses were peaked when savoring authentic Syrian cuisine at the Grandmother House Restaurant. Time seemed to stop when exploring the opulence of the Al-Azem Palace and immersing myself in the archaeological wonders of the National Museum, I felt a profound connection to the vibrant culture and storied history of this remarkable city. The experiences were not just about visiting sites, but about discovering the essence of Damascus—a place where tradition, hospitality, and the beauty of the past merge seamlessly, creating memories that will forever remain etched in my heart.

As I stood on the precipice of completing a lifetime dream, emotions swirled within me, like a kaleidoscope of colors and profound feelings. I had accomplished something that very few people ever get the chance to do, **I had visited every known country on earth**. The intensity of pride mingled with gratitude, and an overwhelming sense of awe and wonder wrapped me in its embrace. I had become a citizen of the world, forever enriched by the diverse perspectives, the shared joys, and the collective wisdom that only travel can provide, and forever grateful for the extraordinary journey that had reshaped my very essence.

In the end, the emotional intensity and profound pride that welled up within me as I completed this remarkable endeavor, were an affirmation of the limitless capacity of the human spirit. Curiosity, resilience, and an insatiable desire to connect with the world had propelled me forward, breaking down barriers and opening my heart to the wonders that awaited. The journey had ignited a sense of purpose, a flame of appreciation for the extraordinary mosaic of our planet, and a responsibility to nurture and protect it for generations to come.

> "WE TRAVEL NOT TO ESCAPE LIFE, BUT FOR LIFE NOT TO ESCAPE US."
> - Anonymous

I HAD VISITED EVERY COUNTRY ON EARTH

Bomb scars left behind by the war

=="THE WORLD IS A BOOK AND THOSE WHO DO NOT TRAVEL READ ONLY ONE PAGE."==
- Saint Augustine

TÜRKIYE

Türkiye is one of my favorite places to visit, and it truly has it all! From the warmth of the locals to its incredible natural attractions, UNESCO World Heritage archaeological sites, rich history and culture, stunning beaches, and uniquely delicious cuisine, this is a destination that cannot be missed.

My trip to Türkiye was an extraordinary experience that encompassed the country's rich history, stunning natural landscapes, vibrant culture, and warm hospitality. Situated at the meeting point of Europe and Asia, this transcontinental nation offered a fascinating fusion of Eastern and Western influences. Embarking on this immersive journey allowed me to delve into the diverse facets of Türkiye. With a history spanning thousands of years, Türkiye stood as a land where ancient civilizations had left an indelible mark, and their legacies could be witnessed through remarkable ruins, breathtaking architecture, and enduring cultural traditions.

During my visit, I explored various cities in Türkiye, including Istanbul, Cappadocia, Ephesus, Pamukkale, and Antalya.
Istanbul, the enchanting city that straddles Europe and Asia, proved to be a captivating blend of history, culture, and modernity. It was a place where ancient wonders coexisted harmoniously with contemporary marvels. My stay in "Sultanahmet", the historic heart of the city, provided easy access to iconic landmarks. One of the highlights was the awe-inspiring **Hagia Sophia**, a Byzantine architectural masterpiece. Stepping inside this majestic structure, I was instantly transported back in time, marveling at its grand domes, intricate mosaics, and the ethereal play of light filtering through stained glass windows. Many of the original religious icons were painted over when Hagia Sophia transitioned to an Islamic Mosque. Amazingly, this actually helped preserve these artistic marvels to be enjoyed today saving them for the ages.

Another architectural gem and a must see is the nearby, **Blue Mosque;** an exquisite example of Ottoman design. Its stunning domes, slender minarets, and intricate blue Iznik tiles created a serene and peaceful atmosphere. Immersing myself in the bustling ambiance of the **Grand Bazaar**, one of the world's oldest and largest covered markets, was a sensory delight. Wandering through its labyrinthine alleys, I discovered a treasure trove of goods, from traditional carpets and kilims to intricately crafted ceramics, spices, and jewelry. The vibrant colors, aromatic scents, and the melodic cadence of merchants beckoning me to explore their wares added to the enchantment.

Taking a cruise along the **Bosphorus Strait**, the waterway that separates Europe and Asia, offered a breathtaking perspective of Istanbul's skyline. Majestic palaces, Ottoman-era mansions, and picturesque waterfront neighborhoods adorned the shores. Passing under the iconic Bosphorus Bridge, I marveled at the shimmering waterway dotted with fishing boats, cargo ships, and elegant yachts. Another notable stop was the **Topkapi Palace**, once the residence of Ottoman sultans. Its opulent halls, landscaped gardens, and serene courtyards provided glimpses into the empire's imperial past. Exploring the palace's museum allowed me to witness dazzling treasures, including the renowned Topkapi Dagger and the Spoonmaker's Diamond. Additionally, I ventured into the Harem section, a labyrinth of chambers that offered insight into the secluded lives of the sultans and their concubines.

A "once in a lifetime" highlight of my Turkish adventure was riding a **hot air balloon in Cappadocia**. It was an unparalleled experience that transported me to a world of wonder and enchantment. As the first rays of sunlight bathed the extraordinary landscape, a sense of awe and excitement welled up within me. The adventure began in the early hours of the morning as I made my way to the launch site. The crisp air and the atmosphere filled with anticipation added to the thrill. Upon arrival, I witnessed the bustling activity of the balloon crew preparing the magnificent balloons for flight. The sight of colorful fabric inflating and the roar of burners igniting sparked a surge of excitement.

Stepping into the wicker basket, I experienced a mix of nerves and exhilaration. The pilot provided a brief safety briefing, and as the last connections were secured, the balloon began its gentle ascent. A feeling of weightlessness enveloped me as we rose higher, leaving the ground behind. The extraordinary landscape of Cappadocia unfolded beneath me like a surreal painting. The unique rock formations, known as fairy chimneys, majestically rose from the earth, showcasing intricate shapes and vibrant hues. Carved by centuries of volcanic activity and erosion, these ancient geological formations created a landscape unlike anything on earth I had ever seen before.

The thrill intensified as the sun made its appearance on the horizon. The soft golden light illuminated the valleys, casting long shadows and accentuating the intricate details of the rock formations. The landscape seemed to come alive, bathed in a warm and ethereal glow. The beauty combined with the serene silence of the early morning created a truly magical ambiance. As the hot air balloon glided effortlessly through the sky, I was captivated by the ever-changing vistas. The pilot skillfully maneuvered, guiding us through valleys, over vineyards, and above quaint villages that dotted the Cappadocian countryside. Each turn revealed a new perspective, a fresh angle to admire the breathtaking beauty surrounding us. The tranquility of the experience was mesmerizing, allowing me to fully immerse myself in the moment. Apart from the occasional blast of the burner, silence prevailed, enabling deep reflection and appreciation for the natural world.

As the hot air balloon began its descent, a wave of gratitude washed over me. I felt grateful for the privilege of witnessing such natural splendor, for the skilled pilot who guided our journey, and for the opportunity to create lasting memories. Touching down gently on the ground, I stepped out of the basket with my heart still racing from the adventure. The memories of riding a hot air balloon in Cappadocia lingered long after the ride itself. The incredible sunrise, the surreal chimney rocks, the breathtaking landscapes, and the exhilarating sense of adventure combined to form an unforgettable experience. It was a moment that stayed with me, forever etched in my mind and heart, serving as a reminder of the boundless beauty of the world and the capacity for joy and wonder within me.

My next visit was to the historical port city of **Ephesus**, Türkiye was an enchanting journey that transported me back in time, allowing me to witness the grandeur of an ancient civilization. Ephesus holds immense historical significance and is mentioned many times in the Bible, and its archaeological remains provided a captivating window into the cultural, social, and architectural achievements of the past. Established as an Ionian Greek settlement around the 10th century BC, Ephesus flourished over the centuries, becoming a prominent city and a thriving center of trade and commerce.
The ancient cityscape of Ephesus was adorned with magnificent structures and monuments that showcased the power and opulence of its rulers. Among these, the Library of Celsus stood out as an iconic symbol. Built in the 2nd century AD and dedicated to the Roman senator Tiberius Julius Celsus Polemaeanus, the library housed an extensive collection of books and scrolls. Its imposing facade, adorned with statues and intricate reliefs, served as a testament to the city's intellectual and cultural achievements.

Adjacent to the library, I explored the Agora, a vibrant marketplace where merchants from across the Mediterranean would gather to trade their goods. Walking through the ancient streets, remnants of commercial buildings, shops, and bustling stalls reminded me of the vibrant atmosphere that once filled this place. The Agora not only served as a hub for commerce but also as a center for social and political gatherings, fostering discussions, debates, and the exchange of ideas. Another remarkable structure was the Theater of Ephesus, an immense amphitheater capable of seating over 25,000 spectators. As I stood amidst its grandeur, I could almost hear the echoes of past performances, envisioning the lively plays, music concerts, and gladiatorial contests that once captivated the audience.

The religious significance of Ephesus added another layer of intrigue to my visit. The city was home to the Temple of Artemis, one of the Seven Wonders of the Ancient World. Although only fragments remain today, the temple was a revered place dedicated to the Greek goddess of the hunt, Artemis. Pilgrims from far and wide would journey to Ephesus to pay their respects and seek the blessings of the deity. Additionally, Ephesus played a crucial role in early Christianity, with the apostle Paul believed to have spent time there. The ruins include several early Christian basilicas, such as the Basilica of St. John, which stands on the traditional site of his tomb.

Venturing to **Pamukkale** was a truly awe-inspiring experience that introduced me to a natural wonder unlike anything I had ever seen. Situated in southwestern Türkiye, Pamukkale was a testament to the power and artistry of nature, leaving me utterly amazed. As I approached, the sight of dazzling white terraces cascading down the hillside greeted me. These terraces, formed by mineral-rich deposits of travertine, resembled a frozen waterfall or a cotton castle, giving rise to the name "Pamukkale," meaning "cotton castle" in Turkish. The surreal appearance of the terraces, with their glistening white and turquoise hues, defied belief.
Stepping onto the terraces, I felt as if I were walking on clouds. The travertine terraces were the result of warm, mineral-rich water flowing from thermal springs that emerged from the ground. Over time, the water deposited calcium carbonate, creating the stunning white terraces that stretched before me. Beyond their visual splendor, the mineral-rich water was believed to possess healing properties, adding to the allure of Pamukkale.

One of the highlights of my visit was exploring the ancient city of Hierapolis, situated atop the terraces. This UNESCO World Heritage Site showcased well-preserved ruins and archaeological treasures, providing a fascinating glimpse into the past. I wandered through the ancient theater, imagining the performances that once captivated audiences, and I could almost hear the echoes of applause that once reverberated through the air.
Both Ephesus and Pamukkale left an indelible impression on me, deepening my appreciation for the wonders of history and nature. The journey through the ancient ruins and magnificent landscapes sparked a sense of wonder and curiosity within me, reminding me of the rich tapestry of human civilization and the enduring beauty of the natural world.

My next visit to **Antalya** was nothing short of a dream come true. Nestled on the picturesque Turkish Riviera, this coastal city enchanted me with its harmonious blend of history, natural splendor, and vibrant culture. From the breathtaking beaches to the ancient ruins, and the captivating old town to the bustling markets, Antalya offered an array of experiences that left me in awe.

As I stepped into the old town of Kaleiçi, I felt like I had entered a time capsule. Wandering through its narrow, winding streets, the echoes of history reverberated through the ancient walls. The exquisite Ottoman architecture adorned with intricately carved wooden balconies and vibrant facades caught my eye at every turn. I couldn't resist pausing by the Yivli Minaret, an iconic symbol of Antalya, marveling at its unique Seljuk design. Discovering Türkiye's hidden historical and cultural gems was a delightful surprise, whether stumbling upon secluded courtyards adorned with blooming bougainvillea or finding cozy cafes where I could savor a cup of traditional Turkish tea.

One of the highlights of my extended stay in Antalya was embarking on a boat tour along the mesmerizing coastline. Sailing across the azure waters, I was treated to awe-inspiring views of rugged cliffs, hidden coves, and pristine beaches. A stop at the Blue Cave was a moment of sheer magic, as the sunlight filtering through the water created an ethereal blue glow, casting a spell of tranquility upon the surroundings.

Turkish cuisine, renowned for its diverse flavors and culinary traditions, became a culinary adventure in itself. Influenced by the Mediterranean, Middle Eastern, Central Asian, and Balkan regions, Turkish dishes tantalize the taste buds with a harmonious balance of spices, fresh ingredients, and time-honored cooking techniques.
One particular culinary delight that captured my heart and palate was the mouthwatering **Testi Kebab**. This traditional Turkish dish not only offered an explosion of flavors but also a mesmerizing flame presentation that added a touch of theater to the dining experience. The preparation of Testi Kebab began by marinating tender chunks of meat, such as lamb, chicken, or fish, in a blend of spices, yogurt, and olive oil. The meat soaked up the flavors, tenderizing and infusing it with a rich taste. Meanwhile, a medley of fresh vegetables like tomatoes, onions, and peppers was prepared to accompany the succulent meat.
 The real spectacle unfolded during the cooking process. The marinated meat and vegetables were carefully placed inside a clay pot, which was then hermetically sealed with dough. This seal ensured that the flavors intensified as the dish cooked. With a flourish, the server brought the sealed clay pot to the table and set it ablaze, creating a mesmerizing display of dancing flames. The heat from the fire gradually cooked the Testi Kebab, allowing the aromatic spices and trapped juices to infuse the dish with a depth of flavor. The sizzling sound and tantalizing aroma that filled the air heightened my senses, making the dining experience all the more enticing. Each bite of the Testi Kebab was a journey of taste, showcasing the meticulous craftsmanship and culinary artistry of Türkiye. The flame presentation of Testi Kebab added an element of spectacle to the dining experience, transforming it into an event to be savored and remembered. It ignited a sense of wonder and excitement, creating lasting memories of a meal that went beyond mere sustenance.

Overall, my visit to Türkiye was an enchanting journey that transported me through time, culture, and natural splendor. From the ancient wonders of Istanbul to the mystical landscapes of Cappadocia, and the breathtaking beauty of its coastal regions, Türkiye offered a rich tapestry of experiences. I allowed myself to be captivated by historical sites, indulged in delectable cuisine, and embraced the warmth of Turkish hospitality. A trip to Türkiye was an adventure of a lifetime, leaving me with cherished memories and a deep appreciation for the extraordinary wonders this country has to offer.

Hagia Sophia

The Blue Mosque

Testi Kebab

Grand Bazaar

Pamukkale

Cappadocia

Mesmerizing Cappadocia

Ephesus

AFRICA CONTINENT: 54 COUNTRIES

Flag	Country	Flag	Country	Flag	Country
	Algeria		Eswatini		Namibia
	Angola		Ethiopia		Niger
	Benin		Gabon		Nigeria
	Botswana		The Gambia		Rwanda
	Burkina Faso		Ghana		Sao Tome & Principe
	Burundi		Guinea		Senegal
	Cabo Verde		Guinea Bissau		The Seychelles
	Cameroon		Kenya		Sierra Leone
	Central Africa		Lesotho		Somalia
	Chad		Liberia		South Africa
	Comoros		Libya		South Sudan
	D.R. of the Congo		Madagascar		Sudan
	Republic of the Congo		Malawi		Tanzania
	Cote d'Ivoire		Mali		Togo
	Djibouti		Mauritania		Tunisia
	Egypt		Mauritius		Uganda
	Equatorial Guinea		Morocco		Zambia
	Eritrea		Mozambique		Zimbabwe

AFRICA CONTINENT

The African continent holds a unique place in human history. It is widely believed to be the "cradle of humankind" with the dawn of life brimming between the Tigris and Euphrates rivers and expanding onward. It is here where we find the first evidence of Homo Sapiens and their ancestors and the legacy, they left for all of us. Besides being the birthplace of our species, it is an epic landscape stuffed with wildlife and biodiversity not found anywhere else on earth

The African continent, is a land brimming with endless possibilities and untamed beauty. This mysterious land, calls out to intrepid souls, inviting them to embark on a journey that promises to set their senses ablaze, ignite their spirits, and fill their hearts with an exhilarating rush of joy and excitement. After Asia, Africa is the second largest and second most populated continent on Earth. Africa is home to deserts, tropical rain forests, rugged mountains and fertile grasslands. From the vast, sweeping savannahs to the crystalline waters of coastal paradises, Africa unfolds before you as a realm of enchantment, offering an intoxicating blend of adventure, nature's wonders, and unadulterated delight. As you dive headlong into this unparalleled tapestry of experiences, hold on tight and get ready for the adventure of a lifetime.

The very name "Africa" traces its roots back to the ancient Romans, who used it to describe the lands that now correspond to modern-day Tunisia. "Africa" derives from the Latin word "Africus," which translates to "sunny" or "hot." Originally, it referred to the sun-soaked, arid regions of North Africa, but it eventually expanded its embrace to encompass the entire continent.

As your feet touch the soil of this vast and welcoming continent, you'll be embraced by the warmth of its people, custodians of rich cultural traditions. Africa tantalizes your senses with extraordinary delights, beckoning your taste buds, your ears, your very soul. To truly savor its richness, immerse yourself in its unique music, lose yourself in its mesmerizing dances, and gaze upon its stunning art. The local cuisine, with its diverse array of spices and flavors, is a gastronomic adventure that will tantalize every palate. Let's now plunge headfirst into **whirlwind destinations of the most exciting and joy-filled experiences that Africa has to offer**, etching memories that will forever sear your soul. Our journey kicks off in the captivating and sensory wonderland of North Africa, with Morocco leading the way.

Marrakech, Morocco, is an explosion of sights, sounds, and sensations that will catapult you into a world where every step surges with a unique cocktail of excitement and pure joy. The bustling streets, like a vivid, living tapestry, beckon you to lose yourself in their vibrant markets, known as "souks." The air is alive with the intoxicating aroma of spices that will carry you away on a gust of wonder. Marrakech, with its intricate architecture and mosaic-adorned gates, feels like a city plucked from the pages of a Middle Ages tale. The labyrinthine, bustling alleyways create an atmosphere of enchantment and wonder. If you're a connoisseur of the art of haggling, Marrakech is your playground. Here, you can barter for silver tea sets or marvel at the intricate Moroccan craftsmanship while sipping on cardamom and mint tea in serene courtyards. Marrakech transports you not only to another era but also to a realm of delight that's as infectious as it is unforgettable.

Our next stop is the iconic and fascinating country of **Egypt**, a land where history and grandeur converge, a land that dates back to more than 3500 B.C. It is a land bustling with a population over 105 million people and a literacy rate of over 73 percent. Egypt is also famous for being the home of one of the World's largest dams. The Aswan Dam spans across the Nile river separating Egypt from Sudan and creating Lake Nassar. The capital city of Cairo may initially overwhelm with its hustle and bustle, but brace yourself as Cairo is famous for its places, food, culture and activities and for the famous Pyramids of Giza. Also, imagine wealthy and powerful kings and queens, lost fortunes, endless piles of gold and mystical gods immersed in underground burial chambers and you are finally ready to see these magnificent structures that have withstood the trial and tribulations of time.

The Pyramids of Giza, Egypt, stand as one of the most renowned ancient wonders of the world. A visit to these colossal structures is a plunge into the depths of history and culture. You can also pay homage to the enigmatic Sphinx and indulge in a camelback adventure through the desert. If time allows, stay until the evening for a mesmerizing laser light show. And don't dare to miss the new Egyptian museum, situated majestically on the banks of the Nile River.

We must now leave the mysterious desert and travel southward to the teeming jungles, unique landscapes and magnificent water falls down the Zambezi River to some of the most impressive national parks and animal reserves that only southern Africa can offer. We are not venturing southward through this sprawling continent to Zimbabwe, to the home of some of the world's most incredible natural wonders and wildlife to visit one of the seven natural wonders of the world and one of Earth's most awe-inspiring sites, the majestic and breathtaking Victoria falls!

Victoria Falls, straddling Zambia and Zimbabwe, is a sensory extravaganza like no other. Standing on the precipice of these cascading waters transports you to a realm of pure natural grandeur. The roar of the falls, the enveloping mist, and the kaleidoscope of rainbows dancing in the spray combine to create an immersive sensory overload of sheer awe. If you really want to feel the rush of the waterfalls sign up for a helicopter ride over the falls for a bird's-eye view that rivals the most exhilarating adventures, with the breathtaking vista of this natural wonder as your backdrop. Victoria Falls will not only humble you with its power and beauty but also invigorate you with an infectious sense of joy. Lake Kariba, at the foot of the falls is the largest man-made lake by volume and is a great place to go bungee jumping for those adventurous types. Now, brace yourself for an adventure that will change your life: a visit to the ancient Maasai people in Kenya.

Maasai Mara, Kenya, stands as a testament to the raw power and majesty of the natural world. Witnessing the Great Migration, an epic spectacle of wildebeests and zebras traversing the savannah in search of greener pastures, will set your heart racing with excitement. The sight of predators and prey engaged in a delicate dance of survival will fill you with wonder beyond words. Spotting the iconic "Big Five" animals – lions, elephants, buffalos, leopards, and rhinoceroses – against the backdrop of the Mara's expansive landscape will etch memories of exhilaration into your very soul. Virtually next door lies Tanzania and its crown jewel, Serengeti National Park. Wildlife, beautiful beaches, friendly people, fascinating cultures and Mount Kilimanjaro all make Tanzania a must stop on your way south in Africa. With the highest peak in Mount Kilimanjaro and the lowest floor in Lake Tanganyika, Tanzania has it all. Let's take a look at its most famous wildlife and eco-tourist park.

Serengeti National Park, Tanzania, is a symphony of nature's artistry and unparalleled beauty. Here, you'll have an unparalleled opportunity to witness wildlife in its untamed habitat. The heart-pounding excitement of a safari, with every turn revealing new creatures engaged in the circle of life, will fill you with a profound connection to the natural world. As the sun sets over the savannah, dining under the starlit sky amidst the sounds of the wild will amplify the enchantment of your experience. The Serengeti is a sanctuary of joy for both animal enthusiasts and those seeking a deep connection with nature. Staying in lush, scenic Tanzania, we venture into the Ngorongoro Crater.

Descending into the **Ngorongoro Crater** is like stepping into a realm where nature's wonders converge. The sheer diversity of wildlife, from majestic lions to graceful gazelles, creates an atmosphere of excitement and discovery. Each sighting becomes a source of pure joy, and the realization of being surrounded by a microcosm of life reignites a sense of awe that is both humbling and invigorating. Another astounding destination awaits us – Botswana.

In Botswana's **Okavango Delta**, glide through waterways in a traditional "mokoro" canoe and discover a paradise of tranquility and biodiversity. The joy of silently traversing the water while encountering a symphony of life – from graceful giraffes wading through marshes to playful hippos cavorting in the water – is a testament to the Delta's unique allure. Every moment spent in this pristine wetland ecosystem evokes a sense of wonder and appreciation for the delicate balance of nature. Now, let's venture off the beaten path to marvelous Mozambique!

The Bazaruto Archipelago in **Mozambique** is a realm beneath the azure waters that beckons with vibrant coral reefs and exotic marine life. Snorkeling alongside dolphins and swimming with whale sharks will awaken a sense of childlike wonder and exhilaration within you. The archipelago's idyllic beaches and welcoming locals add layers of joy to your journey, from leisurely beach strolls to lively interactions with the island's inhabitants. And now, it's time for one of my personal favorites, Cape Town, South Africa.

Cape Town, South Africa is located in most southwestern tip of this great continent, here you will find dramatic scenery as endless ocean views and stunning, world-class beaches abound in Cape Town. Take some time to visit "Camps Bay near the city center and through some of the most stunning natural landscapes that mother earth has to offer. Talking about beaches, "Boulder's beach is home to our favorite waddling friends, the endangered African penguins. Cape Town is no doubt the undisputed culinary capital of South Africa and has some of the best seafood anywhere on earth. Cape Town is a vibrant city teeming with culture and history. Ascend the iconic Table Mountain for breathtaking views of the city and the ocean. Take a leisurely stroll through the colorful Bo-Kaap neighborhood, known for its brilliantly hued houses and rich history. Immerse yourself in South Africa's history by visiting Robben Island, where Nelson Mandela was imprisoned for 18 years during the apartheid era. And, of course, don't miss the opportunity to savor the local wines from Stellenbosch and nearby regions – some of the finest wines in the world. Then, crown your African adventure with a visit to the tranquil and mesmerizing beaches of the Seychelles.

The pristine beaches of the **Seychelles** beckon travelers to bask in the sheer joy of relaxation and rejuvenation. Plunging into the crystal-clear waters, swimming alongside gentle sea turtles, and exploring vibrant coral reefs become a dance of bliss and a profound connection with the natural world. Each moment spent on these shores is a testament to the harmonious relationship between humans and nature, a source of endless joy and contentment.

THE BEST TIME TO VISIT AFRICA CONTINENT

Exploring Africa is a journey through a continent of incredible diversity, where the best times to visit are as varied as the landscapes themselves. Here, we delve into each season and reveal more must-see destinations.

Spring (March - May): As the days grow longer and warmer, Southern Africa invites travelers to experience its natural and cultural wonders. In South Africa, Cape Town's Mediterranean climate is at its most inviting during these months. Explore the city's iconic Table Mountain, visit the historic Robben Island, and unwind on the stunning beaches of Clifton and Camps Bay. Further north, the majestic Victoria Falls straddling Zimbabwe and Zambia is a breathtaking sight to behold during the wet season. The falls are at their most impressive in

April, with cascades of water plunging into the Zambezi River, creating a mesmerizing spectacle.

Summer (June - August): The East African savannahs come alive in the summer, and the Serengeti-Maasai Mara ecosystem is a top draw. Witness the Great Migration as millions of wildebeests and zebras make their perilous journey across the plains, creating an awe-inspiring spectacle of nature. Venture to the exotic island of Madagascar, which is often less crowded during the summer months. Explore the Avenue of the Baobabs, go trekking in Andringitra National Park, and discover unique wildlife, such as the elusive lemurs.

Fall (September - November): As the days grow shorter, Southern Africa shines once again. Botswana's Okavango Delta, a UNESCO World Heritage site, is in its prime during the dry season. Glide through the pristine waterways in mokoros and embark on game drives to encounter a wealth of wildlife, including elephants, lions, and hippos. Consider a journey to the ancient city of Marrakech, Morocco, in the fall. The bustling souks, historic palaces, and lush gardens are best explored under the warm but not scorching temperatures of the season.

Winter (December - February): While much of the Northern Hemisphere experiences winter, the Indian Ocean islands of Seychelles and Mauritius are basking in their tropical glory. With idyllic beaches, luxury resorts, and vibrant coral reefs, these islands offer the ultimate winter escape. For a unique winter adventure, head to the Sahara Desert in Morocco. The days are pleasantly cool, making it an ideal time for camel treks over the undulating sand dunes. Spend nights under the starry desert sky in traditional Berber camps, immersing yourself in the magic of the desert. In South Africa's Kruger National Park, the dry and mild winter creates excellent conditions for wildlife viewing. Embark on game drives to spot the Big Five and soak in the beauty of the African bushveld.

These are just a few of the many incredible destinations that Africa has to offer throughout the year. Each season presents its own set of experiences and opportunities, ensuring that there's always something exciting to discover on this vast and captivating continent. Whether you're drawn to the thrill of a safari, the allure of ancient cultures, or the tranquility of tropical beaches, Africa has it all. Think of it, Africa has all the big things in nature. It has the largest desert in the World, the Sahara Desert, it has the longest river in the World, the Nile River, it has the highest free-standing mountain in the World and one of the seven summits-Mount Kilimanjaro. It also has the largest living land animal, the African elephant and the World's largest wildlife migration on Earth and it occurs in Tanzania has I had mentioned before. I hope this gets you excited to start your African adventure tour.

The unique adventures, experiences and photographs in the following pages encapsulate the exhilarating odyssey that was my exploration of the mesmerizing continent of Africa. Every moment, every encounter, every vibrant scene etched in my memory has infused my life with an electrifying surge of experiences and boundless joy. My enthusiasm knows no bounds as I recount the sheer magnificence of the places I traversed and the incredible souls I crossed paths with. I am overflowing with gratitude for the privilege of embarking on this awe-inspiring journey across the astonishing tapestry of Africa. I hope I was able to convey some of the excitement and joy that my adventures have done to transform me and change my view of the amazing world around us.   We are living in a remarkable time and I wish that I can inspire you to see the beauty that is all around you.

Sunset in MASAI MARA

KENYA: THE GREAT MIGRATION

Kenya is known as the world's best safari location with 50 epic national parks and reserves that are home to extremely diverse wildlife and some of the finest scenery in East Africa. There is also Malindi Marine National Park which host rich aquatic lagoons, reefs and coral gardens. Kenya not only has stirring landscapes, wildlife laden plains and an epic natural playground, it simply has too many exciting things to do. A once in a life time experience is observing the "Great Migration", guaranteed to blow your mind.

The Great Migration is a truly incredible natural spectacle. The sheer scale of the spectacle and the raw power of nature on display is awe-inspiring, and it's hard not to feel a sense of joy and excitement when witnessing this incredible event. The Great Migration is an event that occurs annually in the Masai Mara, and it is undoubtedly one of the most spectacular natural events that one can ever witness. The migration is a cyclical journey made by millions of wildebeest, zebras, and gazelles as they travel from the Serengeti in Tanzania to the Masai Mara in Kenya in search of water and pasture. This epic journey spans a distance of over 1,800 miles (2,896 Km) and is an astonishing display of instinct and survival that has been going on for centuries. In addition to the incredible wildlife, Kenya also boasts a rich cultural heritage, with dozens of indigenous communities such as the Maasai living in harmony with the land and preserving their traditions for generations.

My journey to Kenya to witness the Great Migration was truly unforgettable. We started our adventure by driving to **Masai Mara**, a national reserve that is famous for its vast herds of wildlife and stunning landscapes. The road to Masai Mara was rough, with bumpy dirt tracks and rocky terrain, but the journey was worth it. Our campsite was an ecotourist site with all nature-based forms of tourism that allows for tourists to observe and appreciate nature as well as traditional cultures. Mayetta camp, was surprisingly a nice campsite, with each tent having its own housing roof and a concrete slab foundation. The tents were quite spacious, with three beds and their own private bathrooms, complete with hot water and electricity that was on twice a day. The dining hall had a breathtaking view of the mountains, and the camp was just a five-minute drive from Masai Mara National Park.

We embarked on a game drive on our first afternoon in Masai Mara after 4 p.m. The heat of the day had subsided, and the animals were more active. We saw zebras, lions, giraffes, and even witnessed a lion kill a zebra. Seeing a leopard was rare, but we were lucky enough to spot one on this game drive. Witnessing the Great Migration in person is an experience like no other. The wildebeest, with their shaggy manes and distinctive horns, moved in large, tight-knit herds, and their collective power and energy were incredible to witness. The zebras, with their black and white stripes, stand out against the golden grass, their playful antics and distinctive braying calls adding to the joy of the experience. At night, while laid in bed, we were serenaded with the beautiful sounds of nature that lured us to sleep.

The next morning, our adventure began with **an early morning game ride**. As we set out into the cool, fresh air, we were met with the stunning beauty of the Masai Mara. Animals of all shapes and sizes roamed the plains, and it was a breathtaking sight to behold. As we rode through the savannah, I couldn't help but feel a sense of exhilaration. The primal urge driving the animals to migrate in search of food and water was palpable, and the sound of their hooves thundering across the ground echoed through the air. As I stood on the vast plains of Masai Mara, I could see thousands upon thousands of animals moving in unison. The sound of their hooves pounding the ground creates a thundering symphony that echoes across the savannah, while the dust they kick up hangs in the air like a mist, creating an otherworldly atmosphere. As we continued on our ride, we stumbled upon a group of around 200 zebras, one of my favorite animals. The zebras' distinctive black and white stripes stood out against the golden grass, and their playful antics and braying calls added to the joy of the experience.

After our morning game drive, we had the opportunity to visit **the Masai Village**, where we learned about the culture and way of life of the Maasai people. The Maasai are a semi-nomadic ethnic group that has inhabited parts of Kenya and Tanzania for centuries. Their culture has been shaped by tradition, and their way of life is deeply connected to the land and natural environment. Their traditional dress, which consists of brightly colored shukas, is symbolic and represents various aspects such as age, marital status, and social standing. They are also known for their beaded jewelry, which is often worn as a sign of wealth and status. The Maasai people are a pastoralist society, and they have traditionally relied on their herds of cattle, sheep, and goats for their livelihood. They move with their animals in search of water and pasture, and their way of life is closely tied to the rhythms of the natural environment. The Maasai are also known for their jumping dance, which is a display of strength and agility that is performed during ceremonies and celebrations.

In the afternoon, we went on another game drive and witnessed more incredible wildlife, including giraffes, elephants, lions, and even a black rhino. The migration is a treacherous journey for these animals, and they face many dangers along the way. Crossing rivers is particularly perilous, with crocodiles waiting in the waters for their next meal, and predators like lions, leopards, and cheetahs lying in wait. Despite the dangers, watching the Great Migration unfold in person is a deeply exhilarating experience and one that you will remember for the rest of your life. The sight of so many animals moving in unison is awe-inspiring, and the sounds they make as they move through the savannah add to the sensory experience.

One of the most incredible aspects of the Great Migration is the way it underscores the interconnectedness of all living things. The wildebeest, zebras, and gazelles are not only moving in search of food and water, but they also play a vital role in the ecosystem. As they move through the savannah, they fertilize the soil with their droppings, supporting the growth of new grass. They also provide food for predators like lions and hyenas, which are themselves crucial to maintaining a healthy ecosystem. In witnessing the Great Migration, we gain a deeper appreciation for the intricate web of life that exists in the natural world. As the sun began to set, our group made our way back to the campsite after a thrilling day spent exploring the natural wonders of a vast national park. We sat around the fire pit outside the dining hall, enjoying the company of good friends and reflecting on the incredible experiences we had shared. The peaceful evening atmosphere combined with the excitement of the day made for a perfect ending to a perfect day.

The following day, we embarked on a long-distance drive to a massive national park spanning over 1510 square kilometers. Our journey was filled with excitement as we witnessed the majesty of various animals such as zebras, wildebeests, giraffes, and several lions feasting on a freshly killed zebra. The sound of bones being chewed by the lions was a spine-tingling reminder of the circle of life. We were fortunate enough to spot a big black rhino in the open savannah, which was a rare sight to see. The constantly changing landscape of open savannah, palm trees, and bushes provided breathtaking views at every turn.

We drove to a hillside to witness the incredible sight of millions of wildebeests migrating in search of food and water. Along the migration routes, we watched as baby wildebeests were born, taking their first steps and joining their parents on their journey. This was a touching reminder of the beauty and wonder of nature. Then we drove to the riverside, where we saw wildebeests, hippos, and crocodiles waiting for a chance to cross the river. Although they didn't cross, it was still an amazing sight to see these majestic creatures in their natural habitat. We stopped under a big tree for some shade and enjoyed a relaxing picnic lunch, sipping on wine and savoring the peaceful atmosphere. After lunch, we continued our game drive and were thrilled to encounter many other animals, including giraffes, elephants, wildebeest, zebra, lions, and leopards. Being so close to these magnificent creatures was an unforgettable experience.

The Great Migration is a celebration of life and the beauty of nature, and there is something deeply satisfying about witnessing such a grand and magnificent spectacle. It's a reminder that despite all the chaos and uncertainty in the world, there is still wonder and magic to be found in the natural world. Witnessing the Great Migration is a humbling and unforgettable experience that reminds us of the beauty and power of the natural world. It's a reminder that despite all of our technology and modern conveniences, we are still just a small part of a much larger and more complex system. This grand celebration of life and the magic of nature is the experience I will never forget.

Kenya is a country of great diversity, both physically, culturally, and environmentally. Kenya has it all, blissful Indian Ocean, beaches, craggy, deep mountains, wildlife-rich savannahs, fascinating culture, all beckoning the visitor to come, taste and see! Let your hair down and walk on the wild side and visit unforgettable Kenya.

WITNESSING
THE GREATEST SHOW ON EARTH

"TRAVEL FAR, TRAVEL WIDE, AND TRAVEL DEEP WITHIN YOURSELF."
-Unknown

Flamingoes at Lake Nakuru

Hippos swimming in the water

Giraffes

White Rhinoceros

Lilac Breasted Roller Bird

Zebras

The Masai Chief

The Masai People

The Masai Children

Black Rhinoceros

The Lion

The Lion made a kill

MADAGASCAR

Madagascar, situated off the coast of southeastern Africa in the Indian Ocean, stands as the world's fourth largest island. Its remarkable geographical location has fostered a diverse ecosystem teeming with unique flora and fauna found nowhere else on the planet. The island's isolation from mainland Africa, coupled with its diverse climate and topography, has given rise to an unparalleled biodiversity. Over the course of more than 80 million years of separation from the African continent, Madagascar has become a sanctuary for an extensive range of species.

The island boasts an impressive collection of lemurs and reptiles, housing over 300 species, including chameleons and geckos. Additionally, it is home to more than 200 species of amphibians, featuring vibrant frogs and toads. Furthermore, Madagascar is renowned for its rich avian population, comprising over 100 endemic species, such as the elusive Madagascar fish eagle.

Embarking on a journey to Madagascar was a once-in-a-lifetime experience that left me filled with awe and wonder. The island's abundance of plant and animal life, much of which is exclusive to this location, captivated my senses from the moment I set foot in **Antananarivo, the capital city**. Despite the chaotic traffic and challenging road conditions, the striking beauty of the landscape was impossible to ignore. Our path from Antananarivo Airport to **Andasibe National Park** led us through meandering roads that traversed mountains and valleys, treating us to breathtaking vistas at every turn. Finally arriving at Vakona Lodge, it felt as if I had stepped into a completely different world. Excitement filled the air as we settled in for the night, eagerly anticipating the adventures that awaited us.

Over the next few days, I had the privilege of visiting numerous national parks and nature reserves, each surpassing the previous one in terms of beauty and sheer grandeur. Andasibe National Park, a haven for lemur enthusiasts, stood out as one of the most remarkable locations. The park boasts 11 lemur species, which serve as its primary attraction. Within the lush rainforest of Andasibe National Park, we spent hours exploring and marveling at the exotic trees, vines, and orchids. The overwhelming biodiversity of the park left an indelible impression, and I felt incredibly fortunate to witness it firsthand. Lemurs, extraordinary primates found exclusively in Madagascar, revealed themselves in their natural habitat, each species adapted to a specific area within the park.

The Indri Indri, the park's largest and most renowned lemur species, captivated me with its black and white coloration and an impressive weight of up to 9.5 kilograms. Being arboreal creatures, the Indri Indris spend most of their time high up in the trees, using their unmistakable and haunting calls that resonate for several kilometers. I vividly recall hearing the distant echoes of their calls throughout the park, an otherworldly experience that intensified the sense of awe. Another popular lemur species found in Andasibe National Park is the "diademed sifaka". These lemurs possess a striking white fur coat and a distinctive black "crown" on their head. Renowned for their unique locomotion style known as vertical clinging and leaping, diademed sifakas can leap up to 10 meters in a single bound, utilizing their tails for balance. Additionally, the park is home to the black and white ruffed lemur, characterized by its thick fur coat and boisterous vocalizations. These social animals often gather in groups of up to 16 individuals. The grey bamboo lemur, named for its bamboo-based diet, also resides in the park, boasting a reddish-brown coat and exhibiting exceptional agility in the treetops. Our knowledgeable guide at Andasibe National Park possessed expertise in the park's lemur species. She skillfully spotted these lemurs and provided invaluable insights into their behavior, diet, and social habits.

The following day, our expedition took us to **Lemur Island**, a place that completely mesmerized me. Also known as Vakona Private Reserve, Lemur Island is a small, captivating oasis nestled within Andasibe National Park in Madagascar. This remarkable sanctuary is inhabited by a diverse array of lemur species, including the enchanting black and white ruffed lemur, the delightful brown lemur, and the agile bamboo lemur. Exploring Lemur Island in Andasibe National Park became one of the most memorable highlights of my journey through Madagascar. As an ardent lover of nature and a passionate enthusiast of animals, I was thrilled at the prospect of being able to observe these extraordinary creatures up close.

Upon our arrival at the island, I was handed a bunch of bananas to feed the lemurs. The moment I witnessed these lively lemurs leaping and frolicking about, an overwhelming sense of joy and excitement enveloped me. Amongst the lemurs on the island, the black and white ruffed lemurs stood out as the most active and sociable. They fearlessly climbed onto my lap and shoulders, eagerly reaching for the fruit. The experience of feeling their soft fur and observing them from such proximity was truly awe-inspiring. The brown lemurs, although more reserved compared to their ruffed lemur counterparts, were equally delightful to interact with. Approaching me with cautious curiosity, they would gaze up at me with their large, captivating eyes before gently accepting the offered fruit from my hand. The bamboo lemurs, being more elusive, required patience and keen observation to spot. However, the moment I caught sight of them was nothing short of magical. Their graceful agility and effortless leaps from tree to tree resembled a mesmerizing dance.

Interacting with the lemurs on Lemur Island brought me immense joy. Witnessing them in such close quarters, engaging with them in their natural habitat, left an indelible impression of wonder and gratitude within me. The island itself exuded stunning beauty, with lush greenery and towering trees providing a cool and serene refuge. The air was crisp and pure, while the harmonious symphony of lemurs and other wildlife contributed to the peaceful and tranquil atmosphere around us.

Another aspect that made the visit to Lemur Island truly special was the conservation efforts it supported. The lemurs residing on the island had either been rescued or rehabilitated, living in a secure and protected environment. The island forms part of the Vakona Forest Lodge, a dedicated institution focused on conservation and education initiatives in Madagascar. This island nation is home to a myriad of unique flora and fauna, including numerous lemur species found nowhere else on Earth. Unfortunately, these extraordinary species face threats such as habitat loss, climate change, and poaching. Safeguarding these species and their habitats is of utmost importance to the survival of Madagascar's exceptional biodiversity. The proceeds from visits to Lemur Island contribute directly to the support of conservation efforts in Andasibe National Park and other protected areas throughout Madagascar. This funding aids research, education, and habitat protection, allowing visitors like myself to play a vital role in preserving Madagascar's incredible wildlife.

Throughout my journey, I was constantly reminded of the unparalleled uniqueness and significance of Madagascar. Nearly 80% of the island's animal and plant species cannot be found anywhere else on the planet, and lemurs, in particular, are exclusive to Madagascar's wilderness. It was an undeniable blessing to explore this remarkable island and encounter its natural wonders firsthand. Nonetheless, the tourism industry in Madagascar is not without its challenges. The country grapples with issues such as deforestation, illegal hunting, and overfishing, all of which pose threats to the island's unparalleled biodiversity. Numerous conservation organizations are tirelessly working to address these challenges and promote sustainable tourism practices that both support local communities and protect the environment. Despite these hurdles, Madagascar remains an alluring and captivating destination that offers a glimpse into a world of wildlife and culture unlike any other on Earth.

Overall, Andasibe National Park serves as an extraordinary destination for anyone seeking to observe lemurs in their natural habitat. The park's diverse lemur species, knowledgeable guides, and breathtaking natural landscapes make it an essential visit for anyone venturing to Madagascar. Furthermore, my visit to Lemur Island within Andasibe National Park was an absolutely incredible and joyous experience. It allowed me to forge a profound connection with nature, to marvel at the beauty and wonders of the world, and to contribute to vital conservation endeavors. It served as a powerful reminder of the importance of protecting our natural environment and the extraordinary animals that call it home. The memories of my time spent on Lemur Island and the sheer bliss it brought me will forever hold a cherished place in my heart.

Indri Indri Lemur

BEFRIEND WITH
LEMURS

Ring-Tailed Lemurs

Vakona Lodge

Indri Indri Lemurs

Andasibe National Park

Lemur Island

Grey Bamboo Lemur

Brown Lemurs

MOROCCO

Mesmerizing Morocco offers a diverse range of experiences. You can start your day riding a camel in the Sahara Desert, explore vibrant and intricately decorated souks in the afternoon, discover a UNESCO World Heritage ancient city, or unwind with a rejuvenating hammam in the evening, concluding with a delightful dinner in the Kasbah - all in a single day. In a nutshell, Morocco is an incredible place to visit.

Setting foot in the captivating land of Morocco was an extraordinary experience that transported me into a realm of vibrant colors, exotic aromas, bustling souks, and ancient traditions. From the moment I arrived, it was evident that Morocco was a destination that awakened the senses, overwhelmed the mind, and left me spellbound with its sheer beauty and cultural richness. Every step of my journey through this enchanting country was an adventure filled with excitement, cultural immersion, and a sensorial overload like no other.

One of the first things that struck me about Morocco was the sheer diversity of landscapes it had to offer. From the golden sand dunes of the Sahara Desert to the snow-capped peaks of the Atlas Mountains and the stunning coastal stretches along the Atlantic and Mediterranean, Morocco boasted a kaleidoscope of natural wonders that left me in awe and with lasting timeless memories.

As a passionate traveler, Morocco holds a special place in my heart, and I have had the opportunity to explore several cities and regions within the country. From the bustling streets of Marrakech to the historic wonders of Fez, the coastal charm of "Essaouira", the modernity of "Casablanca", the capital city of "Rabat", the vibrant energy of "Tangier", the blue enchantment of "Chefchaouen", and the majestic beauty of the Sahara Desert, each destination offered a unique and unforgettable experience.

"Fez", known as the intellectual and spiritual heart of Morocco, was a treasure trove of architectural marvels and ancient traditions. It is the oldest city in Morocco and was first established in 789. Its sprawling medina, recognized as a UNESCO World Heritage site, was a labyrinth of narrow alleyways where donkeys ambled past artisans practicing age-old crafts. The city's ancient madrasas, grand palaces, and historic mosques created a mesmerizing journey through its rich history. One of the most captivating sights in Fez was its famous leather tanneries, where vibrant dyeing vats created a sensory overload of colors and scents, visible from the terraces of surrounding shops. Exploring the medina's intricate mosaic work, beautifully carved wooden doors, and hidden treasures felt like stepping back in time and immersing myself in a living museum.

On the other hand, **Casablanca**, the economic powerhouse of Morocco, presented a fascinating blend of tradition and progress. The city exuded a cosmopolitan vibe, exemplified by the iconic "Hassan II Mosque", which stood as a symbol of Morocco's blending of Islamic heritage with contemporary architecture. The mosque's stunning minaret reached towards the sky, making it one of the tallest religious structures in the world. Imagine scenic ocean waves crashing under the mosque in perfect natural symmetry amidst beautiful and timeless mosaic structures and you begin to see the uniqueness of this beautiful designed Islamic structure unlike any other in North Africa.

While Casablanca boasted bustling boulevards, designer boutiques, and a vibrant nightlife, it still preserved glimpses of the country's rich past. Exploring the Corniche, a palm-lined coastal promenade, or wandering through the historic district of "Habous", this economic powerhouse of a city revealed its diverse facets and unique charm.

Marrakech, with its bustling medina and vibrant souks, was a true sensory playground. The city's beating heart lay in the iconic **Jemaa el-Fnaa** square, recognized as another UNESCO World Heritage site. By day, the square buzzed with activity as performers captivated audiences with skillful displays. Snake charmers mesmerized onlookers with their enchanting dance, while musicians filled the air with the rhythmic beats of traditional Moroccan music. Acrobats defied gravity with daring feats, and henna artists adorned hands with intricate designs. The square came alive with vibrant textiles, spices, and fruits, creating a feast for the eyes. As the sun set, Jemaa el-Fnaa underwent a mesmerizing transformation. The square turned into a playground of culinary delights as food stalls emerged from the shadows. The air became filled with the enticing aromas of sizzling kebabs, fragrant tagines, and freshly squeezed orange juice. I found myself taking a seat at one of the bustling food stalls, immersing myself in the lively atmosphere, and indulging in a feast of flavors that transported my taste buds to new heights of delight. Adjacent to Jemaa el-Fnaa, the entrance to the souk beckoned, offering a labyrinthine wonderland promising endless excitement and discovery. Stepping into the souk felt like entering another world, where vibrant colors, intricate designs, and rich textures surrounded me at every turn. A quiet cup of tea on the terrace of an adjacent café provided me with a spectacular aerial view of the bustling square below and was like a time machine allowing my imagination to take me back in time as well.

Another city that left an indelible mark on my soul was **Chefchaouen**, known as the renowned Blue City of Morocco. It was an experience that transcended all expectations. As I approached the mesmerizing town, a stroke of magic unfolded before my eyes. The blue-washed buildings began to emerge, dotting the landscape in hues that ranged from the softest baby blue to the deepest azure. It felt as though **the entire town had been designed with my love for the color BLUE in mind.**

Every step I took through the enchanting streets of Chefchaouen intensified my excitement. The blue-painted facades created a symphony of shades that danced harmoniously together, forming a visual feast for my eyes. The walls seemed to whisper stories of artistic expression and cultural significance, reminding me that this was more than just a color choice—it was a symbol of tradition, spirituality, and community. Strolling through the narrow alleys of the medina, I couldn't help but feel a sense of wonder and joy. The cobalt blue walls created a serene and tranquil atmosphere, transporting me to a realm where time slowed down and worries melted away. It was an immersive experience, as if I had stepped into a living painting, where every turn revealed a new masterpiece of blue hues. The attention to detail was astounding. Intricate doorways adorned with handcrafted motifs invited me to explore what lay behind them. Flower pots overflowing with vibrant blossoms added pops of contrasting colors, further enhancing the blue backdrop. The interplay of light and shadow created a dynamic and ever-changing canvas that kept my eyes engaged at every moment.

Embarking on a journey to the **Sahara Desert** was an experience that will forever be etched in my memory. From the moment I set foot in "Merzouga", a small village serving as the gateway to the desert, I was captivated by the towering sand dunes that surrounded me. The colors of the landscape were a mosaic of vibrant greens, rugged mountains, and the vast expanse of golden sand. The anticipation built with each passing mile, and as I ventured deeper into the desert on the back of a camel, my heart filled with excitement and gratitude.

Riding through the ever-shifting sands was a surreal experience. The rhythmic sway of the camel and the gentle footsteps created a soothing rhythm that allowed me to fully immerse myself in the magic of the desert. The vastness of the Sahara unfolded before my eyes, evoking a profound sense of awe and wonder at the magnificence of nature. As the sun began its descent, the colors of the sky intensified, painting a breathtaking backdrop of fiery reds, burnt oranges, and soft pinks. The golden rays cast an ethereal glow on the dunes, creating a spectacle of light and shadow that was simply awe-inspiring. In that moment, time seemed to stand still as I soaked in the beauty, feeling an overwhelming sense of gratitude for being present in this extraordinary setting.

As darkness descended upon the desert, a whole new world came to life. A bonfire crackled, casting a warm and inviting glow, while laughter and music filled the air. I joined fellow travelers in rhythmic drumming, dancing, and singing—a celebration of life that resonated deep within my soul. Looking up at the night sky, I was greeted by a dazzling display of stars, too numerous to count. The desert's remoteness offered a pristine view of the universe, and I couldn't help but feel humbled and small under this vast canopy. Retiring for the night in a cozy desert camp nestled among the dunes, I laid back on the soft sand and gazed up at the twinkling stars above. It was a serene moment, surrounded by the stillness of the desert, where I reflected on the incredible journey that had brought me here.

As the first rays of light painted the horizon, I woke up to witness the desert come alive once again. The colors danced across the dunes, rekindling a renewed sense of wonder and excitement. Watching the sunrise in the Sahara Desert was a privilege—a reminder to cherish each day as a precious gift. With a heart full of gratitude and a mind teeming with cherished memories, I bid farewell to the Sahara. The adventure had been nothing short of extraordinary, instilling in me a profound appreciation for the natural wonders of the world and a willingness to embrace the unknown.

Another immersive experience in Moroccan culture was a visit to a **traditional Hamman**. Stepping into this historical place of purification and rejuvenation offered me a profound insight into the customs and traditions that have shaped Moroccan society for centuries.

As I entered the Hamman, a sense of tranquility washed over me. The space was meticulously designed to foster serenity, with its soft lighting, soothing ambience, and the delicate scent of aromatic oils permeating the air. The architectural details showcased Morocco's exquisite craftsmanship, with intricate tile work, ornate mosaics, and domed ceilings that allowed soft natural light to filter through, creating a warm and inviting atmosphere. The Hamman experience was not just about cleansing the body; it was a holistic journey encompassing the mind, body, and spirit.

The ritual began with a steam bath, enveloping me in the warm embrace of moist heat. As the steam gently penetrated my pores, tensions melted away, and a deep sense of relaxation washed over me. This initial phase not only prepared my body for the cleansing process but also symbolized a release of worries and stress, allowing me to be fully present in the moment.

After the steam bath, I was guided to the "gommage" room, where an experienced professional known as a "kessala" attended to me. The kessala, a master of exfoliation, expertly performed a gommage—a traditional body scrub using a coarse mitt called a "kessa" and a special soap made from olive oil and eucalyptus. With skillful movements, the kessala gently sloughed off dead skin cells, revealing a renewed and radiant complexion. This process not only purified the body but also symbolized shedding the old and embracing the new, leaving me feeling revitalized and connected to my inner self. Beyond the physical and spiritual benefits, the Hamman was deeply intertwined with Moroccan culture and societal values. It served as a cherished gathering place, where people of all ages and backgrounds came together, fostering a sense of community and connection. By the way, don't be surprised if someone invites you to drink a famously sweet Moroccan mint tea, hospitality is an integral part of Moroccan culture.

Overall, my journey through Morocco was an immersive experience that enthralled every sense. The vibrant colors of the markets, the rhythmic beats of traditional music, the tantalizing flavors of Moroccan cuisine, the intricate architecture, and the warm hospitality of the locals all combined to create an unforgettable adventure. The trip to the Sahara Desert was a once-in-a-lifetime opportunity to witness the grandeur of nature, immerse myself in the rich traditions of the desert, and feel a profound sense of connection within the heart of the dunes. Exploring Chefchaouen, the Blue City, was a journey that transcended the ordinary—a chance to wander through blue-washed streets, embrace serenity, and become immersed in the culture, traditions, and warm hospitality of the locals. Morocco opened my mind and overwhelmed my senses, between haggling with local merchants and being serenaded by traditional music, the rich scents of the spice markets wafting through the air, all came together to make Morocco a magical adventure that left an indelible mark on my soul.

The Most Beautiful Desert on Earth

"Traveling tends to magnify all human emotions."

—Peter Hoeg

Jemaa el-Fnaa

Food vendors at Jemaa el-Fnaa

A **Hammam in Marrakesh**

Majorelle Garden in Marrakesh

The leather tanneries in Fez

The leather tanneries in Fez

Casablanca Mosque

A Riad in Fez

Goats on an Argan Tree

Bonfire in Sahara Desert

Chefchaouen

The Blue City

RWANDA: GORILLA TREKKING

Rwanda is a country with varied ecosystems, wildlife, and scenic national parks that offer the visitor a wide range of activities. These activities include gorilla trekking, chimpanzee tracking, bird watching and hiking up panoramic volcanoes in different national parks. Rwanda has a rich African history and unique hospitality that is not found in other parts of Africa.

Experiencing the wonders of **Rwanda's gorilla trekking** was an unforgettable opportunity that allowed me to witness these captivating creatures up close and learn about conservation efforts aimed at protecting them. With **less than 1,000 mountain gorillas remaining in the wild**, spotting them in their natural habitat was a rare and valuable moment that left me awestruck. Setting off on my journey to Volcanoes National Park filled me with anticipation, as I woke up bright and early at 7 a.m. to begin my gorilla trekking adventure. Upon arrival at the park, the welcoming staff provided me with a comprehensive briefing on the dos and don'ts during the trek, and my knowledgeable guide was introduced to me. Following the briefing, we joined a group of eight individuals and drove to our next location.

As we embarked on our hike, I was in awe of the breathtaking Rwandan landscape, with its lush forests and rolling hills. We walked through farmland where potatoes and herbs were grown, and the park was an exquisite sight to behold. Moving deeper into the forest, my guide pointed out rare bird species and colobus monkeys, as well as various flora and fauna along the way.

After an hour of steep hiking, something magical happened. We stumbled upon a flat area and **saw a family of 12 gorillas! The Amahoro family**, which means "peace", was a sight to behold, featuring three **Silverback gorillas**, dominant males, along with females and adorable baby gorillas. The youngest was only 9 months old, and we were only a few feet away from them. Observing their peaceful and content demeanor was a surreal experience. The guide explained that gorilla families are social and peaceful animals that form close-knit family units, each with its unique personality. The guide also shared captivating insights into their behavior, hierarchy, and communication, noting that each family is ranked based on the strength and dominance of the silverback.

The similarities between gorillas and humans struck me profoundly. Their facial expressions and mannerisms were strikingly human-like, and I could sense their intelligence and emotions. Gorillas are our closest living relatives, sharing over 98% of their DNA with humans, which means we have many genetic similarities. This includes many of the same genes involved in vital biological processes. Although humans have one fewer pair of chromosomes than gorillas, we share comparable genetic material organization. Humans have a larger cerebral cortex responsible for advanced cognitive abilities, while gorillas have a larger body size and more muscle mass.

Experiencing the majestic gorillas up close and personal was an awe-inspiring moment. The creatures were tranquil and composed, paying no attention to our presence. The encounter was extraordinary, witnessing a mating fight between two Silverbacks and learning about their habitat. Watching the baby gorillas playfully tumbling around while the older ones foraged for food was captivating. The silverback, keeping watch over his family, would occasionally warn us by beating his chest if he felt threatened. Our guide, Francis, was incredibly knowledgeable and ensured that we didn't disturb the gorillas. He communicated with them and asked them to remain calm and peaceful around us. It was remarkable to see how the gorillas went about their daily routine as if we weren't even there. The calmness of their demeanor was awe-inspiring. As we watched the gorillas, I could see the intelligence in their eyes, and I felt a deep connection to them.

Our guide also shared information about Rwanda's conservation efforts to protect the gorillas. The country has implemented strict regulations to safeguard the gorillas and their habitat, and they work closely with local communities to promote sustainable tourism that benefits both the gorillas and the people. It was inspiring to see how much Rwanda had progressed in this area and how much dedication and effort had gone into gorilla conservation. Dian Fossey's groundbreaking conservation work on the mountain gorillas of Rwanda was inspirational and paved the way for modern gorilla conservation efforts.

As our visit came to an end, we said our goodbyes to the gorilla family and trekked back to our starting point. I felt an overwhelming sense of gratitude and humility for having had the opportunity to witness such a rare and precious moment. It was an experience that filled me with joy, excitement, and wonder, and one that I will cherish for the rest of my life.

Gorilla Family

Silverback Gorilla

Baby Gorilla and Mother

Eye to Eye with MOUNTAIN GORILLAS

Silverback Gorilla

Rwanda Cultural Center

THE SEYCHELLES

The Seychelles, an enchanting archipelago consisting of 115 islands, is nestled in the Indian Ocean, off the eastern coast of Africa. This tropical paradise offers a harmonious blend of natural splendor, vibrant culture, and blissful relaxation. Renowned for its unspoiled beaches, azure waters, and lush greenery, the Seychelles beckons those seeking respite from the hectic pace of everyday life, providing an immersive connection with nature. I had the privilege of exploring the breathtaking Seychelles for a few days, embarking on a journey that commenced on Mahe Island, the largest of the Seychelles islands, and subsequently venturing to Praslin and La Digue.

To reach Praslin, we opted for a swift 15-minute flight instead of the hour-long ferry ride due to turbulent seas. Upon arriving in Praslin, we embarked on a ferry to La Digue, where we rented bicycles from the ferry station. Cycling on La Digue proved to be a captivating experience as bicycles stood as the primary mode of transportation for most of the island's inhabitants.

Praslin Island, a popular destination renowned for its magnificent natural landscapes and distinctive cultural encounters, captivated my senses. A significant attraction on the island is the Vallée de Mai Nature Reserve, a UNESCO World Heritage site that shelters the renowned Coco de Mer palm tree. Along scenic trails, I embarked on a hike, immersing myself in the island's remarkable flora and fauna. Praslin also boasts some of the Seychelles' most stunning beaches, such as Anse Lazio and Anse Georgette. These immaculate shores offer crystalline waters, velvety white sand, and awe-inspiring vistas of the surrounding landscape. Beyond its natural splendor, Praslin celebrates a rich culture and history, evident in its local cuisine, music, and traditional dances. I took pleasure in exploring the local markets, savoring traditional Creole dishes.

La Digue Island, though smaller and less developed than Praslin, captivated me with its population of just over 2,000 people. Renowned for its mesmerizing beaches, including the world-acclaimed Anse Source d'Argent, La Digue lured me with its granite boulders and crystalline waters, creating an idyllic setting for swimming, snorkeling, and sunbathing. Additionally, La Digue boasts traditional Creole houses, quaint shops, and local markets, offering a glimpse into the island's distinctive culture and way of life. One aspect that I cherished about Praslin and La Digue was the pervasive sense of tranquility and relaxation that envelops these islands.

Our initial stop was **Anse Source D'Argent Beach**, widely hailed as one of the most photographed beaches in the world. As we approached the beach, the mesmerizing granite boulders strewn along the shoreline immediately caught my attention. These distinctive boulders, shaped by the elements over time, bestow upon the Seychelles their unique and fascinating appearance. They offered an excellent opportunity for capturing photographs, and I ascended their summits to bask in the awe-inspiring views. Descending toward the beach, I was captivated by the beauty of the crystal-clear waters and powdery white sand. The water's clarity allowed me to witness its vibrant marine life, creating an ideal location for snorkeling and underwater exploration. Furthermore, the exceptionally soft and fine sand provided an inviting surface for relaxation and sunbathing. Anse Source D'Argent's tranquility and serenity make it a haven for unwinding, enabling us to appreciate the Seychelles' natural beauty to the fullest. The absence of large crowds fosters an atmosphere of calm, allowing me to immerse fully in the beach's unique ambiance and unwind amidst the Seychelles' natural splendor. Anse Source D'Argent offered a range of activities, including snorkeling, kayaking, and paddle boarding. These waters teem with vibrant marine life, comprising colorful fish, graceful sea turtles, and playful dolphins, making it a paradise for underwater enthusiasts. Another enchanting feature of Anse Source D'Argent is the mesmerizing sunsets that grace the beach. As the sun descended below the horizon, the sky erupted in a kaleidoscope of colors, ranging from deep oranges and fiery reds to delicate pinks and serene purples. This truly magical experience left me with indelible memories that will endure a lifetime.

The following day, we embarked on a bike ride to **Grand Anse Beach**, an equally enchanting destination. As we arrived, I was immediately struck by the immense stretch of the beach. Extending nearly 2 kilometers, it offered an abundance of space to find the perfect spot. The sensation of the soft, powdery sand beneath my feet was exquisite as I strolled barefoot along the shoreline. I spent several hours basking in the sun and indulging in the relaxed island atmosphere.

The allure of Grand Anse Beach extended to its captivating waters. The turquoise blue expanse was remarkably clear and alluring, creating an inviting space for swimming. The gentle current and calm waters provided an ideal environment to relax and float. Bordering the beach were verdant green hills, adding to the picturesque charm of the location. What made Grand Anse Beach truly unique was its seclusion and tranquility. With minimal development, devoid of nearby restaurants or shops, a sense of peace enveloped the area, allowing us to fully immerse ourselves in the beauty of our surroundings. Furthermore, the lack of crowds ensured ample space to revel in the natural splendor of the Seychelles. Another aspect that enhanced the joyous experience of visiting Grand Anse Beach was the sense of community and friendliness among both visitors and locals. The Seychellois people are renowned for their warm and welcoming nature, immediately making us feel at home in their presence. The beach served as a popular gathering spot for locals to unwind and appreciate the natural beauty, providing us with opportunities to connect and gain insights into the local culture.

During our time in Praslin, we ventured to **Anse Lazio**, a serene and extensive sandy stretch that drew considerable tourist attention. After a delightful beachside lunch, we embarked on a leisurely stroll along the shore, taking in the captivating scenery. Our exploration also led us to "Vale de Mer", an excursion that immersed me in the breathtaking natural beauty of the islands. "Vale de Mer", nestled within Praslin and often referred to as the "Garden of Eden," encompasses a secluded valley. The valley's crowning jewel is the famed Coco de Mer palm tree, a remarkable species native to the Seychelles. The Coco de Mer is renowned for producing the largest seed in the plant kingdom, bearing a striking resemblance to the female pelvis, earning it the namesake "Coco de Mer" or "Coconut of the Sea."

Journeying through **Vale de Mer**, I found myself surrounded by lush vegetation and verdant landscapes. The air carried the intoxicating fragrance of tropical flowers, while the harmonious melodies of birds and rustling leaves created a serene ambiance. Along the well-maintained trails, I had the privilege of observing a variety of plant species endemic to the Seychelles, including the majestic Coco de Mer. These towering palms, reaching heights of up to 30 meters (98 feet), featured fronds that gracefully swayed with the gentle breeze. Witnessing these awe-inspiring trees left me with a feeling of amazement at nature's beauty and diversity. Mature female Coco de Mer trees bore large, double-lobed nuts, weighing up to 25 kilograms (55 pounds) each, highly sought-after as cherished souvenirs. Within Vale de Mer, I also encountered diverse wildlife species that called this sanctuary home. The striking Black Parrot, Seychelles' national bird, frequently graced the area, alongside avian companions such as the Seychelles Bulbul and the Seychelles Sunbird.

Visiting the Seychelles proved to be an extraordinary and once-in-a-lifetime experience. The allure of Anse Source D'Argent Beach on La Digue Island, with its stunning granite boulders, crystal-clear waters, soft white sand, and breathtaking sunsets, left an indelible mark on my memory. Exploring Grand Anse Beach offered a joyous and delightful encounter, enabling me to connect deeply with the natural beauty of the Seychelles. The expansive shoreline, clear turquoise waters, and captivating views made it an ideal destination for relaxation and appreciation. Moreover, the visit to Vale de Mer and the encounter with the Coco de Mer trees showcased the wonders of the natural world, leaving me with an enduring memory of a truly enchanting place that epitomizes the Seychelles' beauty. Overall, my journey to the Seychelles remains a cherished and unparalleled experience, as the stunning beaches, laid-back lifestyle, and exquisite natural scenery etched an everlasting impression upon my soul.

Beach Anse Source D'Argent

Seychelles Beach

Beach Anse Source D'Argent

Beach La Digue

Female Coco De Mer

Male Coco De Mer

Anse Source D'Argent

Anse Source D'Argent

③ NORTH AMERICA CONTINENT: 23 COUNTRIES

Flag	Country	Flag	Country
	Antigua & Barbuda		Haiti
	The Bahamas		Honduras
	Barbados		Jamaica
	Belize		Mexico
	Canada		Nicaragua
	Costa Rica		Panama
	Cuba		Saint Kitts & Nevis
	Dominica		Saint Lucia
	Dominican Republic		Saint Vincent & The Grenadines
	El Salvador		Trinidad & Tobago
	Grenada		The United States
	Guatemala		

NORTH AMERICA CONTINENT

North America has it all! Big vibrant cities, rolling prairies wild verdant forests, luxurious beaches, desert heat, Arctic cold and everything in between. It is also a melting pot and meeting place of many world cultures. North America is the third largest continent with amazing diversity to show for it. Weather ranges from icy Greenland to tropical beaches of the Caribbean and ancient forests and amazing national parks not found anywhere else on earth.

The North American continent is a vast and diverse continent, beckoning travelers with a plethora of captivating destinations and innovative gastronomy. From its stunning natural wonders to vibrant cities and the tropical paradises of the Caribbean. This continent promises unforgettable experiences for all, its nature, raw, wild and untouched promises memories of a lifetime. The very name "America" has its origins in the Latin version of "Amerigo," derived from the Italian explorer Amerigo Vespucci, whose voyages in the late 15th and early 16th centuries helped realize that the lands discovered by Christopher Columbus constituted a separate continent from Asia. The German cartographer Martin Waldseemüller was the first to suggest naming these newfound lands after Amerigo Vespucci, bestowing the name "America" upon the continent to honor Vespucci's significant contributions.

Starting our journey through North America, one must not miss the iconic **Grand Canyon**, located in Arizona. This awe-inspiring natural wonder boasts breathtaking canyon walls that change hues as the sun dances upon them. Hiking along the rim offers a closer look, or soar above it all on a helicopter tour for a bird's-eye perspective. Equally mesmerizing is **Niagara Falls**, straddling the Canadian and U.S. borders. Feel the mist on a boat tour as you approach the roaring cascade or opt for a helicopter ride for panoramic views. Adventure enthusiasts will find solace in **Banff National Park** in Canada, nestled in the Canadian Rockies. Here, hiking, skiing, and snowboarding amid stunning landscapes abound, along with the chance to rejuvenate in soothing hot springs.

For urban explorers, the bustling metropolis of **New York City** awaits. Known as the "City That Never Sleeps," it offers world-class museums, dazzling Broadway shows, and a gastronomic scene that rivals the world's best. Stroll through Central Park and pay homage to iconic landmarks like the Statue of Liberty and the Empire State Building. Another vibrant city to visit in North America is **San Francisco**. Located in California, this city offers stunning views of the bay and the Golden Gate Bridge. Take a walk along the waterfront and visit the famous Fisherman's Wharf. Take a cable car up the steep hills for a thrilling ride and breathtaking views of the city.

For those interested in history, a visit to **Washington D.C.** is a must. The capital of the United States offers a wide range of museums, monuments, and government buildings. Visit the Smithsonian museums and learn about everything from space exploration to American history. Take a tour of the **White House** and witness the seat of American power up close. Nearby, are the states of Maryland and Virginia with many of the classic Civil War military sites like Antietam and Manassas to name just a few, beckoning historians and visitors alike to come and share their rich history of freedom and struggle for unity of a nation. Finally, within a two-hour drive is the famous Civil War site of **Gettysburg**, Pennsylvania and the battle of Gettysburg (1863). The town of Gettysburg is known for Abraham Lincoln's Gettysburg address a small town with a rich history and culture all its own. It is here where the Confederate Army reached its highest point in the Civil War and is home to some of the most historic and scenic Civil War sites in the United States. Lastly, for you paranormal enthusiasts the Gettysburg battlefield is said to be one of the most haunted places in the United States.

The West coast of the United States and the many beautiful sites to be seen in **California** and **Oregon** and the coastal drive of Highway one which stretches from southern California and Mexican border to the north all the way up to Canadian border covering some of the most beautiful scenic views on this planet. Stop and have a glass of wine and enjoy the richness of the Mendocino coast, a coastal community, known for its cliffside trails, postcard like beaches and outstanding cuisine.

Onward to Central America, where the region's rich cultural and natural diversity awaits. **Guatemala's Tikal National Park** boasts impressive Mayan ruins amidst lush rainforests, offering an intriguing glimpse into ancient civilizations. **Costa Rica** enchants with its lush rainforests, diverse wildlife, and pristine beaches. Don't miss the **Arenal Volcano**, hot springs, and the captivating **Monteverde Cloud Forest**. Costa Rica is one of the most hospitable places that I have ever traveled to and the people live and breathe their famous saying of "Pura Vida" or simple life. Here in Costa Rica, it is more than just a saying but truly a way of life!

Traveling further south, we arrive in Panama, the **Panama Canal** is a marvel of engineering. Explore its history and witness massive ships navigating this impressive waterway. In Belize, the **Blue Hole**, a giant marine sinkhole, beckons divers to explore its depths, while the ancient city of Caracol provides a glimpse into the rich and perplexing Maya civilization.

Now, let's set our sights on the Caribbean, a tropical paradise that epitomizes relaxation and natural beauty. The **Bahamas** offers stunning beaches, clear blue waters, and vibrant coral reefs. In **Jamaica**, embrace reggae rhythms and explore the lush landscapes, including the iconic Dunn's River Falls.

Cuba, with its rich history and vibrant culture, is a must-visit. Wander through the colorful streets of Havana, where vintage cars and colonial architecture tell a story of a bygone era. The **Dominican Republic** beckons with its diverse landscapes, from serene beaches to lush rainforests. For a taste of French and Dutch Caribbean culture, visit the dual-nation island of **Saint Martin/Saint Maarten**. It offers pristine beaches, water sports, and a unique blend of European and Caribbean influences. Then, the tiny island of **Aruba** is renowned for its white sandy beaches, vibrant nightlife, and warm hospitality.

The North America continent is a mixing bowl of many world cultures and presents a diverse tapestry of must-see destinations, each offering its unique allure, culture, and charm. Contrary to other nations where culture is compact and practical, North Americans prefer a large and luxurious lifestyle and are proud of their unique culture and are generally happy to see visitors and are very willing to share their knowledge of their home and country. Whether you're drawn to the natural wonders of the continent, the rich history of Central America, or the idyllic beaches of the Caribbean, this region promises a lifetime of unforgettable travel experiences.

BEST TIME TO VISIT NORTH AMERICA CONTINENT

North America, a vast and diverse continent, offers a multitude of experiences throughout the year, from the icy wilderness of Alaska to the sunny shores of the Caribbean. Whether you're seeking adventure in the Rocky Mountains, the vibrant culture of New Orleans, or the relaxation of a Caribbean beach, North America has something to offer in each of its four distinct seasons.

Spring (March - May): As winter retreats, North America welcomes the fresh bloom of spring. In Washington, D.C., the National Cherry Blossom Festival transforms the nation's capital into a pink paradise as cherry blossoms burst into full bloom along the Tidal Basin. The vibrant city of New Orleans, Louisiana, comes alive with the sounds of jazz during the New Orleans Jazz & Heritage Festival, a celebration of music, food, and culture. Meanwhile, the Caribbean islands, such as Barbados and Jamaica, offer a tropical escape with balmy temperatures and tranquil beaches perfect for spring getaways.

Summer (June - August): As the days grow longer, North America's natural beauty beckons. The rugged landscapes of Canada's Banff National Park in Alberta offer opportunities for hiking, wildlife spotting, and exploring turquoise lakes during the summer months. In the United States, Yellowstone National Park showcases its geothermal wonders, from erupting geysers to bubbling mud pots. The vibrant city of New York welcomes visitors to Central Park, where outdoor concerts, picnics, and cultural events are in full swing. In the Caribbean, the Bahamas and Turks and Caicos Islands boast some of the clearest waters and pristine beaches for summer relaxation.

Fall (September - November): As the air turns crisp, North America's autumnal beauty takes center stage. The New England region in the United States, including states like Vermont and Maine, is famous for its picturesque fall foliage. Embark on scenic drives through colorful forests and indulge in apple picking and warm cider. The southwestern United States, including Arizona and New Mexico, offers a unique blend of desert landscapes and Native American culture, with events like the Albuquerque International Balloon Fiesta illuminating the skies with hot air balloons. In Central America, Costa Rica's lush rainforests and diverse wildlife are at their best during the fall, offering excellent opportunities for nature enthusiasts.

Winter (December - February):
When winter blankets North America, various regions come alive with unique experiences. Ski enthusiasts flock to Colorado's Rocky Mountains and Utah's world-class resorts for downhill adventures. In Quebec City, Canada, the historic Old Town transforms into a magical winter wonderland during the Quebec Winter Carnival, featuring ice sculptures and traditional activities. Mexico's Riviera Maya offers a tropical escape from the cold, with warm waters for snorkeling and diving in the cenotes and colorful marine life in the Caribbean Sea. Meanwhile, the Caribbean islands, including the Dominican Republic and the Cayman Islands, welcome visitors with balmy temperatures and white-sand beaches during the winter months.

North America is listed as the second most "livable" region in the world just narrowly behind Western Europe and is a continent that offers a rich tapestry of experiences, from natural wonders and cultural festivals to relaxation by the beach. Whether you're an adventure seeker, a culture enthusiast, or a beach lover, these regions invite you to explore, savor, and create unforgettable memories year-round.

Get ready to embark on an extraordinary adventure as I take you on a breathtaking journey through the incredible continent of North America. What awaits you is not just a mere compilation of stories and photographs; they are the vibrant threads woven into the fabric of an unforgettable odyssey. My exploration of North America was nothing short of a grand tapestry of awe-inspiring moments, each more magnificent than the last. From the towering skyscrapers of bustling cities to the pristine wilderness that whispered ancient tales, every step I took was a revelation. The continent's diversity, from the Arctic tundra to the sun-soaked beaches of the Caribbean, mirrored the diversity of its people, each encounter a chapter in the book of my life. Venturing through the bustling streets of North America's iconic cities, discovering hidden gems in remote corners, and immersing myself in its rich cultural tapestry, I realized that this journey was an exploration of not just geography but also the very essence of humanity. Every interaction, every meal shared, every smile exchanged was an invitation to experience the soul and the essence of the continent.

"TO TRAVEL IS TO LIVE"

-Hans Christian Andersen

CANADA

Canada, a vast and awe-inspiring country, is renowned for its breathtaking natural wonders, dynamic cities, and diverse cultural experiences. From the majestic snow-capped peaks of the Rocky Mountains to the bustling urban streets of Toronto and the enchanting charm of Montreal, Canada offers something extraordinary for every visitor. Personally, I have been incredibly fortunate to not only live and work in Canada but also to have had the opportunity to visit the country multiple times. Each visit left me captivated by its astounding natural beauty, warm and friendly people, and the countless unique cultural encounters it has to offer.

One aspect of Canada that never fails to amaze me was its stunning landscapes. The country boasts some of the most awe-inspiring natural wonders in the world, and its national parks provide visitors with an unparalleled opportunity to experience them up close. Alberta's **Banff National Park**, with its mesmerizing turquoise lakes, snow-capped peaks, and majestic glaciers, is a beloved destination. Jasper National Park, also located in Alberta, is renowned for its rejuvenating hot springs, remarkable wildlife sightings, and untouched wilderness. Other notable national parks, such as Gros Morne in Newfoundland and Labrador, Yoho in British Columbia, and Fundy in New Brunswick, each possess their own distinctive features, ranging from rugged coastlines to magnificent waterfalls. These parks offer a chance to reconnect with nature and immerse oneself in their unrivaled beauty.

Furthermore, Canada's vibrant cities not only showcase modern amenities but also provide a wealth of cultural experiences. Toronto, Vancouver, Montreal, and Ottawa are popular urban destinations, boasting historical landmarks, world-class museums, enticing restaurants, and bustling nightlife. Each city possesses a unique character and a wide array of attractions. For instance, **Toronto** is home to the iconic CN Tower, an architectural marvel that grants breathtaking views of the city and Lake Ontario. On the other hand, Montreal captivates visitors with its charming cobblestone streets, rich historical architecture, and world-renowned museums like the Montreal Museum of Fine Arts.

However, what truly sets Canada apart and resonates with me the most, is its celebration of multiculturalism. The country serves as a melting pot of diverse cultures, allowing visitors to partake in a wide range of cultural traditions and festivals throughout the year. Alberta's Calgary Stampede, a renowned celebration of cowboy culture, features exhilarating rodeos, captivating parades, and electrifying concerts. The Toronto International Film Festival showcases the finest works of global cinema, while the Montreal Jazz Festival attracts acclaimed musicians from around the world.

Personally, I have had the pleasure of attending numerous festivals in Canada, and I am consistently moved by the warmth and hospitality of its people. Canada truly embraces and cherishes its diversity, making it a place where cultures converge and flourish.

No discussion of Canada would be complete without mentioning its exceptional culinary scene. The country's emphasis on locally sourced ingredients and regional specialties is renowned. Classic Canadian dishes, such as poutine—a delectable combination of french fries, cheese curds, and gravy—are a delight for the taste buds. Seafood enthusiasts can indulge in the freshest lobster, scallops, and salmon. Moreover, Canada's craft breweries and wineries, particularly in regions like British Columbia's Okanagan Valley and Ontario's Niagara region, produce award-winning wines, adding to the country's gastronomic appeal.

Canada holds a special place in my heart. Through my visits to various cities and natural wonders, each experience has brought me immense joy and happiness. Among the many captivating cities in Canada, **Montreal** stands as my favorite. Having been fortunate enough to reside there for several years due to work, the city swiftly became my second home. Montreal's rich history, magnificent architecture, and vibrant cultural scene consistently left a lasting impression. **The enchanting Old Montreal district**, with its cobblestone streets, resplendent buildings, and charming boutiques, offered a nostalgic journey back in time. Not to be missed is the Notre-Dame Basilica, a captivating attraction adorned with exquisite Gothic Revival architecture and intricate interior designs. Another gem in Montreal is Mount Royal, a sprawling hill providing breathtaking panoramic views of the city and the St. Lawrence River. Whether hiking or biking to its summit or simply enjoying a leisurely picnic in the park, the experience is truly invigorating. Lastly, the Montreal Botanical Garden, one of the world's largest, serves as a serene oasis nestled within the heart of the city, featuring over 190 acres of lush greenery and an astounding 22,000 plant species. Montreal's culinary scene further enhances the city's allure, with a diverse range of delicacies from classic poutine to mouthwatering smoked meat sandwiches and delectable maple syrup treats. Moreover, the city's thriving coffee culture and burgeoning craft brewery scene, marked by numerous microbreweries and cafes scattered throughout, add to Montreal's vibrant atmosphere.

One of the greatest sources of joy for me is the vibrant festival scene in Montreal. This city is a vibrant hub of life, culture, and diversity. What truly captivates me about Montreal is its unwavering commitment to celebrating art and music. With approximately 100 festivals taking place each year, the city showcases a remarkable array of art forms, music genres, culinary delights, and cultural traditions. Among the most renowned festivals in Montreal, **the Montreal International Jazz Festival** stands out. As one of the largest jazz festivals worldwide, it attracts over two million visitors annually. Spanning 11 days in late

June and early July, the festival boasts more than 500 concerts featuring 3,000 artists from around the globe. This includes both established musicians and rising talents. With a mix of free outdoor performances and ticketed indoor concerts, the festival ensures that people from all walks of life can revel in the magic of jazz.

Another festival that infuses immense joy into Montreal is the **"Just for Laughs"** comedy festival. Held every summer, this event showcases the talents of over 1,500 comedians from across the globe, ranging from established names to emerging performers. Stand-up comedy shows, improv performances, and galas featuring renowned comedians are just a few highlights of this laughter-filled extravaganza. The festival also spills out onto the streets of Montreal with captivating street performances and outdoor events, making it an engaging and amusing experience for all.

One of the most awe-inspiring spectacles in Montreal is **the Montreal International Fireworks Competition**, which illuminates the summer nights. This competition showcases dazzling pyrotechnic displays from top fireworks companies worldwide. Set to captivating music, the displays unfold over the majestic St. Lawrence River, creating a breathtaking backdrop. The competition features live music and other forms of entertainment, ensuring an unforgettable evening of visual splendor and auditory delight.

While Montreal shines brightly in its own right, it also serves as an ideal gateway to explore the rest of Quebec. A short journey from Montreal leads to **Quebec City**, a charming and historically significant city renowned for its cobblestone streets, French-inspired architecture, and cultural heritage. The heart of Quebec City lies in its UNESCO World Heritage site, Old Quebec. This exceptionally preserved historic district showcases a wealth of landmarks and architectural gems. Meandering through the narrow cobblestone streets of Old Quebec evokes a sense of stepping back in time to the city's French colonial era. The district is home to numerous museums, boutiques, and restaurants, creating a delightful atmosphere for leisurely exploration. Among the notable landmarks is Chateau Frontenac, a historic hotel that has become an iconic symbol of Quebec City. Built in the late 19th century, it stands as a testament to the city's allure and historical heritage.

Overall, Canada as a whole, offers a cornucopia of experiences for every traveler, from its bustling cities and captivating national parks to its thrilling outdoor adventures, rich cultural encounters, and delectable culinary offerings it is a must see for any traveler. Personally, my encounters with Canada have been overwhelmingly positive, leaving me filled with happiness and a sense of fulfillment. Exploring the natural wonders of Banff National Park, immersing myself in the vibrant cultural tapestry of Montreal, and discovering the historic charm of Quebec City have all contributed to my deep appreciation for this remarkable country. Whether through festivals, natural beauty, or cultural immersion, Canada has an abundance of treasures waiting to be experienced, and I consider myself incredibly fortunate to have witnessed it firsthand.

Exploring BANFF NATIONAL PARK

Holi Festival in Montreal

Niagara Falls

Chateau Frontenac in Quebec City

Spring in Montreal

Notre Dame de Montreal

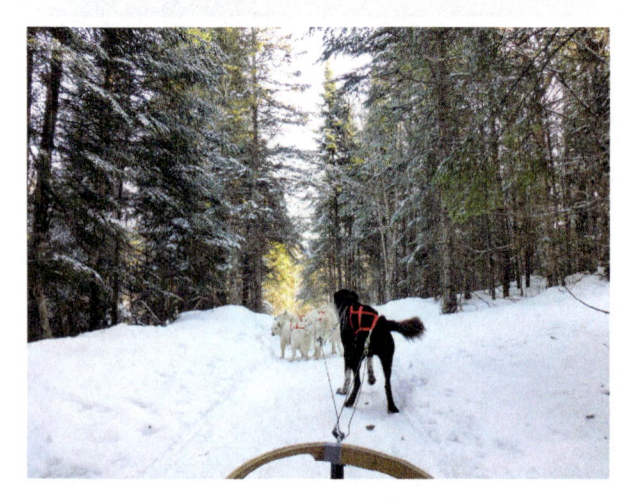

Dog sledding in Quebec City

The Ice Hotel in Quebec City

Jasper National Park Icefield

Glacier Skywalk, Banff

Lake Louise, Banff National Park

A Festival in Montreal

The Jazz Festival in Montreal

Summer Fun

HAITI

My visit to Haiti proved to be an extraordinary and enriching adventure, as I immersed myself in a country brimming with a profound cultural heritage and awe-inspiring natural beauty. Situated in the Caribbean, Haiti occupies the western portion of the island of Hispaniola, and it captivates visitors with its lively music and dance scene, vibrant artistry, and delectable cuisine.

Engaging with the local community stands out as a paramount aspect of visiting Haiti. Renowned for its deep-rooted history and culture, Haiti's people exude warmth and hospitality. During my time there, I had the incredible opportunity to forge connections with the locals, acquiring a profound understanding of their nation and its people. Naturally, it is crucial to remain mindful of safety concerns while traveling in Haiti. The country has faced political instability and endured natural disasters in recent years, necessitating caution and precaution to ensure our well-being.

As my departure to Haiti approached, I couldn't help but harbor a hint of apprehension about traveling alone. Fortunately, my gym buddy Joe decided to accompany me, immediately alleviating my concerns with his reassuring presence. On the flight to Port-au-Prince, we found ourselves seated next to an extraordinary woman named Natasha, hailing from Haiti and having served in the U.S. military. Natasha had undertaken two deployments to Iraq and had recently relocated to New York with aspirations of establishing an orphanage. Armed with a background in social work, she proved to be an amazing companion, and our conversations with her were both enlightening and captivating.

As we descended into **Port-au-Prince** and made our way to the Hotel Keenan in Petonville, I was immediately struck by the area's breathtaking beauty. This upscale suburb boasted a charming gingerbread motif, with the hotel itself showcasing an enchanting design. I was fortunate to have a lovely room overlooking a glistening swimming pool, further enhancing the allure of the surroundings.

The following morning, we embarked on a visit to an orphanage, laden with school supplies, teaching materials, soccer jerseys, and footballs. Accompanying us were Natasha, her brother Hans, and her sister Mondy, as well as Willie, an individual who had been selflessly working in the area since 1998. The journey to the Foyer de Sion au Croix des bouquets orphanage consumed approximately an hour, and along the way, we witnessed several tent cities where people still endured dire living conditions.

Upon arrival at the orphanage, we were warmly received by the manager, who graciously guided us through the premises and introduced us to the children. These remarkable youngsters, aged between 5 and 9, numbered forty in total. We had the opportunity to explore the baby room, the classroom, and the dormitory, and we were deeply impressed by the seamless operation of the orphanage. Over the course of several hours, we engaged with the children, participating in games and singing heartwarming melodies. Hans even brought along an electronic keyboard, which instantly attracted the children, who gathered around him as he played. Amongst the children, there was a specially-abled individual, and witnessing the others embracing him and including him in their activities touched me profoundly. Together, we danced and sang, forging memories that will forever be etched in my heart. Witnessing the radiant joy on the children's faces as we distributed pens, pencils, books, crayons, jerseys, and soccer balls filled my heart with warmth. As we bid farewell, the children expressed their heartfelt gratitude for the impact we had made on their lives, leaving me feeling incredibly blessed to have been able to make a positive difference.

Back at the hotel, I took a moment to reflect upon the events of the day. It had been a day of inspiration, a day dedicated to making a genuine impact, and a day of forging connections with newfound friends. Overwhelmed with emotion, I acknowledged the abundance of goodness in my own life, from the blessings I enjoyed to the remarkable individuals who graced my journey. It truly was a perfect day.

The following day brought another remarkable encounter as I had the chance to meet a woman from Ohio who dedicated her time to working at a nearby church. Engaging in conversation with her, I immediately felt a profound connection. Later on, I strolled over to the town square, intending to capture some snapshots of the Scouts who were diligently cleaning up the St-Pierre park. It was during this time that I crossed paths with a young boy named Roody. Despite being a mere fifteen years old, Roody had already faced adversities that most of us can hardly fathom. Abandoned by his father, he lived with his mother, who lacked the financial means to send him to school. Having only completed third grade, Roody yearned to acquire English and computer skills. I felt an overwhelming urge to assist him, and so I brought him to the church, introducing him to the woman from Ohio. With her invaluable connections, she was able to provide him with the educational resources he needed, while I contributed some funds to support his course fees. Though a modest gesture, I sincerely hope that my actions made a lasting difference in Roody's life.

The subsequent day, we embarked on a journey to the picturesque beach in **Jacmel**. The anticipated two-hour drive, however, took an unexpected detour through downtown. Our path intersected with the Champ de Mars, now transformed into a tent city, and the crumbling remnants of the **President's Palace**, scars left behind by the earthquakes. The city remained ensnared in chaos, with people bustling about in every direction. Yet, amidst the ruins, a resolute spirit and energy pervaded the atmosphere. The market continued to thrive, and individuals persevered in makeshift tents. Continuing our expedition, we bore witness to further evidence of the earthquake's devastation. We traversed through the town of Legion, a place where a significant number of earthquake casualties originated. The entire town lay in ruins, including the once-grand university. Nevertheless, upon arriving in Jacmel, a semblance of normalcy emerged. We sought solace at a family beach, indulging in the tantalizing flavors of grilled fish. The beach exuded vitality, teeming with both locals and tourists reveling in the moment. It served as a poignant reminder that even amidst chaos and destruction, life presses on.

Upon returning to Natasha's family home, we relished in the bonds we had forged. Hans graced us with his piano melodies, and together, we sang and danced in perfect harmony. It was a beautiful moment, characterized by a profound sense of connection and unadulterated joy. The family expressed their heartfelt gratitude for our visit and the benevolent acts we had undertaken.

Reflecting upon the trip, my heart overflows with gratitude for the privilege of serving the people of Haiti. I was able to make a tangible impact on Roody's life and forge meaningful connections with numerous individuals along the way. Despite initial concerns regarding safety and security, everything seamlessly fell into place. I found myself embraced by a surrogate family, savoring delectable local cuisine, and sharing a common purpose with the remarkable people I encountered. The journey surpassed all expectations, etching an indelible mark upon my soul—one that I will forever cherish.

Jacmel Beach

President's Palace after the earthquake **Children at the Orphanage**

Children singing **A bus in Port au Prince**

The Scouts cleaning up St-Pierre park **Delicious grilled fish at Jacmel beach**

HONDURAS: PRIVATE ISLAND

The thought of **renting a private island** fills my heart with overwhelming excitement and joy! It's a cherished aspiration that has captivated the dreams of countless individuals, and I consider myself incredibly fortunate to have transformed that dream into a tangible reality. For years, I pursued this extraordinary goal with unwavering determination, fueled by a desire to experience something truly exceptional. Joined by my five trusted friends, we embarked on an adventure of a lifetime, exploring the vast and breathtaking Caribbean region in search of the perfect island that would meet our exacting criteria and affordable. After days upon days of dedicated search and exploration, our efforts were rewarded beyond measure. We stumbled upon a small, secluded sanctuary—a hidden gem nestled away from the rest of the world. This remarkable place exuded an aura of tranquility, beauty, and serenity. Time seemed to stand still as we marveled at its untouched natural splendor, leaving us in absolute awe of the magnificent wonders of the world. Renting a private island is far more than an extravagant luxury; it transcends the realm of the ordinary. It is an experience that testifies to the boundless possibilities that await those who dare to dream. It serves as a reminder that with unwavering determination, unwavering support, and a touch of serendipity, the world can become our playground—a vast canvas upon which we paint our most extraordinary adventures.

Embarking on the odyssey to reach our destination proved to be an adventure in itself. Commencing from Washington Dulles, I undertook two flights, first from there to San Salvador, El Salvador, and then from San Salvador to San Pedro. However, fate had different plans in store. Soon after takeoff from San Salvador, an acrid scent of smoke permeated the cabin, setting off alarm bells in my mind. The flight attendant valiantly attempted to dissipate the smoke, while the captain gravely announced the need to execute an immediate turnaround and emergency landing due to a malfunction. It was an anxiety-inducing ordeal, yet providentially, we managed to touch down safely. After a two-hour wait, we finally boarded another aircraft, eventually arriving in San Pedro. From there, we embarked on a two-and-a-half-hour taxi ride to Le Ceiba. Finally, we reached the ferry terminal, procured our tickets, and eagerly awaited the voyage to Utila, Honduras. Although the day had been fraught with unanticipated challenges and restlessness, our determination to set foot on our dream island remained steadfast.

The following day marked the pinnacle of our expedition—the private island itself. We had arranged for a boat ride with George, the island's proprietor, who expertly piloted us on a 15-minute journey to our destination. With each passing moment, my excitement soared exponentially as the private island loomed closer. This was the long-awaited instance when I would bask in the splendor and tranquility unique to such an exclusive locale.

As our vessel neared the island's shores, we were instantaneously captivated by the awe-inspiring beauty that enveloped us. Everywhere our eyes wandered, crystal-clear waters, unspoiled beaches, and verdant foliage greeted us. Eager to explore and immerse ourselves in the wonders of this ethereal place, we could hardly contain our anticipation. Our boat docked, and we disembarked, eager to set foot on the island that spanned approximately 2 acres of land. It boasted a main house and a guest house, nestled amidst the tropical paradise. The main house featured three bedrooms, three bathrooms, a fully-equipped kitchen, and a dining room. The guest house, on the other hand, offered a bedroom and two bathrooms. Towering palm trees dotted the landscape, while two inviting hammocks beckoned us to unwind. Facilities such as a generator room, a barbecue pit, and a porch were thoughtfully provided, enhancing our experience. The island relied on solar power for its lighting needs and sourced water from a rainwater tank. Throughout our stay, we utilized solar power solely for illumination during the night, while water was sourced from the rainwater collection.

The ensuing days spent on the island provided us with unparalleled serenity and rejuvenation, constituting the most blissful experiences of my life. My daily routine consisted of leisurely strolls encompassing the entire island, leisurely reclining in a hammock, and engrossing myself in captivating books while admiring the turquoise waters and pelicans gracefully diving for fish. This tranquil escape from the rigors of everyday life proved to be nothing short of perfection.

One of our initial escapades took us **snorkeling at the reef** situated right in front of the house's pier, etching an indelible memory in our hearts. Submerging ourselves in the pristine waters, we were instantly enveloped by a vibrant aquatic ecosystem teeming with life. Schools of brilliantly colored fish danced around us, while intricate coral formations added to the mesmerizing spectacle. For hours, we swam and explored, awestruck by the sheer beauty of this underwater realm. When we resurfaced, a breathtaking sunset greeted our senses, casting a painter's palette of pink, purple, and orange hues across the sky.

Throughout the days, we delighted in observing the graceful pelicans diving fearlessly into the water to seize their piscine prey. We dedicated countless hours attempting to capture the perfect photograph of these majestic creatures in motion. As twilight descended each evening, we made our way to the beach, eager to relish a delectable dinner beneath the canopy of stars. We reveled in the soothing ambiance, savoring fresh seafood and reveling in the company of cherished friends. Even the **hermit crabs** joined us for these nightly feasts, scurrying along the sand and adding a touch of enchantment to the experience.

On one particularly enchanting evening, we chose to recline on the dock, allowing the gentle symphony of ocean waves to wash over us. The night sky stretched above, a tapestry of shimmering stars visible in its entirety. In that transcendent moment, we felt as if we had been transported into a reverie. It was an instance of pure enchantment, forever etching itself in our memories. In fact, the allure of the celestial spectacle compelled me to set up a mattress outdoors and **slumber beneath the stars**. That night, as the gentle ocean breeze lulled me into a peaceful sleep, the twinkling stars illuminated the heavens, creating an ambiance of serenity and rejuvenation.

As the days slipped by, we found ourselves increasingly immersed in the island's serenity and magnificence. We whiled away the hours exploring the azure depths, idling in the comforting embrace of hammocks, and relishing the warmth of genuine camaraderie. One afternoon, we embarked on a boat excursion, venturing out to explore the surrounding areas. Our path led us to a hidden cove, secluded from the vast expanse of the open ocean. We stood entranced, captivated by the pristine, crystal-clear waters and the kaleidoscope of colorful fish gliding effortlessly before us.

Amidst all the thrilling adventures, some of the most cherished moments of our trip arose from the simplest pleasures. We gathered along the shoreline, marveling at the slow descent of the sun, as it bathed the sky in a symphony of hues. By nightfall, we congregated around a crackling **bonfire**, roasting marshmallows and sharing tales that wove threads of laughter and warmth. And for countless hours, we enjoyed each other's company and reveled in conversations and mirth, embracing the gift of true friendship.

As the time drew near to bid farewell to the island, we realized that we had all experienced a profound sense of relaxation and rejuvenation. The stress and worries of our everyday lives had faded away, replaced by a deep sense of peace and contentment. Renting a private island had been a dream come true, but it was the joy, relaxation, nature, and friendship that we experienced there that truly made the trip unforgettable and forever hold a cherished place in our hearts. As we said goodbye to the island and each other, we knew that we would always carry the memories of this special time with us, and that we would cherish them for years to come.

"TRAVEL IS NOT A LUXURY, IT'S A NECESSITY FOR THE SOUL."

- Unknown

Island Dreaming:
OUR PRIVATE ISLAND

Our house on the private island

Crackling bonfire, roasting marshmallows

Hermit Crabs

MEXICO: THE MONARCH BUTTERFLY MIGRATION

Mexico is a diverse and beautiful country that offers visitors a wealth of cultural and natural attractions to explore. With its rich cultural heritage, beautiful landscapes, and warm hospitality, Mexico is a destination that will leave visitors with unforgettable memories. One of the amazing memories was witnessing the monarch butterfly migration. The monarch migration in Mexico is truly a phenomenon that fills scientists with wonder and amazement. How do these beautiful creatures find their way back to the same forest, the same trees, year after year? It was a mystery that I simply had to witness for myself. So, I embarked on a journey to Mexico City and then to **Angangueo**, a small town near the butterfly sanctuaries.

For centuries, **the monarch butterflies have been traveling over 3,000 miles (4,800km) from Canada and the United States to their wintering grounds in Mexico**, where they congregate in large numbers in just a handful of sanctuaries. What's even more remarkable is that these butterflies return to the same trees year after year, using a combination of genetic and environmental cues to guide them on their journey. It's a mystery that still fascinates scientists to this day. The migration is a spectacular sight to behold, as the butterflies fly in large swarms and create a beautiful and colorful display. The journey is a treacherous one, and the monarchs must navigate harsh weather conditions and avoid many predators along the way. It is estimated that only about half of the butterflies that start the journey will make it to Mexico. Scientists still do not fully understand how the monarchs navigate their way to Mexico, but they believe that the butterflies use a combination of the sun's position, the Earth's magnetic field, and visual cues to guide their journey. Once they arrive in the **Oyamel fir forests**, the butterflies huddle together in large clusters to conserve heat and protect themselves from predators.

My adventure started early in the morning, and we went to the **El Rosario monarch butterfly sanctuary**. As we walked up the steep and winding steps, workers were sweeping the area, ensuring that the sanctuary was in pristine condition for visitors. The hike was challenging, but as we approached the forested area, we saw trees that were full of sleeping butterflies, clumped together in groups of thousands. The sight was awe-inspiring, and I couldn't help but feel a sense of wonder at the sheer number of monarchs that were nestled in the trees. As the morning wore on, we explored different parts of the sanctuary and saw more and more butterflies fluttering along the trails. As the day wore on, the butterflies became more and more active, and we watched as they fluttered about, exploring their surroundings and enjoying the warmth of the sun on their wings. We walked along the trail, marveling at the sight of millions of monarchs taking flight around us, their bright orange wings a brilliant contrast against the blue sky above. By noon, the butterflies had started flying around, and we saw them drinking water from mud pots and puddles to warm up. When the sun finally emerged from behind the clouds in the early afternoon, the forest was illuminated with golden light, and the butterflies took flight en masse. It was a breathtaking sight, with thousands upon thousands of orange butterflies filling the sky, like confetti raining down from the heavens.

Despite the crowds of people around us, it felt as though we were the only ones there, lost in the awe-inspiring beauty of this natural wonder. I couldn't help but feel a deep sense of gratitude for the opportunity to experience such a magnificent sight, and for the scientists and researchers who continue to study the monarch migration and try to unravel its mysteries. As the sun began to set and the day drew to a close, we reluctantly made our way back down the trail, our minds still filled with the incredible sight we had witnessed. It was a moment that would stay with us for a lifetime, a reminder of the breathtaking beauty and wonder of the natural world.

Over the course of the day, we learned more about the monarch migration and how it takes five generations for the butterflies to complete their journey. We also discovered that one generation of monarchs, known as the Musathrlah, can live up to nine months – the equivalent of 525 years in human terms. It was fascinating to see how nature had found a way to ensure the survival of this species, and I felt grateful for the opportunity to witness it firsthand.

The next day, we visited another sanctuary, **Sierra Chincua Sanctuary**, which was a newer butterfly sanctuary that had opened in 1970. The hike was longer and more challenging than the one at El Rosario, but the vista was just as beautiful. As we walked through the forest, we saw more and more butterflies on the trees, and when we reached an area that was sunnier, the butterflies started flying around in a frenzy. It was like being in the middle of a snowstorm, except with butterflies instead of snowflakes. We sat on a log and watched the magic unfold, feeling a sense of calm and contentment as we took in the natural beauty of the moment. As we made our way up to the forest where the monarchs roosted, we marveled at the incredible sight of thousands upon thousands of butterflies clinging to the trees, their bright orange wings creating a vivid tapestry against the green foliage. We spent hours in this forest, watching as the butterflies took flight and danced about in the warm sunshine, and we felt our hearts swell with wonder and gratitude for the privilege of being able to witness such a magnificent sight of nature.

On our final day, we returned to **El Rosario Sanctuary**, eager to see more of the monarchs as they took flight in the warm sunshine. We arrived early and made our way up to the sanctuary, where we watched millions of monarchs on the trees as the sun rose higher in the sky. In the afternoon, we witnessed a breathtaking display of monarchs taking flight, with their orange wings shimmering in the sunlight. We talked to locals and other visitors, and everyone we met was friendly and welcoming. As the day drew to a close, we lay on the grass and watched as they filled the sky with their brilliant orange wings, and we marveled at the sight of millions of butterflies fluttering about, their beauty and grace a testament to the incredible power of nature. The monarch butterfly population has been in decline in recent years due to habitat loss, climate change, and the use of pesticides. Conservation efforts are underway to protect the butterfly's habitat and raise awareness about the importance of this incredible migration.

As our trip came to an end and we made our way back to our homes, we felt a sense of deep gratitude and awe for the experience we had just had. We knew that we had been privileged to witness something truly remarkable, a natural wonder that few people ever have the opportunity to see. It was a moment that filled us with a sense of wonder and awe, and that reminded us of the incredible beauty and power of the natural world. It also reminds us of the importance of protecting our planet's fragile ecosystems and preserving the diversity of life on Earth. We are grateful for the opportunity to have had such an incredible experience, and we will always treasure the memories of that magical trip to Mexico.

Thousands of butterflies on Oyamel fir trees

El Rosario monarch butterfly sanctuary

Clusters of Butterflies on **Oyamel fir trees**

Butterflies warming up in warm mud puddle

Butterflies on Oyamel fir trees

Thousands of butterflies filling the sky

THE UNITED STATES OF AMERICA

Ah! America, the home of the Brave and the Free! Being one of the most important and developed countries in today's world, the USA is one of the most beautiful and fascinating countries to explore and visit. There is such a wide range of things to see and do, you could travel the entire 50 States for a lifetime and not get bored. With natural and man-made attractions and scenic beauty visible nowhere else in the World

I consider myself extremely fortunate to call Washington D.C. home. Ever since I was young, I harbored a lifelong dream of embarking on an extraordinary quest to **explore all 50 states comprising the United States of America**. This monumental undertaking promised a once-in-a-lifetime adventure, and as I eagerly awaited its commencement, my heart swelled with unparalleled excitement, boundless curiosity, and uncontainable joy. I envisioned the journey as an opportunity to traverse the country's vast landscapes, immerse myself in its rich history, experience the vibrancy of America's diverse cultures, and partake in unique adventures, all of which would leave an indelible mark on my soul.

As I prepared for this momentous journey, I couldn't help but marvel at the sheer breadth and diversity that awaited me within the borders of my own country. The United States, with its staggering natural beauty, rich historical tapestries, and vibrant cultural expressions, beckoned me with open arms, inviting me to unravel its countless complexities and uncover its hidden treasures.

My adventure began in the **eastern states**, a deliberate choice due to their proximity to my beloved hometown, Washington D.C. Massachusetts, steeped in history, captivated me with the hallowed grounds of Lexington and Concord, where the fires of the American Revolution ignited. Walking the cobblestone streets of Boston, I was transported to the birthplace of the nation, and the iconic Freedom Trail guided me through American history's very heart. Boston is the capital of Massachusetts and is full of history, food, unique neighborhoods and amazing museums and is one of the most walkable downtowns in America. This city is best known for its baked beans, Boston Marathon, Fenway Park and of course the famous bar from the TV show "Cheers". However, if you dig deeper, you will find a treasure of history and culture like the "USS Constitution" the oldest commissioned warship that is still afloat today and is best known by her nickname "Old Ironsides" and fought bravely in the American Revolutionary War and the Museum of Fine Arts just to name a few.

Just a brief 30-minute train ride from Boston is the enchanting and historic town of Salem, Massachusetts which is most famous for its Salem witch trials of 1692 and its famous author Nathaniel Hawthorne of "Scarlet Letter" fame.

Being in Salem, it was easy to lose, myself in the captivating narratives of the past and its rich colonial architecture and world-class museums. Venturing further, I succumbed to the irresistible pull of New York City. Amidst the towering skyscrapers, I marveled at the city's ceaseless energy and the kaleidoscope of cultures interwoven within its fabric. Times Square's luminous spectacle and Central Park's serene beauty left me enchanted and wanting more as the city pulls you into its lively core. As the old adage goes New York is a city that never sleeps and you feel this energy the moment you there. Broadway with its lively shows and artistic prowess will tempt you to stay and visit longer as its sights and sounds are like nowhere else on Earth.
From nightlife attractions like Time Square, Statue of Liberty, its many World-class Museums and art galleries, New York City has it all and is a must see city to put on your "Bucket List".

With wanderlust in my heart, I journeyed **southward**, immersing myself in the soul-stirring landscapes and rich cultural heritage of the region. In Louisiana, the seductive melodies of jazz washed over me, intertwining with the mouthwatering aromas of Creole and Cajun cuisine. In the heart of New Orleans, the city of eternal celebration, I danced to the rhythm of life itself, surrendering to the intoxicating allure of Mardi Gras and the soulful sounds of blues. Moving to Tennessee, the cradle of American music, welcomed me with open arms. Nashville, the illustrious capital of country music, resonated with a harmony that transcended time, while Memphis, the birthplace of blues, sang its sorrowful melodies deep into my soul. I reveled in the exuberance of live performances, tapping my feet to the infectious beats that echoed through the vibrant streets. The allure of the South's sun-kissed beaches and many famous attractions like Walt Disney World, Universal Studios, Kennedy Space Center just to name a few, all drew me to the enchanting shores of Florida. With its glistening turquoise waters and powdery white sands, the Sunshine State exuded an irresistible charm. From the vibrant art deco architecture of Miami Beach to the idyllic tranquility of the Florida Keys, I surrendered myself to the caress of the ocean breeze, allowing the serenity of the coast to wash away the cares of the world.

Eager to explore new horizons, I embarked on a **westward** journey, each mile revealing a breathtaking transformation of the landscapes before me. As I ascended the majestic peaks of the Rocky Mountains in Colorado, a sense of awe enveloped me. The crisp mountain air filled my lungs as I embarked on thrilling outdoor escapades, hiking along rugged trails with the Rockies as my backdrop. Arizona, adorned with a crown of natural wonders, left me breathless. Standing on the precipice of the awe-inspiring Grand Canyon, I gazed into the abyss, my mind grappling with the sheer magnitude and beauty of nature's handiwork. The vermilion cliffs of Sedona painted a surreal backdrop, while the mystical allure of Monument Valley carried me into a realm of timeless wonder.

Continuing my westward odyssey, California unveiled a world of contrasts. Its rugged coastlines kissed the vastness of the Pacific Ocean, and majestic redwood forests stretched towards the heavens. Yosemite National Park, a testament to nature's grandeur, overwhelmed my senses as I stood in the shadow of towering sequoias and witnessed the thunderous roar of cascading waterfalls.

Heading **northward**, the picturesque coasts of Oregon and Washington beckoned me with their ethereal beauty. The dramatic cliffs, adorned with emerald forests, plunged into the churning waters of the Pacific, creating a symphony of crashing waves and salty sea spray. The quaint coastal towns dotted along the way exuded a charm that seemed frozen in time, inviting me to savor their tranquility and partake in their maritime heritage. But the call of the untamed wilderness proved irresistible. Alaska, the Last Frontier, awaited me with open arms. Here, I found myself immersed in a world of staggering glaciers, untouched landscapes, and wildlife that roamed free. From the icy majesty of Glacier Bay to the untamed vastness of Denali National Park, I marveled at the pristine beauty that unfolded before my eyes, forever etching its splendor into the depths of my being.

The allure of paradise beckoned, and I answered its call by crossing the vast expanse of the **Pacific Ocean** to the Hawaiian Islands. A cascade of vibrant hues greeted me as I set foot on this archipelago of natural wonders. From the fiery glow of active volcanoes on the Big Island to the tranquil serenity of Maui's golden beaches, Hawaii enveloped me in its warm embrace. I immersed myself in the rich tapestry of Polynesian culture, experiencing the grace of hula dances, tasting the exotic flavors of traditional cuisine, and forging connections with the islanders who embodied the spirit of aloha.

Throughout my transformative journey, **the warmth and hospitality of the people** I encountered along the way became an integral part of my experience. From the friendly locals in small towns to the passionate guides who generously shared their knowledge, each encounter added depth and meaning to my adventure. I was welcomed into communities, invited to embrace local traditions, and gifted with cherished memories of human connection.

The cuisine of each state also captivated my heart—it was the tantalizing flavors that varied from state to state. In Illinois, I savored the mouthwatering indulgence of a deep-dish pizza, while in Maine, I delighted in the succulent sweetness of lobster rolls. The smoky aromas of Texas-style barbecue tantalized my senses, and the coastal states offered a cornucopia of delectable seafood that celebrated the bounty of the ocean. Every meal became a celebration of local flavors, a delightful chapter in the ever-evolving narrative of my travels.

As the final leg of my journey came into view, a profound sense of accomplishment filled my heart. I stood at the precipice of a remarkable milestone—I had traversed the vast expanse of the

United States, revealing hidden gems and embracing iconic landmarks that collectively defined the captivating essence of this nation. Through my adventures, I had borne witness to the diverse tapestry of landscapes, cultures, and histories that wove the fabric of each state, forging a deeper understanding and appreciation for the astonishing breadth and depth of my extraordinary homeland.

Visiting all 50 U.S. states transcended the realm of physical exploration—it became an emotional and transformative journey that forever expanded the horizons of my soul. It was an opportunity to embrace the unknown, to forge connections with fellow travelers and locals alike, and to celebrate the incredible diversity that makes America so remarkable. The infectious excitement and boundless joy that accompanied every step of this grand adventure left an indelible mark on my being, igniting within me a lifelong passion for exploration, discovery, and the insatiable pursuit of knowledge.

As I reflect upon my odyssey through the 50 states of America, I am filled with an overwhelming sense of gratitude. Gratitude for the vast tapestry of landscapes that unfolded before me, gratitude for the richness of history and culture that I had the privilege to witness, and gratitude for the countless souls who enriched my journey with their warmth, kindness, and stories. For it is through these experiences that I have come to understand that the true beauty of travel lies not just in the places we visit, but in the acquaintances, we forge, the perspectives we gain, and the deep appreciation we develop for the world and its people. The United States of America, with its myriad wonders and captivating spirit, will forever hold a special place in my heart, a testament to the profound impact of exploration and the transformative power of wanderlust.

CHERRY BLOSSOMS
IN WASHINGTON D.C.

The White House

Cherry Blossoms in Washington DC

Cherry Blossoms in Washington DC

Chicago

Miami

Maine

Hawaii

Hawaii sunset

Oregon

Mount Rushmore, South Dakota

The Grand Prismatic Hot Spring

④ SOUTH AMERICA CONTINENT: 12 COUNTRIES

🇦🇷	Argentina	🇬🇾	Guyana
🇧🇴	Bolivia	🇵🇾	Paraguay
🇧🇷	Brazil	🇵🇪	Peru
🇨🇱	Chile	🇸🇷	Suriname
🇨🇴	Colombia	🇺🇾	Uruguay
🇪🇨	Ecuador	🇻🇪	Venezuela

SOUTH AMERICA CONTINENT

Welcome to the home of the World's biggest rainforest, the largest river and the tallest waterfall. That is just the beginning when you travel to the beautifully exotic South American continent. South America, the land of breathtaking natural wonders, is a continent that beckons travelers with its diverse landscapes, rich history, vibrant cultures and an unparalleled number of plants and animal species. South America's extremely rich biodiversity is unique among the world's continents. It also prides itself on a primary mountain system, the Andes, which is also the world's longest, with the range covering over 5500 miles.

It is a place where lush rainforests teem with exotic wildlife, where soaring mountain peaks touch the heavens, and where sun-kissed beaches invite relaxation. The name "South America" was bestowed upon this landmass in honor of Amerigo Vespucci, differentiating it from its northern counterpart and identifying it as the continent located to the south of the equator. As you explore this captivating continent, you'll encounter a people known for their passion, warmth, and a deep-rooted connection to their ancestral lands.

South America's cultural tapestry is a vivid mosaic, woven together by indigenous traditions and the influence of immigrants from around the world. The vibrant celebrations of music, dance, and art reflect this rich diversity. And when it comes to cuisine, South America offers a gastronomic journey like no other, with each region boasting its unique flavors and spices. Now, let's delve deeper into **some of the must-see destinations** and experiences that await you in South America.

Our journey begins in **Machu Picchu, Peru**. This ancient Incan citadel, nestled high in the Andes Mountains, is undoubtedly one of the most iconic destinations in South America. You can reach Machu Picchu's summit either by train or by trekking the famous Inca Trail. Once there, you'll not only enjoy stunning panoramic views of the surrounding landscapes but also experience a profound sense of awe at the incredible engineering and architectural feats achieved by the Incas. While in Peru, the historic city of Cusco, the former capital of the Inca Empire, beckons with its wealth of historical sites, including the impressive Sacsayhuaman fortress and the mesmerizing Qorikancha temple. As you stroll through Cusco's narrow streets to admire its colonial architecture and bustling markets. Be prepared for the high altitude at Cusco and Machu Picchu, as many tourists are surprised by the debilitating effects of the thinner air and often require oxygen to assist them. The Inca citadel sits at 2430 meters above sea level, while the city of Cusco where the tour to Machu Picchu begins is located 3400 meters above sea level. Most people start to feel the effects of altitude sickness once they are above 6561 feet or 2000 meters and it can happen regardless of age or fitness level. Still, Machu Picchu and Cusco are worth the visit and should be on everyone's bucket list.

Next on our journey are the **Galapagos Islands, Ecuador**. This is an experience of a lifetime and the current environmental conditions make the Galapagos a definite must see! Despite being located at the equator, the Galapagos Islands are kept cool by the cool ocean currents that caress these islands and make it a strange mix of tropical and temperate climates, perfect for all types of flora and fauna. For wildlife enthusiasts, the Galapagos Islands are a paradise. Located off the coast of Ecuador, these islands are home to an astonishing array of unique species, including giant tortoises, marine iguanas, and the famous blue-footed boobies. Embarking on a boat tour allows you to witness these remarkable creatures up close in their natural habitat—an experience that will stay with you forever.

Our journey then takes us to **Iguazu Falls, Brazil, and Argentina**. Often referred to as "The Jewel of the Forest," the Iguazu Falls are among the most stunning natural wonders in South America. Straddling the border between Brazil and Argentina, these falls consist of over 250 individual cascades, surrounded by lush rainforest. You can get up close and personal with the falls by taking a boat tour or embarking on hikes along the surrounding trails to soak in the breathtaking views.

Our adventure leads us to **Patagonia, spanning Chile and Argentina**. Adventure seekers will find their haven in Patagonia, a region that offers a plethora of outdoor activities, including hiking, mountaineering, and glacier trekking. Marvel at the awe-inspiring landscapes, including the magnificent Perito Moreno Glacier and the pristine beauty of Torres del Paine National Park. Patagonia promises a series of unique experiences that will test your limits and ignite your spirit of adventure.

Next, we venture to the colorful and exciting city of **Rio de Janeiro, Brazil**. If vibrant culture and an electrifying nightlife are what you seek, a visit to Rio de Janeiro is a must. This bustling city is known for its colorful festivals, beautiful beaches, and lively music scene. Don't miss the iconic Christ the Redeemer statue atop Corcovado Mountain, and be sure to take a cable car ride to Sugarloaf Mountain for panoramic views of this captivating metropolis.

The journey continues to **the Amazon Rainforest**. Explore the heart of the Amazon rainforest, which spans across several South American countries. Here, you can discover unique flora and fauna, witness vibrant biodiversity, and experience the incredible beauty of the world's largest tropical rainforest. From wildlife safaris to canopy walks, the Amazon offers an array of unforgettable adventures.

Our journey then leads us to **Buenos Aires, Argentina,** one of Latin America's largest sea ports and home to incredible national parks and UNESCO

World Heritage sites throughout the city. When you think of visiting Buenos Aires you immediately remember delicious cuisine, incredible wines and some of the hemisphere's most dramatic cityscapes. The restaurants along the river are some of the best places to dine anywhere on earth and Buenos Aires is a relatively safe city to visit and enjoy. Immerse yourself in the rich cultural tapestry of Argentina's capital city. Enjoy passionate tango performances, savor mouthwatering Argentine steaks, and explore historic neighborhoods like San Telmo and La Boca, known for their colorful buildings and vibrant street art.

We then venture to the wine country of **Mendoza, Argentina**. Wine connoisseurs will find paradise in Mendoza. This region is renowned for its vineyards and wineries, offering wine tastings and tours amidst stunning mountain scenery. You can taste some of the world's finest Malbec wines while taking in the picturesque landscapes.

Our next destination is the **Museo del Oro in Bogotá, Colombia**. Delve into the history of pre-Columbian cultures at the Museo del Oro, one of the world's most renowned museums for gold artifacts and archaeological treasures. This cultural gem offers a fascinating glimpse into Colombia's rich heritage.

Our journey continues to **Easter Island, Chile**. Located in the remote Pacific Ocean, Easter Island is known for its enigmatic Moai statues. These massive stone figures, shrouded in mystery, are a testament to the island's intriguing history and unique Polynesian culture.

South America is a continent of boundless wonders, each destination offering a unique blend of natural beauty, cultural richness, and adventurous spirit. As you embark on your journey through this mesmerizing continent, you'll be touched by the warmth of its people, the splendor of its landscapes, and the depth of its history, leaving you with memories that will last a lifetime.

THE BEST TIME TO VISIT SOUTH AMERICA CONTINENT

South America is a vast continent that spans over 17 million square kilometers and offers a wide range of experiences for travelers. The best time to visit South America depends on the region you plan to visit and the activities you want to do. Here are some examples of specific places to visit and when it's best to go:

Spring (September-November)
Spring is a great time to visit South America for nature and wildlife enthusiasts. One of the most iconic spring destinations is Argentina's Iguazu Falls, which is at its peak in October and November. Visitors can witness the stunning waterfalls and lush rainforest scenery while hiking or taking a boat tour. The weather is also more comfortable during this time, with mild temperatures and fewer crowds. Another great spring destination is Chile's Atacama Desert, which comes to life with blooming wildflowers after the winter rains. Visitors can enjoy hiking, stargazing, and exploring the unique geological formations. The temperature is also more mild during the spring months,

making it an ideal time for outdoor activities.

Summer (December-February) Summer is the peak season in South America, with warm and sunny weather that's perfect for outdoor activities and festivals. One of the most popular summer destinations is Brazil, which boasts stunning beaches, vibrant culture, and some of the world's most famous festivals. The most famous of these is Carnival in Rio de Janeiro, held in February or March. The city comes alive with colorful parades, samba music, and parties that last into the early hours of the morning. Another great summer destination is Argentina, where visitors can explore the natural wonders of Patagonia. The summer months offer longer days and more mild temperatures, making it the perfect time for hiking in Torres del Paine National Park or visiting the Perito Moreno Glacier.

Fall (March-May) Fall is a great time to visit South America for outdoor activities and cultural experiences. One of the most iconic fall destinations is Peru, where visitors can explore the ancient ruins of Machu Picchu. March and April are great months to visit as the rainy season has just ended, and the landscape is lush and green. The weather is mild, making it ideal for hiking and exploring the surrounding area. Another great fall destination is Chile's wine region, which is at its peak in April and May. Visitors can enjoy wine tasting and tours, as well as exploring the charming towns and stunning scenery. The harvest season also takes place during this time, making it an excellent opportunity to witness the traditional grape-picking and wine-making processes.

Winter (June-August) Winter is a great time to visit South America for winter sports and wildlife viewing. One of the best winter destinations is Chile's ski resorts, such as Valle Nevado and Portillo. Visitors can enjoy skiing, snowboarding, and other winter activities while taking in the breathtaking Andes mountains. The winter season also offers a chance to see the stunning landscape covered in snow. Another great winter destination is Ecuador's Galapagos Islands, where visitors can see unique wildlife like giant tortoises, penguins, and sea lions. June to August is a great time to visit as it's the dry season and the waters are calmer for snorkeling and diving. The temperature is also cooler, making it more comfortable for outdoor activities.

South America's seasons provide a colorful palette of experiences, from the pulsating energy of Rio's Carnival to the tranquil beauty of Patagonian landscapes. Whether you seek adventure, cultural immersion, or natural wonders, South America invites travelers to explore, savor, and create unforgettable memories.

Step into the realm of unbridled adventure as I unveil the most spellbinding stories and awe-inspiring photographs that encapsulate my extraordinary expedition across the mesmerizing continent of South America. What lies ahead is not just a mere collection of narratives and images; they are the vibrant strokes of a masterpiece painted by the vibrant hues of this magnificent continent. My journey through South America was nothing short of an epic odyssey, an exhilarating dance with the extraordinary. From the towering peaks of the Andes, where I felt on top of the world, to the pristine Amazon rainforests that whispered secrets of the ancient Earth, every moment was a profound revelation. The continent's breathtaking diversity, from lush jungles to arid deserts, mirrored the diversity of its incredible people, whose warmth and hospitality welcomed me with open arms.

As I ventured through the bustling streets of South America's vibrant cities, explored its hidden corners, and immersed myself in its rich cultural tapestry, I discovered that this journey was more than just sightseeing—it was a soul-stirring odyssey. Every encounter, every interaction, every taste of its delectable cuisine was an invitation to partake in the soul of the continent. The joy and enrichment that emanated from my South American sojourn are beyond measure. It was as though the continent had beckoned me into its embrace, sharing its ancient wisdom and contemporary wonders alike. To have had the privilege of exploring this astounding continent has forever transformed my perspective on life and the world. My heart swells with immeasurable gratitude for the boundless gifts that South America has bestowed upon me, and I am utterly exhilarated to have embarked on this remarkable journey of a lifetime.

HIKING ON ICE:
THE PERITO MORENO GLACIER

ARGENTINA

Argentina is a vast and diverse country that spans across much of South America. One of the most popular destinations in Argentina is the vibrant and cosmopolitan city of Buenos Aires. Buenos Aires is a bustling metropolis that is full of life and energy. The city has a long and rich history that is reflected in its architecture, food, and music. But what makes Buenos Aires stand out is its tango culture.

Tango is an important part of Argentine culture and is celebrated throughout the country. The dance originated in the Rio de la Plata region of Argentina and Uruguay in the late 19th century. It is known for its passionate and melancholic rhythms, and its complex and intimate choreography. Tango dancers in Argentina are renowned for their skill and artistry. They are trained in a variety of techniques, including close embrace, fluid footwork, and improvisation. The dance requires a deep connection between partners, with the goal of creating a seamless and harmonious movement. One of the most famous tango dancers in history was Juan Carlos Copes, who helped to popularize tango around the world in the 1980s and 1990s. His innovative choreography and stylish performances captivated audiences and helped to modernize the dance. However, learning about tango culture is one thing, experiencing it is another. My experience of learning tango in Buenos Aires was one of the most memorable experiences of my life. The city is full of tango schools and milongas where locals and tourists can learn and experience the thrill of tango dancing. I took lessons at one of the schools, and it was truly an immersive experience. I learned not only the dance steps but also the cultural significance of tango in Argentine society. I got to meet and interact with locals who shared their passion for tango with me.

Aside from tango, Buenos Aires is also a foodie's paradise, with a cuisine that reflects the city's diverse history and cultural influences. Argentine cuisine is centered around meat, and one of the most popular dishes is asado, a type of barbecue that is popular throughout Argentina. Asado is typically prepared on a grill known as a parilla and is made up of various cuts of beef, lamb, and pork. The cuisine was another highlight of my trip to Argentina. I tried different cuts of meat that I had never tasted before, and they were all delicious.

During my trip to Argentina, I also visited **the Mendoza region**, which is renowned for its stunning natural beauty, rich culture, and world-famous **Malbec wines**. The region is located at the foothills of the Andes Mountains and is Argentina's premier wine region for wine lovers and foodies alike. The Malbec grape is the star of Mendoza's wine industry, and the region produces some of the world's finest Malbec wines. I visited a few wineries and vineyards that are scattered throughout the region and learned about the winemaking process and sampled some of the region's finest wines. Some of the most popular wineries in Mendoza include Bodega Catena Zapata, Bodegas Salentein, and Finca Decero.

Another breathtaking place to visit is **Patagonia**! Patagonia is a vast and breathtaking region located at the southern end of South America, spanning across Argentina and Chile. The region is known for its dramatic landscapes, ranging from snow-capped mountains to glacial lakes and vast steppes. One of the most iconic destinations in Patagonia is the **Perito Moreno Glacier**, located in Los Glaciares National Park in Argentina. This glacier is one of the largest and most impressive glaciers in the world, spanning over 250 square kilometers. I had the opportunity to **hike on the Perito Moreno Glacier** twice during my trips to Argentina, and it was an experience that is unlike any other. The journey began with a boat ride around the glacier's base to witness the calving of icebergs from the glacier's face. The sound of ice cracking and falling into the water was incredible to hear. Once we arrived at the site, I was equipped with crampons on my shoes and followed knowledgeable guides to hike on the glaciers ice field and explore its crevasses and ice caves.

The hike was physically demanding, but it was an unforgettable experience that provides a unique perspective on the glacier's stunning beauty. We hiked up and down the glaciers and experienced the beauty of the glaciers. Many parts of the glaciers were so blue, it was almost surreal. We crossed some streams of melted glaciers, and I took a drink of this fresh, sweet, cold glacier water. It was the best tasting water I have ever tasted, pure and refreshing. The views from the top of the glacier are truly breathtaking, with majestic panoramic vistas of the surrounding mountains and lakes. It was a once-in-a-lifetime experience to be standing on the glacier and to see the immense beauty of the region from that unique vantage point. After an hour of hiking, we celebrated our hike with local rum and 400-year-old glacier ice in the drink, and savoring the awe-inspiring view of these amazing glaciers.

Aside from the Perito Moreno Glacier, Patagonia is home to a number of other natural wonders that are well worth a visit. Torres del Paine National Park in Chile is known for its stunning mountain scenery and hiking trails. The park is also home to a variety of wildlife, including guanacos, pumas, and condors. The Valdes Peninsula in Argentina is a UNESCO World Heritage Site and a haven for marine wildlife such as whales, sea lions, and penguins. Witnessing these creatures in their natural habitats is an experience that can't be replicated anywhere else. Hiking is a popular activity in Patagonia, and for a good reason. The hiking trails in Patagonia offer some of the most stunning vistas in the world, with snow-capped mountains, crystal-clear lakes, and verdant forests providing the backdrop for the region's natural beauty. The most popular hiking trails in Patagonia include the W Trek in **Torres del Paine National Park** and the Fitz Roy Trek in Los Glaciares National Park.

My trips to Argentina are an unforgettable experience that gave me memories to last a lifetime. From exploring the city's rich history, immersing myself in the tango culture, indulging in the incredible cuisine, exploring the many vineyards and wineries, hiking on the Perito Moreno Glacier, exploring Torres del Paine National Park, or experiencing the country's natural wonders, Argentina has given me many joyful moments to savor for a long time.

Hiking on Perito Moreno Glacier

Iguazu Falls

La Boca, Buenos Aires

The Pink House

The Obelisk, Buenos Aires

Tango dancers at the weekend market

BRAZIL

Brazil is a country that is simply breathtaking and a must-visit destination for anyone looking to immerse themselves in vibrant cultures, warm communities, and stunning landscapes. From the moment I arrived, I was struck by the country's welcoming spirit and the vibrancy of the Brazilian people. It was like stepping into a world of color and warmth, where every person I met was eager to share their culture and traditions with me.

Having worked with Brazil for many years, I was fortunate to have built many friendships that have lasted for years. One of the things that I loved most about Brazil was the strong sense of community and family that permeated everything. Whether I was attending a festival or just wandering through a local market, I felt like I was part of a larger family. The warmth and kindness of the people were infectious, and it made me feel more connected to the world around me than I ever had before.

The diversity of the country was something that amazed me, with its mix of indigenous, African, and European cultures coming together to create something truly unique. From trying new foods to experiencing the everyday rhythms of Brazilian life, I loved wandering through the neighborhoods and soaking up the beauty of this incredible country. The natural beauty of Brazil was nothing short of breathtaking, from the endless miles of pristine beaches to the lush rainforests and towering waterfalls. There was no shortage of awe-inspiring landscapes to explore, and I felt more alive and connected to the earth than ever before.

There were many incredible experiences that stand out in my mind, but the Carnival and the New Year's Eve celebration were definitely highlights. **Celebrating the new year in Rio de Janeiro** was a very special day for me. The event attracts thousands of people every year and is known as "Réveillon" in Portuguese. On New Year's Eve, after having dinner, we walked to Copacabana beach to join three million new friends to celebrate the new year. The streets were filled with people dressed in white, which is believed to bring good luck in the new year. The atmosphere was electric, and people were in high spirits, ready to welcome the new year with joy and excitement.

New Year's Eve is a significant celebration in Rio de Janeiro, and the people of Rio de Janeiro follow many unique traditions to welcome the new year. Some of the most popular traditions include paying tribute to the God of the Sea. Honoring the God of the Sea, Lemanjá, is an essential part of New Year's Eve celebrations in Rio de Janeiro. People dress in white and head to the beaches to make offerings of flowers, candles, and other small gifts to the goddess. It is believed that by making these offerings, Lemanjá will bring good luck, happiness, and prosperity in the coming year and jumping over seven waves is an exciting tradition that can bring good luck and ward off evil spirits.

As we approached midnight, the countdown began, and the sky was exploded with a stunning display of fireworks over the ocean. The firework display was accompanied by music, adding to the festive atmosphere. The fireworks were launched from various points along the coast, creating a stunning visual display that was unforgettable. Sharing this awe-inspiring site with three million people was a truly incredible experience.
The celebration continued beyond the beaches and parks, with restaurants, bars, and nightclubs hosting special events and parties to mark the occasion. The party continued well into the early hours of the morning, with people dancing and celebrating until the sun came up.

Another popular event that captured my heart was **the carnival in Rio de Janeiro**, Brazil. It is an annual festival of music, dance, and color that is a celebration of Brazilian culture and tradition. The carnival is an elaborate and spectacular display that takes place in the city every year and attracts thousands of visitors from all over the world. As someone who was fortunate enough to experience it firsthand, I can confidently say that it was a once-in-a-lifetime experience that left me in awe.

The carnival in Rio de Janeiro is organized around samba schools, which are community-based organizations that represent different neighborhoods in the city. It is a festival of music, dance, and color that takes place in the city every year, attracting thousands of visitors from all over the world. These schools prepare for the carnival for months in advance, with preparations starting immediately after the previous year's carnival ends. They create elaborate floats, costumes, and dance routines, with each school trying to outdo the other in the parade competition. The parade competition takes place at the Sambadrome, a purpose-built stadium that can seat up to 90,000 people.

The carnival parade is the highlight of the carnival, with the samba schools competing against each other in a spectacular display of music, dance, and color. Each samba school has a theme or story that they present through their floats, costumes, and dance routines. The parade is divided into several sections, with each samba school having about an hour to perform their routine. I was lucky enough to attend several nights of the carnival parades and can say that I had many sleepless nights from the excitement and joy. Aside from the parade, there are also block parties or "**blocos**" that take place throughout the city during the carnival. These street parties are organized around a particular theme or music genre and attract large crowds of locals and tourists.

Another beautiful place to visit is **the Iguazu Falls**. Visiting the extraordinary Iguazu Falls in both Brazil and Argentina was an exhilarating adventure filled with boundless joy and excitement. From the moment I arrived at this natural marvel, I could sense that I was about to witness something truly extraordinary. As I approached the falls, the air became filled with anticipation and the distant rumble of water crashing against rocks grew louder. The surrounding lush greenery added to the sense of mystery and wonder, as if nature itself was preparing to reveal its grandest masterpiece. The anticipation in my heart reached its peak as I caught my first glimpse of the falls, and my breath was taken away. The sight before me was beyond anything I could have imagined. Countless waterfalls cascaded down from towering heights, forming an intricate network of plunging torrents. The sheer power and magnitude of the falls were awe-inspiring, and I found myself unable to tear my eyes away from this awe-inspiring spectacle.

To explore the falls, I followed the well-maintained paths that wound their way through the national parks on both sides of the border. The path took me through dense rainforests teeming with life, providing a vibrant backdrop to the thunderous roar of the waterfalls. As I walked along the trails, I encountered a symphony of tropical birdsong and the occasional sighting of colorful butterflies fluttering in the air. One of the highlights of my visit was reaching the Devil's Throat, the most iconic and impressive part of Iguazu Falls. The sheer scale of this colossal U-shaped waterfall was simply breathtaking. Standing on the platform overlooking the abyss, I could feel the immense power of nature vibrating through my being. The thunderous sound of water plunging into the abyss below echoed in my ears, creating a sensory experience that was both thrilling and humbling.

To get an even closer look at the falls, I decided to take a boat ride along the river. As the boat approached the cascades, I could feel the mist on my face and the anticipation building within me. The boat ventured bravely towards the falls, navigating through the swift currents with skill and precision. As we drew nearer, the spray engulfed us, drenching our clothes and filling the air with an invigorating freshness. The sheer force of the water was exhilarating, and I couldn't help but let out shouts of excitement and awe. Exploring the falls from different vantage points allowed me to appreciate their diverse beauty. Each viewpoint offered a unique perspective, showcasing the falls' various shapes, sizes, and angles. From the panoramic vistas that stretched as far as the eye could see to the intimate viewpoints that brought me face-to-face with the cascading water, I was constantly in awe of the natural grandeur that surrounded me.

Beyond the falls themselves, the national parks encompassing Iguazu Falls provided a myriad of opportunities for further exploration. I embarked on hikes through the verdant rainforests, following trails that wound their way through the dense foliage. The lush green canopy above me offered respite from the sun's rays, while the rich aromas of damp earth and wildflowers filled the air. Along the way, I encountered exotic wildlife, such as colorful toucans, playful monkeys swinging from tree to tree, and vibrant butterflies fluttering gracefully.

As the sun began to set, painting the sky with hues of orange and pink, I took a moment to reflect on the immense privilege of being able to witness such a natural wonder. The joy and excitement I felt during my visit to Iguazu Falls were unmatched, and I knew that this experience would forever hold a special place in my heart.

Brazil is a country that simply captivates and left me spellbound. Its welcoming people, diverse cultures, stunning landscapes, and the Carnival and New Year's Eve celebrations in Rio de Janeiro were the most amazing events I have ever experienced. They were a showcase of Brazilian culture and traditions that left me feeling both amazed and grateful to have been a part of it. These events truly captured my heart and will forever be etched in my memory as an incredible experience that I will never forget. The visit to Iguazu Falls was an unforgettable journey that exceeded my wildest expectations. The joy and excitement I felt throughout my time there were unparalleled. The sheer power, beauty, and immensity of the falls left an indelible mark on my soul, reminding me of the incredible wonders that our planet has to offer. It was a journey that I will gladly recount with joy and excitement for years to come.

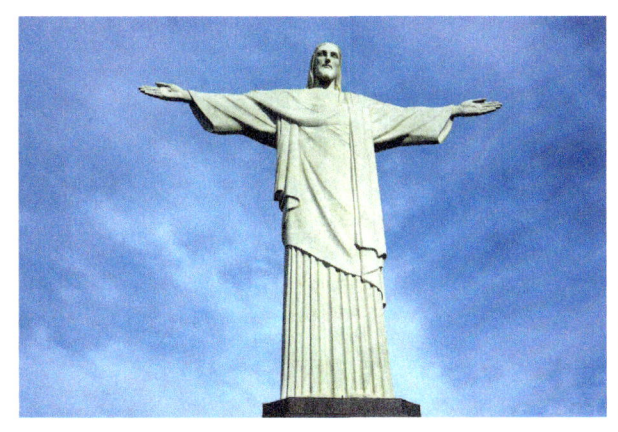

Christ Redeemer

Sugarloaf mountain, Rio de Janeiro

Ipanema Beach

Ipanema Beach

Brasilia Cathedral

Oscar Niemeyer's creation

Ipanema Beach

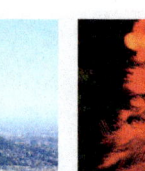

Copacabana Beach

Sugarloaf Mountain

The Carnival

The Carnival in Rio de Janeiro

The Carnival in Rio de Janeiro

ECUADOR: THE GALAPAGOS

The Galapagos are a must see. There is no place on earth quite like it and it is truly an adventure of a lifetime. The archipelago is a remote paradise, located approximately 1,000 kilometers (620 miles) off the coast of Ecuador in the Pacific Ocean. The islands are a melting pot of marine, terrestrial, and avian wildlife, and it's no wonder that they have been dubbed "a living laboratory of evolution." The Galapagos Islands are famous for their unique wildlife, such as the giant tortoises, marine iguanas, and blue-footed boobies. Each species has evolved in isolation, resulting in fascinating adaptations that make them perfectly suited to their environment. The archipelago is also home to a variety of landscapes, from volcanic craters to pristine beaches. Each island has its own distinct character and offers unique opportunities for exploration.

I was filled with excitement as I stepped off the plane onto the tarmac of Baltra Island's airport. This was the start of my long-awaited journey to the Galapagos Islands. From the moment I arrived on **Baltra Island**, I was greeted with breathtaking views of the ocean and the stunning landscapes that make up this incredible archipelago. But it was not just the scenery that left me in awe, it was the wildlife that truly stole my heart.

As I made my way from the airport to my hotel, I was in awe of the stunning scenery around me. The road was lined with tall cacti and lush green vegetation, and as we drove, the driver stopped several times to show us giant tortoises that were roaming the streets. It was an incredible sight to see these gentle giants up close and personal.

My first stop was on **Isabella Island**, where I was blown away by the sheer beauty of the landscape. The island was home to several active volcanoes, and the rugged terrain provided a stark contrast to the crystal-clear waters that surrounded it. During my time on Isabella Island, I hiked through the stunning landscapes, explored the local wildlife, and even had the chance to swim with sea turtles and manta rays.

The following day, I ventured to **Puerto Ayora**, where I embarked on a leisurely walk to Tortuga Bay. While the trail was paved with bricks, the scenery was still breathtaking. The beach was absolutely stunning, with white sand and crystal-clear water. I will never forget the moment when I first saw the marine iguanas swimming in the ocean. It was a sight that I had never witnessed before, and it filled me with a sense of wonder and amazement. These unique creatures were truly fascinating, and watching them forage for food in the water was something that will stay with me forever.

Continue on my journey, I visited **Charles Darwin Research Station in Puerto Ayora**, Santa Cruz Island. This renowned research center is dedicated to the study and preservation of the unique ecosystem that inspired Charles Darwin's theory of evolution. The center itself is a hub of scientific activity, with numerous laboratories, exhibits, and educational facilities that showcase the ongoing research and conservation efforts.

One of the main attractions of the Charles Darwin Research Center is its giant tortoise breeding program. The Galapagos Islands are famous for their giant tortoises, and the research center plays a crucial role in protecting and restoring their populations. I observed these magnificent creatures up close, learning about their biology, behavior, and the ongoing conservation initiatives aimed at preserving their habitats. The research center also offers the opportunity to explore informative exhibits that delve into the rich biodiversity of the Galapagos Islands. These exhibits showcase the unique flora and fauna found on each island and explain the significance of the Galapagos as a living laboratory for scientific research. I learned about the ongoing projects and initiatives undertaken by researchers, as well as the challenges faced in preserving this fragile ecosystem.

In addition to the exhibits and educational displays, the Charles Darwin Research Center also serves as a base for scientists and researchers from around the world. Many experts studying various aspects of the Galapagos ecosystem work here, and I had the chance to interact with them, gaining firsthand knowledge about their research and the importance of their findings. Beyond the scientific endeavors, the research center is actively involved in community outreach and education programs. They collaborate with local communities, schools, and organizations to raise awareness about conservation and sustainability. This engagement not only helps to protect the Galapagos Islands but also fosters a sense of stewardship among the residents and visitors alike. Visiting the Charles Darwin Research Center is not only an opportunity to witness the ongoing scientific research but also a chance to appreciate the incredible natural wonders that inspired Charles Darwin's groundbreaking theory of evolution. It serves as a reminder of the delicate balance of nature and the importance of preserving these unique ecosystems for future generations.

During my visit to **North Seymour Island**, I was blown away by the diversity of wildlife that I encountered. From sea lions to blue-footed boobies, every animal seemed to be more incredible than the last. However, it was the male frigate birds with their bright red balloons on their necks that truly stole the show. Their unique appearance was absolutely breathtaking, and watching them soar through the sky was a true privilege.

On the third day, I embarked on a snorkeling trip to **Pinzon Island**. I stopped at the dive shop to rent equipment, and then we set out on a boat to Pinzon. During the first snorkeling experience, the water was rough, however; things quickly improved when I spotted several massive turtles and then a group of approximately 20 sharks. It was an unforgettable experience to see these creatures up close and personal.

Next up was **San Cristobal Island**, which was home to an incredible variety of wildlife. From the moment I arrived, I was greeted by the sight of sea lions lounging on the beach, and as I explored the island further, I was amazed by the diversity of birds and reptiles that called this place home. One of the highlights of my time on San Cristobal Island was visiting the giant tortoise breeding center, where I learned about the efforts to protect these incredible creatures. But the highlight of my time on San Cristobal was visiting the stunning Cerro Tijeretas viewpoint. From this spot, I could see sea lions lounging on the rocks below and frigate birds soaring overhead.

What sets the Galapagos Islands apart from other tourist destinations is the way that they have been preserved. The Ecuadorian government has implemented strict regulations to protect the fragile ecosystems and prevent over-tourism. Visitors to the islands must be accompanied by a licensed guide and must follow a set of guidelines to minimize their impact on the environment. This ensures that the islands remain pristine for generations to come.

Visiting the Galapagos Islands is an experience that will stay with me for a lifetime. From the incredible wildlife to the stunning landscapes, there is something special about this remote paradise. Throughout my journey, I was constantly inspired by the natural wonders of the Galapagos Islands. From the incredible landscapes to the diverse and unique wildlife, this is a place that truly captures the magic of our world. It is an experience that I will never forget, and I hope that one day I will be able to return and once again bask in the sheer wonder of this incredible place.

Frigate Bird

The Blue footed Booby

Marine Iguanas

Seals

Penguins

Marine Iguana

Dinner on the street, Baltra Island

ANTARCTICA CONTINENT 5

Antarctica is one of the most extraordinary travel destinations in the World. One of the farthest away, yet exquisitely untrammeled, starkly beautiful, and unique places on this Blue Marble we call home. Antarctica is a very unique and special place with its icy landscapes, unique wildlife and no permanent human habitation.

Antarctica, the mesmerizing frozen wilderness at the very bottom of our planet, is a destination that defies description. It is the last great frontier of travel, a place that beckons the intrepid explorer with its pristine natural beauty, towering icebergs, and unique, otherworldly landscapes. Visiting Antarctica is not merely an adventure; it's an exhilarating journey into the heart of the unknown, an experience that leaves an indelible mark on your soul.

The name "Antarctica" carries with it an aura of ancient mystique, hailing from the Greek word "antarktikos," which translates to "opposite to the Arctic." The ancient Greeks, with their vivid imagination and boundless curiosity, believed in the existence of a southern counterpart to the Arctic regions. But it took the courage and determination of early 19th-century explorers to confirm the existence of this vast, icy continent.

The moment you step onto the frozen shores of Antarctica, you become part of a select few who have had the privilege of witnessing this untouched realm. The thrill of standing amidst a landscape where the boundaries of ice and sky merge into an ethereal, infinite horizon is unlike any other. It's a sensory overload of nature's grandeur that awakens a profound sense of wonder.

And then there's the wildlife. Oh, the wildlife! From the comical antics of penguins to the majestic grace of whales, Antarctica boasts a cast of characters that could rival any blockbuster movie. Picture yourself watching Adélie, chinstrap, and Gentoo penguins waddling across the icy terrain, seals basking on glistening ice floes, and colossal whales breaching the surface of frigid waters. Each encounter with these creatures is a symphony of nature's marvels.

In Antarctica, there are no permanent residents, but the inhabitants are a unique community of scientists, adventurers, and explorers who brave the harshest conditions on Earth. Here, survival is an art, and exploration is a way of life. It's a culture deeply rooted in respect for the environment and an unwavering commitment to the principles of stewardship.

One of the most exhilarating activities in Antarctica is **wildlife spotting**. The continent is a living testament to the power of evolution, with a mesmerizing array of animals, including penguins, seals, whales, and seabirds. Imagine the sheer joy of witnessing penguins in their playful splendor, seals lazing in the sun, and the sheer spectacle of whales breaking the surface with a thunderous splash. These wildlife encounters will forever be etched in your memory.

But there's more. **The South Pole,** that iconic spot at the southernmost tip of our planet, stands as a symbol of human achievement and exploration. Visit the Amundsen-Scott South Pole Station, a scientific research outpost staffed year-round. Stand at the very spot that marks the Earth's axis, and capture that historic moment in a photograph—a memento of your journey to one of the most remote places on Earth.

For those who crave adventure, **kayaking** in Antarctica offers an experience that defies description. Paddle through icy waters, gliding past colossal glaciers and icebergs. Listen to the hauntingly beautiful sounds of ice as it breaks off from the glacier, plunging into the frigid abyss. It's a thrilling adventure that will make your heart race and leave you feeling truly alive.

Camping on the ice is another extraordinary experience that allows you to spend a night in a remote location, surrounded by the ethereal beauty of Antarctica. As you sleep under a canopy of stars, you'll hear the soft whispers of wildlife in the distance. And when you wake up, you'll be greeted by a stunning sunrise over the vast, untouched landscape. It's a night you'll cherish forever.

THE BEST TIME TO VISIT ANTARCTICA CONTINENT

Antarctica, the southernmost continent on our planet, calls to adventurers during the austral summer months, which span from November to March. During this magical season, the sea ice retreats, and the weather becomes milder, making it the perfect time to explore this majestic land and its surrounding waters.

November marks the beginning of the Antarctic summer, a time when you can witness penguins and other wildlife in their full glory. Penguins return to their breeding grounds, and the ice starts to break up, allowing ships to navigate around the continent. It's also a fantastic time to explore the South Shetland Islands, known for their breathtaking landscapes and diverse wildlife.

December brings the enchantment of the midnight sun, with daylight extending into the wee hours of the morning and night. It's the time when whale activity picks up, offering the chance to witness humpback, minke, and orca whales in their natural habitat.

January and February are the peak months for experiencing Antarctica's incredible biodiversity. These are the best times to observe the largest colonies of penguins and seals. Wildlife is in full swing, with penguins hatching and seals tending to their adorable young. The weather is generally calm and mild during these months, making it ideal for outdoor activities like kayaking, camping, and hiking.

As **March** rolls around, it marks the end of the Antarctic summer, offering a different kind of beauty. Icebergs are at their most spectacular, casting a surreal glow in the waning sunlight. The sunsets in March are among the most beautiful of the year. This is also a wonderful time to explore the Falkland Islands, famed for their diverse wildlife, including penguins, sea lions, and albatrosses.

In summary, the best time to visit Antarctica is during the summer months, from November to March. Each month brings its own unique experiences and opportunities for exploration, depending on your interests. Whether you yearn to witness penguins, marvel at whales, or stand in awe of colossal icebergs, Antarctica is a destination that promises to leave you spellbound and with unforgettable memories.

THE BEST TIME TO BOOK A TRIP TO ANTARCTICA CONTINENT

Planning a trip to Antarctica can be an exciting and unique adventure. However, it's important to note that travel to Antarctica is only possible during the southern hemisphere summer months, from November to March. Here are some tips on the best time to book a trip to Antarctica:

1. Determine your travel dates: As mentioned, the only time to travel to Antarctica is during the southern hemisphere summer months. Within this timeframe, the best time to travel depends on what you want to see and experience. Early November is a good time to see penguins and seals breeding, while mid to late December is great for seeing whale activity. January and February are the warmest months and the best time for kayaking and camping. March is the best time to see migratory whales.

2. Choose a cruise company: There are several cruise companies that offer trips to Antarctica. It's recommended to research and compare the various companies to find the best fit for your needs and budget. Some factors to consider include the size of the ship, the length of the trip, the itinerary, the level of comfort, and the onboard activities and amenities.

3. Book in advance: Antarctic cruises are often booked up to a year in advance, so it's recommended to start planning and booking as early as possible. This will give you the best chance to secure your preferred travel dates and cabin type. Some cruise companies may offer early booking discounts, so it's worth checking for any deals or promotions.

4. Be flexible: It's important to be flexible with your travel dates and itinerary as weather conditions can be unpredictable in Antarctica. Some cruise companies may offer alternative itineraries or activities if weather conditions prevent planned activities.

5. Consider additional costs: In addition to the cost of the cruise, there may be additional costs for flights, visas, travel insurance, and gear rental. Make sure to factor these costs into your budget when planning your trip.

6. Consult with a travel agent: If you're unsure about planning a trip to Antarctica, consider consulting with a travel agent who specializes in polar travel. They

can help you with the booking process and provide additional information and advice.

Overall, only a fraction of the population of our planet has been to Antarctica and no war has ever been fought there. It is a fragile place that is rapidly changing and the best time to book a trip to Antarctica is as early as possible to secure your preferred travel dates and cabin type. By considering the above tips and doing thorough research, you can plan a memorable and enjoyable trip to this unique continent.

And now, as I prepare to share with you the enchanting tales and captivating photographs from my unforgettable Antarctic adventure, I'm overwhelmed with gratitude for the privilege of setting foot on this extraordinary continent. Brace yourself for a journey of a lifetime—a voyage that will not only fill your heart with boundless joy but also profoundly enrich your life in countless ways. I am ecstatic, humbled, and profoundly thankful for the incredible privilege of experiencing the magic of Antarctica!

MY ANTARCTICA JOURNEY

Antarctica, the southernmost continent on earth, is a place of extraordinary beauty and wonder, a land of ice, snow, and stunning natural landscapes that are unlike any other on our planet. For those seeking adventure, there is no better way to experience this incredible place than by embarking on a journey by ship, crossing the infamous Drake Passage, and setting foot on the frozen continent itself.

My adventure started in **Ushuaia, Argentina**. Walking through the town of Ushuaia, buying wine for the cruise, and putting on my seasick patch were all just steps towards my ultimate adventure. As we went through security and boarded the ship, my home for the next eleven days, my heart raced with anticipation. The afternoon tea, safety briefing, and meeting the expedition team and scientists only fueled my excitement. Then the ship slowly pulls away from the dock, and I feel a sense of anticipation building as I watched the shoreline fade into the distance. As our ship set out from Ushuaia, the southernmost city in the world, we entered **the Beagle Channel**, a narrow waterway that separates the archipelago of Tierra del Fuego from the southernmost tip of South America. The scenery was stunning, with the snow-capped mountains towering over us, and the crystal-clear waters shimmering beneath the sunlight. As we sailed deeper into the channel, we encountered an abundance of marine wildlife, including pods of playful dolphins, humpback whales breaching, and adorable penguins waddling along the shoreline.

The next day, as we crossed **the Drake Passage**, a notoriously rough stretch of water that separates South America from the Antarctic Peninsula. The journey across the Drake was challenging, with waves that reached over 30 feet high and winds that could gust up to 100 miles per hour. But for those brave enough to make the crossing, the rewards are well worth the effort. As we make our way across the Drake, the ship rocks and rolls with the waves, and I couldn't help but feel a sense of awe at the power of the ocean. I felt a bit queasy at first, but with the help of seasickness patches and medication, I soon adjusted to the motion of the ship and was able to fully enjoy the experience. During the crossing, there was plenty to keep me occupied, from lectures on the wildlife and environment of Antarctica to games and activities organized by the ship's crew. And as we sailed further south, the excitement builds as we draw closer to the frozen continent itself.

Finally, after two days of sailing in a vast ocean, and what seems like an eternity, I caught the first glimpse of the **Antarctic Peninsula** on the horizon. As we approached the Antarctic Peninsula, the landscape became even more breathtaking, a jagged line of snow-covered mountains rising out of the sea. The glaciers and icebergs were like nothing I had ever seen before, and the vast expanse of white and blue stretched as far as the eye could see. The air was crisp and clean, and the silence was almost overwhelming. The wildlife encounters were equally awe-inspiring, with penguins and seals and whales everywhere we looked. I was humbled by the power and resilience of these creatures, who managed to survive and thrive in one of the harshest environments on earth. As the ship glided closer, and I could see massive icebergs floating in the water and colonies of penguins gathered on the rocky shoreline. As we sailed towards the continent, I felt more and more grateful for this once-in-a-lifetime experience.

The following day, we arrived at **Shetland Island** and we took a small Zodiac to go ashore. Visiting Antarctica is a privilege and comes with great responsibility. To protect the unique environment and fragile ecosystem, there are strict rules that all visitors must follow. First and foremost, the tour company must obtain permission from the relevant national authorities and adhere to their guidelines. Once on the continent, we were not allowed to leave anything behind, including food, and trash. We must also not take anything, including rocks, fossils, or wildlife, as these can upset the delicate balance of the ecosystem. We were also required to follow specific protocols to avoid introducing non-native species to Antarctica. Before disembarking on the continent, we must disinfect our clothing, shoes, and equipment to prevent the spread of any unwanted organisms. Additionally, we were required to stay at least fifteen feet (five meters) away from all wildlife, including penguins, seals, and whales. This was not only for our safety but also to avoid disturbing the animals and disrupting their natural behavior.

As I step off the zodiac and onto the continent itself, I was filled with a sense of wonder and amazement. The air is crisp and clean, and the landscape was otherworldly, with towering glaciers, deep blue ice formations, and expanses of snow and ice stretching out as far as the eye can see. I saw penguin colonies, and took part in organized activities that allowed me to fully immerse myself in the beauty and majesty of Antarctica.

Our landing at **Palmer Station** was a fascinating opportunity to talk to US researchers living in isolation on the remote continent. The station is home to scientists studying a wide range of topics, including oceanography, glaciology, and ecology. We took a tour of the facilities, learned about the research being conducted, and interacted with the scientists. We also had opportunity to visit other research centers. These centers offered a glimpse into the challenges of living and working in such a remote and extreme environment. We learned about the important research being conducted on topics such as climate change, marine biology, and geology. The next day, we visited the mainland at **Neko Harbor**, the stunning mountains and sounds of an active volcano left me speechless. Neko Harbor in Antarctica is truly an awe-inspiring place. It's hard to describe the feeling I got when standing in front of such a majestic landscape. The mountains were massive and impressive, and the ice fields were a beautiful shade of blue. The quietness and peacefulness of this place were something that everyone should experience at least once in their lifetime. As I walked around, I could see different shades of white and blue everywhere I looked. The glaciers and icebergs were massive and beautiful, and the sound of them creaking and cracking was a truly unforgettable experience. The air was fresh, crisp, and clear, with no signs of pollution or civilization. The air was so fresh that I wish I could bottle the air and take it home. There were no signs of human development, and the wildlife was abundant. The penguins, seals, and whales were all living in their natural habitat, undisturbed by human activity. It was a humbling experience to see nature in its purest form. Neko Harbor was a place of wonder and beauty. It was a reminder of how incredible and vast our planet is and how much we have to cherish and protect. Visiting this place was an experience that will stay with me forever.

Each day brought new adventures, from sailing through **the Lemaire Channel** to exploring **Peterman Island** and **Port Lockroy**. **Whaler's Bay** and **Deception Island** felt like walking on the moon with their dramatic landscapes, and I even took **a polar swim on Deception Island** and it was invigorating. Our group were eager to take the plunge into the icy waters, and we had been preparing ourselves mentally and physically for weeks leading up to the trip. As we donned our swimsuits and prepared to jump into the freezing water, my heart was pounding with a mix of excitement and trepidation. I could feel the chill in the air and the sting of the wind on my skin, but I was determined to take the plunge and **experience the polar swim** in all its glory. With a deep breath, I took the leap into the icy water, and the shock of the cold hit me like a ton of bricks. The water was so cold that it took my breath away, and I could feel the adrenaline pumping through my veins as I swam through the crystal-clear waters. I knew that this was a once-in-a-lifetime experience that I would cherish forever. The thrill of being in the water, surrounded by the breathtaking scenery of Antarctica, was like nothing I had ever experienced before. Then **Christmas Eve**'s arrival brought a sense of excitement. The **Christmas dinner** with the crew, the captain and staff were very special, singing Christmas songs with my fellow travelers was joyful. The sense of camaraderie and community that developed among the passengers and crew on board the ship was very special. We bonded over shared experiences and shared wonder, and we laughed and celebrated together as we explored the wonders of Antarctica. Sharing these special moments and reflecting on an incredible journey brought us so much joy and memories. And as the ship sets sail once again, leaving the frozen continent behind, I couldn't help but feel a sense of gratitude and awe for the incredible experience I have just had. I knew this incredible journey to Antarctica would stay with me forever. From the breathtaking scenery and fresh air to the wildlife encounters and sense of adventure, I was inspired to cherish this wild, untouched place even more. This was truly the trip of a lifetime, and I am forever grateful for the experience.

Crossing the Drake Passage to Antarctica

Floating Iceberg

Floating Iceberg

Midnight Sunset in Antarctica

Disinfect station before disembarking on the Antarctica continent

Seven Sisters Mountains

Floating Ice Sculptures

A Colony of Penguins

Floating Icebergs

Deception Island

SMILE for the Camera!

EUROPE CONTINENT: 44 COUNTRIES

	Albania		Hungary		Poland
	Andora		Iceland		Portugal
	Austria		Ireland		Romania
	Belarus		Italy		Russia
	Belgium		Latvia		San Marino
	Bosnia & Herzegovina		Liechtenstein		Serbia
	Bulgaria		Lithuania		Slovakia
	Croatia		Luxembourg		Slovenia
	Czech Republic		Malta		Spain
	Denmark		Moldova		Sweden
	Estonia		Monaco		Switzerland
	Finland		Montenegro		Turkiye
	France		The Netherlands		Ukraine
	Germany		North Macedonia		United Kingdom
	Greece		Norway		

EUROPE CONTINENT

Europe, a continent teeming with awe-inspiring history, captivating culture, architectural marvels, world-class museums, and delectable cuisine that tantalizes the taste buds, awaits us. But before we embark on this whirlwind adventure through Europe's most wondrous destinations, let's delve into the intriguing origins of the very name "Europe."

In the rich tapestry of Greek mythology, Europa, a Phoenician princess, found herself at the center of a timeless tale—an abduction by none other than Zeus, the almighty king of the gods, who cleverly assumed the form of a magnificent bull. This mythical escapade gave birth to the term "Europe," initially coined to describe the region Europa called home. With time, this appellation expanded its horizons, ultimately coming to represent the entire continent. Remarkably, the ancient Greeks themselves didn't perceive Europe as a distinct entity; it was the tireless work of geographers and cartographers that breathed life into this name.

As we immerse ourselves in Europe's treasures, we cannot help but be enchanted by its diverse and welcoming people, who hold tradition dear and have an innate knack for turning every occasion into a celebration. The cuisine, a symphony of flavors and spices that dances through various regions, promises an unforgettable culinary journey. And then there's the music and art of Europe—a rich tapestry woven over centuries and still celebrated with boundless enthusiasm. So, let's embark on a thrilling journey through Europe, promising not just excitement but a deep sense of gratitude for the wonders that await.

Our electrifying adventure transports us to the heart of romance and beauty—**Paris, France**. The City of Light, with its stunning architecture and intimate cafes, invites us to take a leisurely stroll along the enchanting Seine River. Here, the iconic Eiffel Tower stands tall, the Louvre Museum houses treasures beyond imagination, and every corner unveils a piece of Parisian charm. Savor a café au lait and croissant in a quintessential café, visit the awe-inspiring Notre-Dame Cathedral, stroll through the serene Luxembourg Gardens, or indulge in a shopping spree along the famed Champs-Élysées.

Next, we venture to **Rome, Italy**, a city steeped in history and grandeur. Here, the Colosseum, Roman Forum, and Pantheon remind us of the ancient world's majesty. A pilgrimage to Vatican City reveals the breathtaking Sistine Chapel, St. Peter's Basilica, and the Vatican Museums. And, oh, the culinary delights of Rome—from mouthwatering pizza and pasta to heavenly gelato—promise an unforgettable gastronomic journey.

Barcelona, Spain, awaits with its vibrant energy and enchanting architecture. The city beckons us with awe-inspiring landmarks like the Sagrada Familia, a masterpiece designed by the visionary Antoni Gaudi, and the bustling La Rambla, a promenade teeming with life and excitement. We soar to Montjuic Castle in a cable car, explore the historic Gothic Quarter, and bask in the sun on the beautiful beaches of Barcelona.

Our journey then leads us to the mesmerizing **Venice, Italy**, a city unlike any other—a floating marvel set atop tranquil waters. Gondola rides along the Grand Canal, the stunning Piazza San Marco, and the iconic Rialto Bridge reveal Venice's unique charm. Visits to the Doge's Palace and the Basilica di San Marco, or shopping for treasures in the local markets and boutiques, promise unforgettable experiences.

Then, we arrive in **Santorini, Greece**, a paradise known for its natural beauty and charm. The striking contrast of whitewashed buildings crowned with blue-domed roofs against the backdrop of the Aegean Sea creates a picture-perfect setting. Exploring the island by boat, witnessing the mesmerizing sunset from Oia, and savoring delectable Greek cuisine are just a few of the enchanting experiences that await. Whether hiking along scenic trails, uncovering the ancient Akrotiri ruins, or unwinding on the black sand beaches of Perissa, Santorini promises moments of pure bliss.

THE BEST TIME TO VISIT EUROPE CONTINENT

Europe, a continent steeped in history and adorned with diverse landscapes, offers a kaleidoscope of experiences throughout the year. Each season paints a different picture, inviting travelers to explore its rich culture, stunning scenery, and historic treasures.

In **Spring (March - May),** as winter's grip loosens, Europe awakens in a symphony of colors and fragrances. Paris, the City of Love, is at its most charming during spring, with cherry blossoms gracing its iconic landmarks, including the Eiffel Tower and Notre-Dame Cathedral. The serene Seine River, lined with blossoming trees, invites leisurely cruises, while the city's art galleries and cafes beckon with their timeless allure. In the heart of the Mediterranean, the Greek islands, such as Santorini and Mykonos, begin to emerge from their winter slumber. With pleasant temperatures and fewer crowds, it's an ideal time to explore ancient ruins, relax on pristine beaches, and savor Greek cuisine under the Mediterranean sun.

Summer (June - August) arrives, and Europe's diverse landscapes beckon. The Amalfi Coast in Italy, with its dramatic cliffs, turquoise waters, and charming villages, becomes a haven for sun-seekers. From Positano to Capri, the region's beauty shines under the Mediterranean sun. Croatia's Dalmatian Coast offers a blend of history and natural beauty. Explore the historic city of Dubrovnik, sail the Adriatic Sea, and discover hidden coves and islands. For those seeking northern adventures, Norway's fjords are a summer delight. Cruise through the majestic

Geirangerfjord or hike the dramatic trails of Nærøyfjord for awe-inspiring vistas of rugged cliffs and cascading waterfalls.

As **Fall (September - November)** sets in, Europe's historic cities and countryside come alive with autumnal splendor. The ancient city of Rome, Italy, basks in a warm and golden light, enhancing its historic treasures like the Colosseum and the Roman Forum. Enjoy the harvest season with Italian cuisine and wine in cozy trattorias. The Scottish Highlands, with their rolling hills and shimmering lochs, are at their most picturesque during fall. Explore the stunning landscapes, encounter Highland cattle, and discover the haunting beauty of Eilean Donan Castle. In Spain's Andalusia region, the historic city of Seville dazzles with its autumn festivals, such as the Feria de Abril and the Bienal de Flamenco. Stroll through its historic neighborhoods and savor tapas in lively markets.

Winter (December - February) blankets Europe in snow, ushering in a different kind of enchantment. Vienna, Austria, embodies the magic of winter with its Christmas markets, where sparkling lights, festive music, and the aroma of roasted chestnuts fill the air. Visit the opulent Schönbrunn Palace and indulge in Sachertorte at historic coffeehouses. In the Swiss Alps, ski resorts like Zermatt and St. Moritz provide thrilling winter sports against a backdrop of breathtaking mountain scenery. Explore picturesque villages, take a ride on the Glacier Express, and unwind in thermal spas. Prague, Czech Republic, becomes a winter wonderland with its charming Old Town Square and iconic Charles Bridge dusted with snow. Warm up with hearty Czech dishes and mulled wine.

Europe's allure is timeless and ever-changing, offering a tapestry of experiences in every season. Whether you seek romance in Paris, adventure in the Norwegian fjords, cultural immersion in Rome, or the enchantment of Vienna's winter markets, Europe invites travelers to explore, savor, and create cherished memories.

Prepare to be transported into a world of sheer wonder and awe as I regale you with the most captivating tales and visually stunning photographs from my exhilarating sojourn across the magnificent continent of Europe. What lies ahead are not just mere stories and pictures; they are the pulsating heartbeats of an adventure that has reshaped my very existence. The landscapes, the cultures, the history, and, above all, the extraordinary people I had the privilege of meeting have collectively woven a fabric of life-changing memories. From wandering the cobblestone streets of ancient cities to standing in awe before the grandeur of centuries-old cathedrals, every moment was a brushstroke on the canvas of my soul. The sheer magnitude of joy and enrichment that this journey bestowed upon me is beyond measure. The privilege of setting foot on this incredible continent is a gift that I will forever cherish, and my heart brims with gratitude for the boundless wonders it has unfurled before me.

CROATIA

Croatia, nestled in Southeast Europe, holds a special place in my heart as a truly enchanting country. Croatia has it all, beautiful beaches, historic cities, hidden coves, and stunning Dalmatian coast. It offers a seamless blend of breathtaking natural beauty and exhilarating experiences that leave a lasting impression. With a coastline stretching over 1,100 miles along the captivating Adriatic Sea, Croatia reveals a world of splendor and excitement waiting to be explored.

One of Croatia's most iconic destinations and a jewel of the Adriatic Sea is **Dubrovnik**, a UNESCO World Heritage Site that exudes charm and history. The city's Old Town is a captivating maze of cobblestone streets, adorned with ornate buildings and fortified by majestic fortresses. As I walked along the ancient city walls, I was greeted by panoramic views of the shimmering Adriatic Sea and the terracotta rooftops below. The experience was nothing short of magical. Dubrovnik was the top location for the "Game of Thrones" series. It has quickly become a favorite of festival goers and travelers alike! It is easy to see that utterly enchanting Dubrovnik is called "Pearl of the Adriatic" and is a must see and a bucket list top travel site.

Having been fortunate enough to visit Croatia multiple times, I have ventured beyond Dubrovnik and discovered other remarkable destinations. Zagreb, the vibrant capital, with its blend of old-world charm and modern energy, captivated me with its lively atmosphere and architectural wonders. Plitvice Lakes National Park, a true natural gem, immersed me in a world of cascading waterfalls and interconnected turquoise lakes nestled amidst lush greenery.

But if there's one city that holds a special place in my heart, it is the city of **Split**. This dynamic city combines ancient history with contemporary living in a remarkable way. At its core lies Diocletian's Palace, a UNESCO-listed site and a testament to Roman architectural brilliance. Exploring its labyrinthine streets, wandering through hidden courtyards, and indulging in local delicacies at the bustling market were experiences that left me in awe. The Peristyle, the palace's central square, stood as a majestic focal point, surrounded by grand columns and ornate carvings. Climbing the bell tower of the Cathedral of St. Domnius rewarded me with breathtaking panoramic views of the city and the glistening Adriatic Sea.

Diocletian's Palace, a true marvel, showcases the grandeur and history of Split. It was originally constructed as a retirement residence for the Roman Emperor Diocletian in the 4th century AD. Stepping through its ancient walls, I felt transported back in time, surrounded by architectural masterpieces that reflected the city's rich heritage. The intricate stone facades, graceful arches, and imposing columns demonstrated the exceptional craftsmanship of that era.

What sets Diocletian's Palace apart is not only its historical significance but also its vibrant atmosphere. It is a living, breathing part of the city where locals and tourists mingle, creating a lively energy that resonates throughout. Cultural events, festivals, and performances bring the palace to life, immersing visitors in the spirit of Split's heritage. It truly stands as a testament to the enduring legacy of the Roman Empire. Croatia's allure extends far beyond its coastline and ancient cities. It is a country that beckons with its natural wonders, warm hospitality, and rich cultural heritage. Each visit reveals a new layer of its splendor, leaving me with cherished memories and a desire to return. Croatia is a treasure trove waiting to be discovered, and I feel truly privileged to have experienced its enchantment firsthand.

My next destination was visiting **Plitvice Lakes National Park**. Plitvice Park is a true wonderland that left me utterly captivated and filled with awe. As I ventured into this magical realm nestled amidst lush greenery, I was greeted by a breathtaking spectacle of cascading waterfalls and interconnected turquoise lakes. The sight was so mesmerizing that it felt like stepping into a fairytale.

Walking along the wooden pathways that wind through the park, I couldn't help but be immersed in the ethereal beauty that surrounded me. The tranquil atmosphere, filled with the soothing sounds of trickling water and chirping birds, transported me to a realm of serenity and natural harmony.

The sixteen interconnected lakes, each more enchanting than the last, displayed a stunning range of colors. The hues of turquoise, emerald, and azure seemed almost unreal, casting a spell of wonder over the entire landscape. It was a symphony of colors that danced before my eyes, creating a truly surreal experience.

Exploring Plitvice Lakes was like embarking on a grand adventure. The wooden walkways led me to magnificent viewpoints where I could witness countless waterfalls cascading down moss-covered cliffs. The most impressive of them all was Veliki Slap, the mighty Big Waterfall, which plunged with such force that its mist sprayed the air with a refreshing coolness.

What fascinated me even more were the charming wooden footbridges that crisscrossed the lakes. As I crossed these bridges, I felt like I was walking on water, surrounded by a magical world where fish glided gracefully beneath the surface and water vegetation swayed with a gentle rhythm. The lush forests that enveloped the park added an extra layer of tranquility, casting dappled sunlight that created a serene ambiance.

But perhaps one of the most unforgettable experiences was my visit to **Hvar Island**. Stepping off the ferry, I was immediately embraced by the Mediterranean charm and the sheer beauty of the island. The elegant waterfront promenade of Hvar Town invited me to immerse myself in its laid-back ambiance, with its delightful cafes, trendy bars, and inviting boutique shops. Climbing up to the Hvar Fortress was an adventure in itself. The scenic hike rewarded me with panoramic views that took my breath away. As I stood atop the fortress, witnessing the magnificent sunset painting the sky in a kaleidoscope of colors, I felt a sense of pure joy and gratitude. It was a moment of complete immersion in the natural beauty and magic of Croatia.

Croatia, with its stunning landscapes, rich history, and warm hospitality, has left an indelible mark on my heart. The blend of natural wonders, captivating cities, and exhilarating adventures created an experience that surpassed all expectations. From Plitvice Lakes' fairy tale-like charm to Dubrovnik's historical splendor and Hvar Island's Mediterranean allure, Croatia beckons travelers with its irresistible charm, promising a journey filled with excitement, beauty, and cherished memories.

TREAD THE PLITVICE BOARDWALKS

The city of Split

The city of Split

Plitvice Park

Plitvice Park

Hvar Island

Hvar Island

Diocletian's Palace

Korcula Island

Dubrovnik

Marco Polo's House in Korcula

Croatia Beach

Zlatni Rat Beach

FRANCE

France is a treasure trove of wonders, offering beautifully historic castles, breathtakingly elegant cities, exquisite cuisine, and some of the world's finest cultural museums. Embarking on a journey to France opens the door to a realm of boundless possibilities, where excitement, beauty, and history converge to weave an extraordinary tapestry of experiences. I was fortunate to call Paris my temporary home for a while, and this experience immersed me entirely in a world brimming with cultural richness, culinary delights, and captivating history. Living in this enchanting city allowed me to unearth its hidden treasures and become fully immersed in the vibrant tapestry of Parisian life.

Paris, often dubbed the "City of Lights" and the "Capital of Culture," is a haven for art enthusiasts. It boasts renowned museums, galleries, and theaters that showcase a diverse range of artistic expressions. During my tenure as a resident, I embarked on numerous cultural journeys, wandering through the grand halls of the Louvre and marveling at iconic masterpieces like the enigmatic Mona Lisa. The Musée d'Orsay, housed in a former railway station, revealed the brushstrokes of Monet and Renoir, bringing their works to life.

Beyond museum walls, the city's streets were adorned with captivating street art, infusing life and colorful art into every corner. The Parisians' innate appreciation for the arts inspired me, propelling my own artistic pursuits. The cobblestone streets, elegant architecture, and grand boulevards served as constant reminders of the city's storied past. The Gothic splendor of the Notre-Dame Cathedral stood as a testament to the enduring craftsmanship of bygone eras. The Château de Versailles, once the opulent residence of French kings, allowed me to step back in time and witness the grandeur of the monarchy.

Moreover, Paris is not just about art and history; it offers a plethora of famous attractions. Strolling through the winding alleys of the Latin Quarter, I retraced the footsteps of writers and thinkers who had profoundly shaped the world with their ideas. A climb to the top of the Eiffel Tower offered panoramic views of the city, a breathtaking experience that highlighted the city's grandeur from above. A visit to Montmartre, with its picturesque streets and the iconic Sacré-Cœur Basilica, provided a glimpse into the artistic heart of the city.

Taking full advantage of the opportunity to explore the country, I ventured beyond Paris to discover the diverse regions of France. Traveling **west**, the lush countryside unfurled before my eyes, revealing enchanting villages and rolling vineyards that dotted the landscape. The Loire Valley, often referred to as the "Garden of France," unveiled its treasure trove of châteaux and lush landscapes, with majestic castles like Château de

Chambord and Château de Chenonceau emerging from the picturesque scenery. As I explored these regal fortresses, I could almost hear history's whispers echoing through their hallowed halls.

Journeying **north** to Normandy, I encountered a region steeped in history and natural beauty. The solemn beaches of Omaha and Utah Beach stood as poignant reminders of the bravery and sacrifices made during the D-Day landings of World War II. Visiting historic sites and museums like the American Cemetery at Colleville-sur-Mer, I paid tribute to the heroes who fought for our freedom. Venturing **south** to the French Riviera, I indulged in sun-drenched beaches and glamorous resorts exuding luxury. The azure waters of the Mediterranean Sea and the picturesque towns of Nice, Cannes, Menton, and Saint-Tropez beckoned me to soak up the sun and revel in the vibrant atmosphere.

During my time in Paris, I also had the opportunity to visit the **lavender fields** in Aix-en-Provence during the summer. It was an immersive and unforgettable experience that transported me to a realm of natural beauty, serenity, and sensory delight. Nestled in the heart of Provence, a region renowned for its captivating landscapes and vibrant colors, Aix-en-Provence provided a picturesque backdrop for the blooming lavender fields that adorned the countryside. Stepping into these fields, a symphony of scents filled the air, enveloping me in the delicate and soothing aroma of lavender. The fragrance was both invigorating and calming, awakening my senses and fostering a sense of harmony and tranquility. Each inhalation brought a renewed sense of calm and a deep connection to the beauty of nature.

The sight that unfolded before me was nothing short of breathtaking. Rolling hills adorned with endless rows of lavender plants stretched out as far as the eye could see, painting the landscape with a stunning tapestry of purples, blues, and greens. The vibrant colors contrasted beautifully against the clear blue sky, creating a visual spectacle that etched an indelible memory in my mind. The sheer expanse of the lavender fields instilled a sense of awe, reminding me of the vastness and majesty of the natural world.

Visiting the lavender fields in Aix-en-Provence is not merely an encounter with nature's beauty; it is also an opportunity to delve deeper into the cultural fabric of the region. Aix-en-Provence itself is a charming city with a rich history and a vibrant arts scene. One of my favorite places to visit there is the **outdoor markets.** These markets are a sensory extravaganza that immerses you in a world of culinary delights, vibrant colors, and infectious excitement. They are a beloved tradition deeply ingrained in the Provencial way of life.

One of the most captivating aspects of the outdoor markets is the extraordinary array of fresh and seasonal produce on display. From juicy tomatoes and plump strawberries to fragrant herbs and crisp greens, the stalls overflow with an abundance of local fruits, vegetables, and herbs. The produce is meticulously arranged, creating a visual feast that showcases nature's bounty in all its glory. As I navigated through the bustling market, I encountered an array of local artisans and vendors passionately sharing their products and expertise. From artisanal cheeses crafted by skilled fromagers to cured meats meticulously prepared by charcutiers, every stall offered a glimpse into the rich culinary heritage of Provence. The vendors were eager to share their knowledge and provided samples, inviting me to taste the distinct flavors and experience the quality that set their products apart.

The outdoor markets in Aix-en-Provence are not just about food; they are a celebration of the region's cultural heritage. The ambiance of the markets is nothing short of magical. The lively chatter of vendors, the laughter of shoppers, and the melodic sounds of street musicians create an atmosphere that is vibrant and joyous. The energy is contagious, spreading from stall to stall as people share stories, exchange recommendations, and revel in the sensory experiences that surround them.

France is a **culinary paradise** and an exquisite journey for the senses. French cuisine is renowned worldwide for its exquisite flavors and meticulous preparation. Indulge in the flaky layers of a freshly baked croissant, savor the creamy richness of a perfectly aged cheese, or delight in the effervescence of a fine Champagne. Living in Paris allowed me to fully savor its culinary delights. From neighborhood bakeries that filled the air with the intoxicating aroma of freshly baked croissants and baguettes to charming bistros serving up classic French dishes, every meal was an opportunity to indulge in the gastronomic wonders of the city.

Living in Paris also provided me with the opportunity to embrace **the city's slower pace of life** and relish in the art of living. Parisians have mastered the balance between work and leisure, understanding the importance of savoring the simple pleasures of life. I learned to appreciate the joy of leisurely strolls along the Seine, pausing to admire the breathtaking views of the city or engage in delightful conversations with fellow flâneurs. The city's parks and gardens, such as the Jardin des Tuileries or the Parc des Buttes-Chaumont, became my sanctuaries, where I could retreat from the hustle and bustle and find solace in nature's embrace. The Parisian way of life taught me the value of slowing down, of relishing a cup of coffee at a sidewalk café, and of immersing myself in the present moment.

Overall, living in Paris was an immersive and transformative experience that enveloped me in a world of beauty, culture, and history. The city's rich artistic heritage, culinary prowess, and palpable sense of history created an atmosphere that was both awe-inspiring and nurturing. As a temporary resident, I had the privilege of unraveling the city's secrets, exploring its hidden corners, and forging a deep connection with the soul of Paris. Living in Paris was an adventure that nourished my mind, body, and spirit, giving me a deeper understanding of the French way of life and leaving an indelible imprint that will forever remain a cherished part of my life.

SAVORING:
THE CITY OF LIGHTS

INHALING A BEAUTIFUL
OCEAN OF LAVENDER
IN AIX-EN-PROVENCE

Louvre Museum

Chateau de Versailles

Chateau de Versailles

Claude Monet's Garden at Giverny

Palais des Papes in Avignon

Mont-Saint-Michel

Bastille Day Celebration in Paris

Champagne Region

Bastille Day in Paris

Arc de triomphe

Market in Nice, France

Market in Nice, France

GREECE

Ah, beautiful, historic, spellbinding Greece. The homes of Plato and Aristotle, along with the birthplace of democracy, philosophy, its rich history, white-washed island towns, and delicious Greek cuisine, are destined to please every palate. A visit to Greece is an extraordinary experience that transports you to a timeless world, where history, culture, and natural beauty seamlessly merge. Situated in southeastern Europe, this captivating country entices millions of visitors each year with its abundance of enchanting encounters. From the ancient ruins of Athens to the breathtaking island vistas of Santorini and the stunning beaches of Crete, Greece is a destination that truly encompasses it all!

Embarking on a journey to **Athens**, Greece's capital, is like embarking on a voyage through history, pulsating with the energy of a bygone era. Renowned as the birthplace of democracy and the cradle of Western civilization, Athens offers an unparalleled opportunity to immerse oneself in the rich tapestry of human history, mythology, and architectural marvels that have captivated the world for centuries. The mere thought of exploring the ancient sites and treading in the footsteps of legendary figures filled me with awe and anticipation.

My first destination was the iconic citadel of **Acropolis**, a UNESCO World Heritage Site, it's on an imposing rocky hill that dominates the city's skyline. It is one of the awe-inspiring architectural marvels of ancient Greece. As I ascended, a sense of wonder grew within me, and the sight of the Parthenon, adorned with its majestic marble columns, left me breathless. Standing in the presence of this ancient masterpiece dedicated to the goddess Athena, I couldn't help but marvel at the ingenuity and craftsmanship of the ancient Greeks. The Parthenon stands as a testament to human achievement, overwhelming my senses with its grandeur and symbolic significance.

Wandering through the ancient streets of Plaka, a neighborhood beneath the Acropolis, a sense of timelessness enveloped me. The narrow cobblestone alleys, adorned with vibrant bougainvillea and charming neoclassical buildings, exuded an enchanting atmosphere. Each step revealed hidden treasures—small shops brimming with handmade crafts, traditional tavernas offering mouthwatering Greek cuisine, and glimpses of ancient ruins peeking through the gaps between buildings. Plaka is a living testament to the enduring spirit of ancient Athens, where the past seamlessly intertwines with the present.

My most recent experience in Athens was spending **New Year's Eve** there. The air was charged with palpable energy as I stood in the heart of the city, preparing to welcome the new year in the shadow of the awe-inspiring Acropolis. The anticipation of midnight mingled with the cool evening breeze, creating an atmosphere brimming with excitement and hope. Bathed in soft lights, the Acropolis stood as a silent witness to the passage of time and the unfolding of history.

As the final moments of the year slipped away, the crowd around me grew animated, their faces illuminated by a mix of anticipation and joy. The air crackled with the collective energy of people from diverse backgrounds, brought together by the shared experience of bidding farewell to the old year and embracing the promise of the new. We stood united, a tapestry woven with various cultures and languages, bound by our shared humanity and the desire to celebrate this special moment together.

And then it happened—a resounding cheer erupted, marking the arrival of the new year. Simultaneously, the night sky was set ablaze with a mesmerizing display of fireworks. Brilliant cascades of light shot upward, illuminating the darkness and casting a kaleidoscope of colors upon the ancient stones. The Acropolis seemed to awaken, infused with the joyous uproar and the vibrant bursts of light that danced across its timeless features. The fireworks soared higher and higher, tracing intricate patterns in the night sky. Each explosion created a symphony of colors, painting the heavens with a breathtaking palette of blues, reds, and golds. The dazzling spectacle reflected off the marble columns and statues, imbuing the ancient site with an otherworldly glow. It was as if the spirits of the past were joining us in our celebration, whispering their blessings and wishes for the year to come.

As the fireworks continued to illuminate the night, I found myself overwhelmed by a mix of emotions. Joy bubbled up within me, intermingling with a profound sense of gratitude for being able to witness such a grand spectacle in this historic setting. I felt an indescribable connection to the generations that had come before, to the countless souls who had gazed upon the Acropolis with reverence and wonder. In that extraordinary moment, time seemed to dissolve, and I felt a profound sense of belonging—a link in an unbroken chain stretching back through millennia. Before leaving Athens, be sure to visit the Acropolis Museum which is next to the Acropolis. It is still an active archeological site which can be viewed through its plexiglass walkways above the site.

One of the most cherished destinations I had the pleasure of visiting in Greece was **Santorini**. Officially called "Thira" in Greek, Santorini is an island in the southern Aegean Sea and the site of one of the largest volcanic eruption in recorded history. This island's geological formation, shaped by a volcanic eruption, presents a breathtaking panorama of towering cliffs adorned with whitewashed buildings that cascade towards the azure sea. The contrast between the vibrant crystal-clear blue waters and the dazzling white architecture creates a sight that feels like stepping into a dream. The picturesque villages of Oia and Fira beckon visitors to explore their narrow, winding streets, where every corner reveals a new facet of the island's undeniable charm.

Santorini's iconic blue-domed churches, majestically perched on cliff edges and surrounded by a steep volcanic caldera, captures the essence of the island's spiritual heritage. These architectural marvels not only served as places of worship but also reflected the islanders' deep-rooted faith. Their azure domes stood in stark contrast to the pristine white buildings, creating a visual symphony that is both serene and awe-inspiring. Exploring the interiors of these churches, I was greeted by stunning frescoes and ornate icons, each telling a story of devotion and faith. Many of these churches have their origin in the Medieval and Ottoman period.

One of the most magical experiences in Santorini was witnessing its legendary sunsets. As the day drew to a close, I found myself seeking out the perfect vantage point to marvel at the kaleidoscope of colors that painted the sky. Whether perched on a cliffside terrace or nestled on a secluded beach, I watched in awe as the sun began its descent, casting a warm golden glow over the island. The sky transformed into a masterpiece of vibrant hues—fiery oranges, rosy pinks, and deep purples—evoking a sense of tranquility and serenity. The moment the sun dipped below the horizon, the island erupted into applause and cheers, as if paying tribute to nature's breathtaking spectacle.

Santorini, with its unique volcanic soil and Mediterranean climate, has earned a well-deserved reputation as a haven for wine lovers. The **island's wineries**, steeped in tradition and innovation, offer an extraordinary experience for those seeking to indulge in the flavors of Santorini's terroir and explore the art of winemaking. The local winemaking tradition in Santorini dates back thousands of years, intertwining with the island's rich history and cultural heritage. The volcanic soil, rich in minerals, imparts a distinct character to the grapes, resulting in wines that are renowned for their complexity and vibrant flavors. The dry, sunny climate, tempered by the cooling sea breeze, provides an ideal environment for grape cultivation, allowing the fruit to ripen slowly and develop exceptional aromatic profiles.

One of the most prominent grape varieties grown on the island is Assyrtiko, a white grape that thrives in Santorini's volcanic soil. Known for its vibrant acidity, mineral-driven character, and citrusy notes, Assyrtiko wines showcase the essence of Santorini's terroir. Whether enjoyed young or aged, Assyrtiko wines captivate the palate with their crispness, complexity, and distinct sense of place.

Apart from Santorini, I had the pleasure of exploring other beautiful Greek islands, such as **Mykonos and Crete**. Mykonos, which has a nickname "Island of the winds" is known for its vibrant and energetic island, boasting stunning beaches against a backdrop of iconic whitewashed buildings adorned with vibrant blue accents. The four windmills of Mykonos City provide a panoramic view of the entire island and are a defining feature of the Mykonos landscape. Paradise Beach and Super Paradise Beach, known for their lively beach parties, were a haven for social butterflies and music enthusiasts, where dancing and revelry continued from day to night. Crete, the largest and most diverse of the Greek islands, left me in awe of its profound cultural heritage. Visiting places like Heraklion, the Palace of Knossos, Chania, and Rethymno allowed me to immerse myself in the history and beauty of the island.

When it comes to culinary pleasures, Greece stands in a league of its own, with a rich culinary heritage and flavors that have delighted palates for centuries. From the sun-drenched islands to the rugged mainland, **Greek cuisine** is a celebration of fresh ingredients, vibrant flavors, and the joy of sharing a meal with loved ones. Greek cuisine is characterized by the use of simple yet flavorful ingredients that are lovingly prepared to create dishes that are both satisfying and memorable. Olive oil, a staple of the Mediterranean diet, forms the foundation of many Greek recipes, adding a luscious and distinctive taste. Fresh vegetables, fragrant herbs, and succulent meats combine to create a harmonious symphony of flavors that pay homage to the country's agricultural abundance. Seafood holds a special place in Greek cuisine, given the country's extensive coastline. Grilled octopus, tender calamari, and succulent shrimp take center stage, capturing the essence of the Mediterranean. Greek cuisine is not just about the food itself; it's a celebration of a way of life—a time to slow down, savor each bite, and enjoy the company of loved ones.

Greece is one of the most beautiful and culturally-rich places in the world! Home of two of seven wonders of the ancient world (Colossus of Rhodes and Statue of Zeus at Olympia). Greece has captured people's imaginations for thousands of years! My visit to Greece was a journey through time and an immersion in a land of rich history, stunning landscapes, delectable cuisine, and warm-hearted welcoming people. It was a destination that effortlessly combined ancient wonders with contemporary delights, leaving me with unforgettable memories. Greek cuisine was a celebration of life, where every meal became a shared experience, filled with laughter, warmth, and the pleasure of savoring the simple pleasures of good food and good company. So raise a glass of ouzo, dig into a plate of mezze, and immerse yourself in the culinary delights of Greece—it's a journey that will leave you nourished in both body and soul. Opa!

"TRAVEL MAKES ONE MODEST. YOU SEE WHAT A TINY PLACE YOU OCCUPY IN THE WORLD"

-Gustave Flaubert

Mykonos Island

Santorini Island

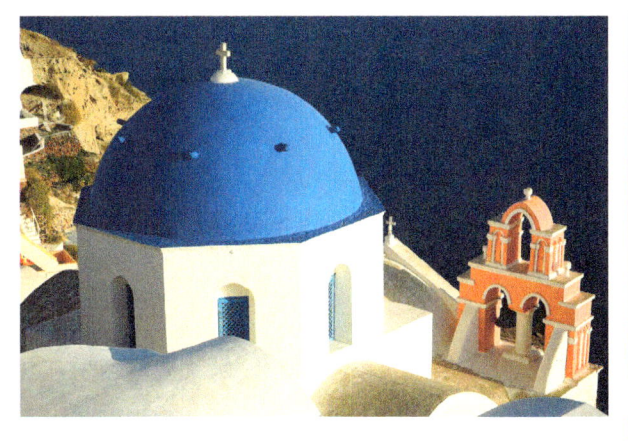

Santorini Island

New Year's Eve Fireworks over Acropolis

Santorini Island

Mykonos Island

Mykonos Island

Santorini Island

The Acropolis

The Acropolis

The Acropolis

The Palace of Knossos in Crete

The Changing Guards

THE NETHERLANDS: AMSTERDAM

One of the most delightful destinations I have ever had the pleasure of visiting in Europe is Amsterdam. I visited there during an enchanting springtime where the tulips were blooming and the streets were alive with tourist. It is an amazing city unlike no others in Europe.

This vibrant city in the Netherlands offers an incredible opportunity to explore its unique historic charm, indulge in various attractions, and immerse oneself in rich cultural experiences. Amsterdam, the capital of the Netherlands, seamlessly combines a captivating blend of history, culture, lively art scene and a friendly welcoming atmosphere. Often referred to as the "Venice of the North," Amsterdam boasts an extensive network of canals. Taking a leisurely stroll along the canal belt, a UNESCO World Heritage site, allowed me to marvel at the charming 17th-century canal houses, picturesque bridges, and beautifully tree-lined streets. The city's architecture effortlessly fuses classic and contemporary styles, featuring noteworthy landmarks such as the Royal Palace on Dam Square, the towering Westerkerk, and the modern Eye Filmmuseum.

As an art enthusiast, Amsterdam is not only an artistic hub, having renown museums and dance venues, art studios and is an absolute art haven for me. The renowned Rijksmuseum showcases masterpieces by Dutch masters like Rembrandt and Vermeer, while the Van Gogh Museum houses the largest collection of the esteemed artist's works. Additionally, the Anne Frank House stands as a significant museum providing profound insights into Anne Frank's life and legacy during World War II. Bicycles are an integral part of Dutch culture, and Amsterdam is truly a cyclist's paradise.

Renting a bike allowed me to explore the city like a local, pedaling through picturesque streets, parks, and alongside the serene canals. The city boasts an extensive network of cycling paths and bike-friendly infrastructure, making it incredibly convenient and enjoyable to navigate on two wheels. It is so delightful to ride along the canals on a bicycle taking in all of the wonderful sights and sounds of Amsterdam.

As a passionate photographer, visiting **Keukenhof** in springtime was an absolute dream come true. It was a truly magical experience that transported me into a world of wonder, where my senses came alive amidst a vibrant tapestry of colors, fragrances, and natural beauty. Keukenhof, located in Lisse, the Netherlands, is one of the most celebrated flower gardens worldwide, offering an unparalleled showcase of floral brilliance and the different aromatic scents will carry you away!

The main attraction at Keukenhof is undoubtedly the breathtaking tulip displays. Spanning over 79 acres, the garden features millions of tulips in various shapes, sizes, and hues. Wandering through the park, I was treated to a mesmerizing kaleidoscope of vibrant reds, yellows, pinks, purples, and even exotic varieties like the Parrot tulips, with their intricately fringed and ruffled petals. The surrounding tulip fields added to the allure, transforming the landscape into a magnificent painter's palette. It is not lost on the people of Amsterdam that years ago in the 17th Century, the tulip once caused a Dutch tulip bulb market bubble known as "tulipmania" and was one of the most famous market bubbles and crashes of all time. Observing these beautiful flowers in their finery makes you realize how people can fall in love with such a beautiful sight.

While tulips steal the show, Keukenhof is also a haven for numerous other flower varieties. Daffodils, hyacinths, orchids, roses, irises, and many more grace the meticulously landscaped gardens. Each section of the park showcases a different theme and design, ranging from formal gardens to more natural and whimsical settings. Keukenhof is not only a visual feast but also a haven for scents. The fragrant aroma of the flowers permeates the air, creating a sensory symphony that enhances the enchantment of the experience. The captivating scent of hyacinths, with their sweet and lingering fragrance, filled the gardens with an intoxicating aroma. Every step I took in "Keukenhof" was a unique olfactory journey, where each breath was a delightful inhalation of nature's perfumes.

Another exhilarating activity for photography enthusiasts during springtime in Amsterdam is the **flower parade**. Known as the "Bloemencorso", the flower parade takes place from "Noordwijk to Haarlem" and is an electrifying event that fills the air with excitement and anticipation. The parade is a celebration that ignites the senses, leaving spectators in a state of pure wonder and exhilaration.

The highly decorated flower floats in the Bloemencorso are a sight to behold. Meticulously crafted with an astonishing array of flowers, each float becomes a symphony of vibrant colors. The blooms in every imaginable shade - from fiery reds and oranges to soothing pastels and brilliant yellows - create a dazzling kaleidoscope of hues that mesmerize the eyes and awaken the spirit. The intensity of the colors establishes an atmosphere of enchantment and joy, infusing me with a sense of childlike wonder.

Moreover, the air is filled with an intoxicating perfume as the floats pass by. The scent of thousands of freshly bloomed flowers intermingles, creating a sensory experience that is nothing short of magical. The fragrance wafts through the crowd, transporting me to a realm where nature's most delicate and delightful aromas reign supreme. It is a symphony of scents that captivate the senses, evoking a sense of harmony and bliss.

The "Bloemencorso" was a testament to the incredible ingenuity and artistic vision of the float designers. Meticulously planned and crafted, each float was a masterpiece in its own right, telling a story or conveying a theme. The attention to detail was simply astounding, with flowers arranged in intricate patterns to form breathtaking images and scenes. Adding to the spectacle, the floats often featured moving parts, lighting effects, and music, elevating the visual experience and generating an extra layer of excitement. The combination of vibrant colors, captivating fragrances, elaborate designs, community spirit, and the festive atmosphere wove together an unforgettable tapestry of emotions and memories. It was a sensory feast that sparked the imagination, inspired awe, and fostered a deep appreciation for the beauty of nature and human creativity. It is truly something to experience as it will leave a lasting memory and bring you close to nature at the same time.

Another exhilarating event to attend in Amsterdam during springtime was the **King's Birthday celebration**, known as "Koningsdag". This vibrant and festive extravaganza captured the hearts of both locals and visitors alike, reflecting the spirited nature of the Dutch people. On "Koningsdag", the streets of Amsterdam are transformed into a sprawling outdoor party venue. The entire city is awash in a sea of orange, the color associated with the Dutch royal family, as people adorned themselves in vibrant orange attire, wigs, hats, and face paint. The festivities commenced early in the morning, with streets lined with stalls and blankets where locals set up their own flea markets, known as the "vrijmarkt". This tradition allowed individuals to sell their second-hand goods, resulting in a massive open-air marketplace.

One of the most iconic features of "Koningsdag" was the spectacular **King's Birthday canal parade**. During this time, the canals of Amsterdam, a UNESCO World Heritage site, come alive with a procession of creatively decorated boats gracefully cruising through the waterways. Private boats, canal tour boats, and barges all participated in this grand display of celebration. Each vessel was adorned with colorful banners, flags, and streamers, creating a mesmerizing visual spectacle. Onlookers lined the canal banks, cheering and waving orange flags as the boats sailed by. The air was filled with music blaring from the boats, further enhancing the excitement as people danced and sang along, generating an atmosphere of unbridled joy.

"Koningsdag" in Amsterdam was a day brimming with live music and performances scattered throughout the city. Numerous stages were set up in public squares and parks, featuring a diverse range of musical genres and artists. From traditional Dutch folk music to contemporary pop and rock bands, the air reverberated with a symphony of melodies.

Enthusiastic crowds gathered around these stages, swaying to the beats, clapping, and singing along. The infectious energy of the performances permeated the streets, captivating everyone in its path. As the sun began to set, the sky over Amsterdam lit up with a breathtaking fireworks display. Fireworks were an integral part of "Koningsdag" celebrations, and multiple locations throughout the city offered grand spectacles that illuminated the night sky.

Families, friends, and strangers gathered in parks, on rooftops, and along the canals, eagerly anticipating the mesmerizing bursts of color and light. The dazzling fireworks provided a dazzling finale, symbolizing the culmination of the day's festivities and leaving spectators in awe.

Amsterdam proved to be an extraordinary city, boasting vibrant cultures, rich history, awe-inspiring art, stunning architecture, and a dynamic atmosphere. Visiting "Keukenhof" in springtime was a truly awe-inspiring experience that delighted my senses and filled me with wonder. The meticulously curated displays, the intoxicating scents, and the lively atmosphere combined to create an ambiance of excitement and beauty. The "Bloemencorso", with its elaborate floats, diverse flower varieties, captivating themes, and the sense of community, was a remarkable celebration of the Netherlands' vibrant floral heritage. It provided a unique opportunity to witness the artistry and creativity involved in showcasing the country's blooming splendor. The parade served as a testament to the profound connection between the Dutch people and their flowers, and it was an experience that left a lasting impression. The King's Birthday celebration in Amsterdam was an unforgettable experience filled with vibrancy, fun, excitement, and a kaleidoscope of colors. It was a day when the entire city came together to celebrate and honor the Dutch monarchy in a joyful and inclusive manner. Koningsdag in Amsterdam promised a truly memorable and lively celebration.

The Flower Parade

Tulip Fields

Van Gogh

A plein-air Artist

Cheese Market

Cheese Market

The Flower Parade

Keukenhof Garden

King's Day Celebration

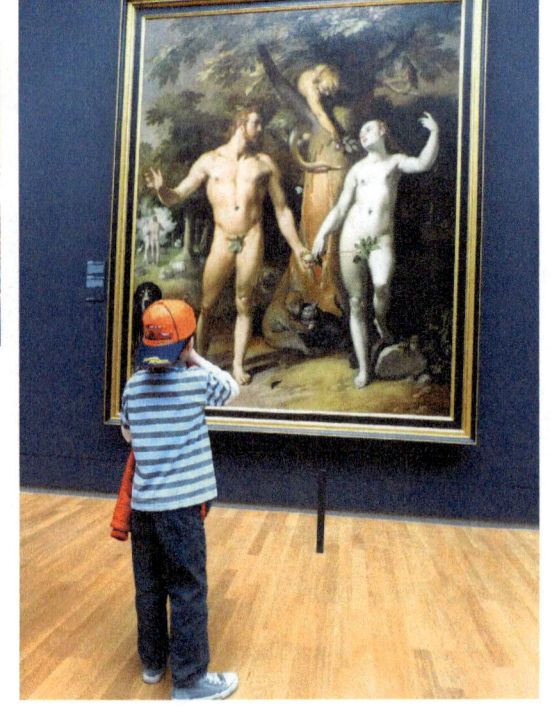

PORTUGAL

Embarking on a journey to enchanting Portugal was an experience that surpassed all my expectations. The country, with its enchanting blend of history, landscapes, hospitality, and cuisine, offers a tapestry of captivating experiences that will forever hold a special place in my heart. Portugal owns some of the most awe-inspiring coastline and stunningly beautiful beaches that are bound to leave you with a very memorable experience. The sunsets are amazing and will move you like no other in their beauty!

As I set foot in **Lisbon**, the vibrant capital city, I was immediately captivated by its unique charm. Situated along the banks of the Tagus River, Lisbon seamlessly combines a rich historical heritage with a modern cosmopolitan atmosphere. Exploring the city's narrow, winding streets became a delightful adventure, particularly in the Alfama district. The colorful houses, hidden squares, and the haunting melodies of fado music created an ambiance that transported me back in time. While wandering through the streets, I stumbled upon iconic landmarks such as the Belém Tower and the Jerónimos Monastery, both of which stand as testaments to Portugal's glorious past. These UNESCO World Heritage sites offered a glimpse into the country's architectural splendor and cultural significance.

To truly immerse myself in Lisbon's unique character, I embarked on a memorable ride aboard Tram 28. This historic tram traverses the city's most enchanting neighborhoods, offering panoramic views and an authentic taste of local life. As I sat on the tram, I marveled at the intricate mosaic pavements, ornate buildings, and the vibrant energy that permeated every street corner. It was an opportunity to witness the city's pulse and appreciate its rich tapestry of cultures and influences.

Yet, Lisbon's allure extends beyond its architectural marvels and lively streets. The city's culinary scene proved to be a delight for the senses. Portuguese cuisine, with its robust flavors and fresh ingredients, took me on a gastronomic journey like no other. I indulged in traditional dishes such as bacalhau à brás, a tantalizing combination of shredded codfish, potatoes, and eggs, as well as grilled sardines and cozido à portuguesa, a hearty Portuguese stew. However, it was my visit to **Pastéis de Belém** that truly left a lasting impression on my taste buds. This iconic bakery has been serving its renowned Portuguese custard tarts since 1837. Stepping into the bakery, I was met with the irresistible aroma of freshly baked tarts. The delicate, flaky pastry encased a creamy, velvety custard filling that tantalized my palate with its perfect balance of sweetness and richness. Each bite transported me to culinary heaven, and I couldn't resist going back for more.

Leaving Lisbon behind, I made my way to **Porto**, a city steeped in old-world charm and famous for its production of Port wine. Situated along the picturesque Douro River, Porto exuded an undeniable allure. As I strolled through the winding streets, the hilly landscape and historic architecture painted a picturesque scene. The Ribeira district, a UNESCO World Heritage site, offered a captivating backdrop for leisurely walks along the riverfront. Crossing the iconic Dom Luís I Bridge provided breathtaking views of the city and the river, adding to the magical ambiance of Porto.

To delve deeper into the world of Port wine, I ventured into the **Douro Valley**, a UNESCO World Heritage region renowned for its terraced vineyards and the production of world-class wines. Exploring the wineries allowed me to witness the passion and dedication that goes into crafting these exceptional wines. The steep terraced vineyards, painstakingly carved into the hillsides, created a stunning mosaic of green and gold. I had the privilege of visiting quintas, centuries-old estates that have been passed down through generations, preserving the winemaking traditions and heritage. Walking through the vineyards, I gained a profound appreciation for the meticulous process of cultivating grapes and the artistry of winemaking. Tasting the renowned Port wines, with their rich flavors and velvety textures, was a true delight for my senses and a testament to the region's winemaking prowess.

Exploring the wineries in Portugal's Douro Valley was an experience that truly delighted my senses. The wines produced in this region, particularly Port wine, captivated my taste buds with their rich and distinctive flavors. During my visit, I had the opportunity to sample various types of Port wine, including Ruby, Tawny, Vintage, and Late Bottled Vintage. Each style had its own unique characteristics, from the vibrant fruitiness of the Ruby to the nutty and complex flavors of the Tawny. It was fascinating to learn about the winemaking process and the meticulous care that goes into crafting these exceptional wines.

In addition to Port, the Douro Valley also produces outstanding still wines. Reds, whites, and rosés made from indigenous grape varieties such as Touriga Nacional, Tinta Roriz, and Malvasia Fina showcased the region's diversity and terroir. Participating in wine tastings at the wineries allowed me to fully appreciate the nuances of these wines and understand how the local climate, soil, and winemaking techniques contribute to their exceptional quality. It was a true celebration of the region's winemaking expertise and a testament to why the Douro Valley is recognized as one of the world's premier wine regions.

Moving on to the **Algarve region**, I found myself immersed in a world of stunning beaches and picturesque coastal towns. Praia da Marinha, with its golden sands and dramatic cliffs, left me in awe of nature's beauty. As I made my way down the stone staircase to the shore, the anticipation of feeling the warm sand beneath my feet and the salty breeze against my skin grew. The cliffs that encircled the beach added an element of grandeur and served as a testament to the region's raw natural beauty. Exploring the hidden caves and alcoves carved by the sea was like uncovering secrets of the coastline, and each discovery filled me with a sense of wonder.

The towns of Lagos and Albufeira offered a glimpse into the rich history and vibrant atmosphere of the Algarve. In **Lagos**, the colorful streets and whitewashed houses adorned with bougainvillea created a picturesque setting that felt like stepping into a painting. Exploring the cobblestone lanes and stumbling upon historic landmarks allowed me to delve into the city's maritime heritage and appreciate its cultural significance. In contrast, **Albufeira** exuded a lively energy with its bustling bars and restaurants. The vibrant colors of the traditional Portuguese tiled buildings added a playful charm to the surroundings, and the inviting beaches tempted me to relax and soak up the sun.

Yet, it was the untamed natural landscapes of the Algarve that truly took my breath away. Hiking along the cliffside trails of the Seven Hanging Valleys was an exhilarating experience. Each turn in the path revealed a new vista of rugged cliffs plunging into the sparkling sea. The crashing waves below created a symphony of nature's power, and the vastness of the horizon reminded me of the world's endless possibilities. Reaching the highest point of the hike, I was rewarded with a panoramic view that stretched as far as the eye could see—a reminder of the region's unspoiled beauty.

My journey through Portugal was a sensory delight that embraced me with its rich history, cultural treasures, natural wonders, and culinary delights. From the vibrant cities of Lisbon and Porto to the tranquil beauty of the Algarve, each moment was filled with discovery and unforgettable experiences. Whether I was savoring the flavors of Port wine in the Douro Valley or basking in the sun on the stunning beaches, Portugal's diverse offerings left an indelible mark on my heart. It is a destination that I will forever cherish, and its memories will continue to inspire my future travels. Truly, Portugal is a place where history comes to life, almost every city has a story to tell, so get ready to experience the rich history, unique culture and stunning architecture and soak in the vibrant atmosphere that only Portugal can offer.

"I SEARCHED FOR HAPPINESS IN EVERY COUNTRY IN THE WORLD, BUT IN THE END, I FOUND TRUE HAPPINESS IN MY HEART"

-Michael David

Monument to the discoveries

View from Belem Tower

Jeronimos Monastery in Lisbon

Lisbon Tram

Pasteis de Belem Bakery

Pasteis de Nata

Sintra

Porto

Aveiro, Portugal

Porto Winery

Lagos, Algarve Region

Algarve Region

UKRAINE

Bordering Russia to the East and the European Union to the West, Ukraine occupies a vast expanse of land and offers a truly unique experience unlike anywhere else! Imagine stepping into a world of boundless excitement and joy when visiting Ukraine before the senseless war. The country was an absolute gem, boasting a rich tapestry of culture, warm hospitality, and breathtakingly beautiful architecture spanning centuries. My journey through Ukraine was a symphony of joy and excitement as I delved deep into its vibrant cultural heritage. One of the most striking aspects of Ukraine was the genuine warmth and friendliness of its people. From the moment I set foot on Ukrainian soil, I was greeted with open arms and a sense of genuine curiosity.

The locals were eager to engage with visitors, share their traditions, and forge connections that transcended language barriers. Conversations with strangers often led to heartfelt exchanges, as Ukrainians shared their stories, aspirations, and the deep love they held for their homeland. Ukraine's cultural identity is a tapestry woven from the threads of music, dance, and art. I had the privilege of witnessing mesmerizing Ukrainian dance performances that left me awestruck. Dancers adorned in vividly colored, intricately embroidered costumes moved with grace and precision, telling stories that spanned generations. The music, often accompanied by the hauntingly beautiful sounds of the bandura, filled the air with an ethereal energy that seemed to resonate with the very soul of the nation.

Exploring Ukraine's cities felt like stepping into a time machine that seamlessly blended history with the modern world. Kyiv, the capital city, epitomized this fusion. Imagine a city with medieval castles and fortresses, perfectly preserved old towns, and the discovery of some of Europe's most offbeat places. That is Ukraine. Among the many remarkable places I visited, one that stood out as a personal favorite was **Saint Michael's Cathedral**. The Saint Michael's Golden-Domed Monastery in Kyiv is an architectural masterpiece and holds immense historical and cultural significance in the hearts of Ukrainians. Located in the heart of Kyiv's historic district, the monastery dates back to the 12th century and was originally built to honor the Archangel Michael, the patron saint of Kyiv. Throughout the centuries, the monastery underwent various reconstructions and renovations, with its golden-domed cathedral becoming an iconic symbol of the city.

Although the original cathedral was destroyed during the Soviet era, the decision was made to rebuild the monastery and restore its former glory after Ukraine gained independence in 1991. The reconstruction project, completed in 2000, aimed to revive the architectural heritage and spiritual significance of the site. The Saint Michael's Cathedral, a true masterpiece of Ukrainian Baroque architecture, showcases a golden-domed roof and an ornate facade that creates a breathtaking sight against the backdrop of Kyiv's skyline. The exterior is adorned with intricate stucco decorations, sculptures, and beautiful frescoes, showcasing the craftsmanship and artistry of the time.

Upon stepping inside the cathedral, I was immediately greeted by a stunning interior filled with religious icons, vibrant murals, and intricate woodwork. The iconostasis, a beautifully carved wooden screen covered in religious icons, separates the altar from the rest of the church. The cathedral's ambiance is serene and awe-inspiring, inviting contemplation and reflection. However, one of the highlights of the Saint Michael's Golden-Domed Monastery was its bell tower, which offered panoramic views of the city. Climbing the tower's stairs rewarded me with breathtaking vistas of Kyiv's ancient streets, the winding Dnipro River, and other architectural gems of the city. It was a perfect spot to capture memorable photographs and appreciate the beauty of Kyiv from above.

Another stunning examples of Ukrainian architecture which left a lasting impression on me was **Saint Andrew's Cathedral**. Visiting this cathedral was like embarking on a journey into the heart of Ukrainian history, spirituality, and architectural magnificence. Perched on a hill overlooking the city, this iconic structure held a special place in the hearts of the locals. Saint Andrew's Cathedral is a striking example of Baroque architecture and was designed by the renowned architect Bartolomeo Rastrelli in the mid-18th century. Its distinctive blue exterior, adorned with white columns and sculptures, stood out against the backdrop of the historic Podil district. The facade of the cathedral was adorned with delicate carvings, including biblical scenes and angelic figures. The cathedral's elegant bell tower added to its grandeur, providing a vantage point to admire the surrounding landscape. Stepping inside, I was greeted by a serene and contemplative atmosphere. The interior was adorned with richly painted frescoes and decorative elements that showcased the skill of Ukrainian artists of the time. The iconostasis, a beautifully crafted wooden screen displaying religious icons, separated the main nave from the altar, further enhancing the sacred atmosphere.

Beyond its architectural beauty, Saint Andrew's Cathedral holds a significant place in Ukrainian folklore and spirituality. According to legend, Apostle Andrew, the patron saint of Ukraine, stood on the hill where the cathedral now stands and prophesied the foundation of Kyiv. This connection to Ukraine's spiritual and historical roots makes the cathedral a pilgrimage site for many believers. It is easy to see the extraordinary pride and patriotism of the Ukrainian people as you explore their long historic roots of old Soviet times to the resurgence of Ukraine's patriotic spirit today.

In addition to exploring these magnificent cathedrals, I had the opportunity to visit the **weekend outdoor market near Saint Andrew's Cathedral** in Kyiv, which showcased the city's rich cultural heritage, local craftsmanship, and delicious culinary delights. Nestled in the historic neighborhood of Podil, this market offered a delightful experience that captured the essence of Kyiv. Every weekend, the area surrounding Saint Andrew's Cathedral came alive with an array of stalls, vendors, and enthusiastic shoppers. The market's lively atmosphere created a sense of excitement and anticipation as people gathered to explore the diverse offerings.

The market proved to be a treasure trove of traditional arts and crafts. Local artisans showcased their skills, presenting a wide range of handmade products. Intricately embroidered textiles, handcrafted jewelry, wooden carvings, ceramics, and other unique creations adorned the stalls. Moreover, the market often hosted live music performances, cultural displays, and entertainment. Local musicians and performers added to the festive ambiance, serenading visitors with traditional melodies and captivating performances. Folk dance groups showcased their talents, providing a glimpse into the vibrant cultural traditions of Ukraine. Not only is Ukraine a country of pleasant surprises but one that is bound to be one of your more memorable adventures as you travel along the country barely discovered by the average traveler.

During my visit, I also had the opportunity to explore the small town of **Zhytomyr**, where my friend's great grandfather hailed from. Taking a train from Kyiv, we arrived in Zhytomyr and ventured through the town with a local map in hand. Zhytomyr offered a captivating blend of history, culture, and natural beauty, boasting charming streets, architectural wonders, a vibrant cultural scene, and warm-hearted people.

While in Zhytomyr, we explored the life city's notable landmarks St. Michael's Cathedral, a grand Orthodox church with golden domes and an intricate exterior, showcasing Zhytomyr's rich religious heritage. Stepping inside, I admired the stunning frescoes, ornate iconography, and the peaceful ambiance that permeated the sacred space. The cathedral was not only a place of worship but also a cultural treasure reflecting the city's deep-rooted spirituality.

As we wandered through the city, we discovered Zhytomyr's well-preserved historic center, a treasure trove of architectural gems. The picturesque Sobornyi Maidan, the main square, was surrounded by elegant buildings representing various architectural styles, including neoclassical, baroque, and art nouveau. We took leisurely strolls, appreciating the intricate details of structures such as the Zhytomyr Regional Administration, exuding grandeur, and the Transfiguration Cathedral, a masterpiece of Byzantine architecture.

Returning back to Kyiv, the capital city of Ukraine, the city came alive with the warmth, hospitality, and genuine kindness of its **friendly people**. It was here that I experienced the true unique spirit of the Ukrainian people. The people of Kyiv were proud of their city and renowned for their strong sense of community, taking great pleasure in showcasing their rich cultural heritage. Engaging in conversations with Kyivites was a delightful experience. They were open-minded, curious, and genuinely interested in cultural exchange. Discussions spanned various topics, from art and literature to politics and history. Their eagerness to learn about other cultures created meaningful connections and fostered a sense of global understanding. Throughout history, Ukraine has often been a battleground due to its strategic location in Europe and its strong determination to be free. Ukrainians have also been renowned for their strong sense of unity and solidarity. In times of celebration or crisis, they have come together to support one another, forming a tightly-knit community. Witnessing this unity firsthand was incredibly inspiring and showcased the resilience and spirit of the people of Kyiv.

Ukrainian cuisine proved to be a true delight for food enthusiasts, offering a rich tapestry of flavors, hearty dishes, and traditional culinary techniques. Rooted in the country's agricultural heritage and influenced by neighboring regions, Ukrainian cuisine showcased a diverse range of ingredients and cooking methods.

One of my favorite dishes was Borscht, perhaps the most famous Ukrainian dish. This hearty beet soup featured a flavorful broth, richly colored from the beets, and a medley of vegetables such as cabbage, carrots, potatoes, and onions. It was often served with a dollop of sour cream, adding a creamy tang to the dish. Varenyky, Ukrainian dumplings similar to pierogies, were another culinary delight. They consisted of a thin dough wrapped around various fillings, ranging from savory options like potatoes, cheese, cabbage, or meat to sweet fillings like cherries, blueberries, or plums. Varenyky were typically boiled and served with melted butter, sour cream, or fried onions.

"Holubtsi", or stuffed cabbage rolls, were a comforting dish made by rolling cabbage leaves around a mixture of ground meat, rice, and spices. The rolls were then simmered in a savory tomato-based sauce until tender and flavorful, often served with a side of sour cream. Deruny, Ukrainian potato pancakes, were crispy on the outside and tender on the inside. Grated potatoes were mixed with flour, eggs, and seasonings, then fried until golden brown. Deruny were often served with sour cream or applesauce and could be enjoyed as a side dish or as a main course. For dessert, Medovik, or honey cake, was a beloved Ukrainian treat. Layers of honey-infused cake were stacked with a creamy filling made from sweetened condensed milk or sour cream. The cake was left to rest, allowing the flavors to meld together, resulting in a decadent and moist dessert.

As I reflect on my visit to Ukraine before the onset of conflict, my heart brims with nostalgia for the unparalleled beauty rich historical heritage of the country and the warmth of its people. Visiting Kyiv was an enchanting experience that immersed me in its fascinating landmarks, allowed me to indulge in delectable cuisine, connect with friendly locals, and embrace a culture rich in history and traditions. While the war has undoubtedly affected the region, it is our hope that peace will prevail, enabling future generations to rediscover the wonders of this remarkable city. The friendly people of Kyiv created an atmosphere of warmth and inclusion, making me feel at home. Their genuine hospitality, curiosity, and willingness to connect made exploring the city an enriching and unforgettable experience. The connections and friendships formed with the people of Kyiv were cherished, as they embody the essence of Ukrainian culture and left a lasting impression in my heart. If you are looking for an adventure of a lifetime and want to travel off the beaten tracks of other travelers to see rich cultural and historic spirit like no where else, Ukraine is the place to go!

SAINT MICHAEL'S CATHEDRAL

"TRAVEL IS THE BEST EDUCATION THAT MONEY CAN BUY"
-Unknown

Saint Andrew's Cathedral

Painted Pysanky Easter Eggs

A wedding in Kyiv

Traditional Music

Independence Square in Kyiv

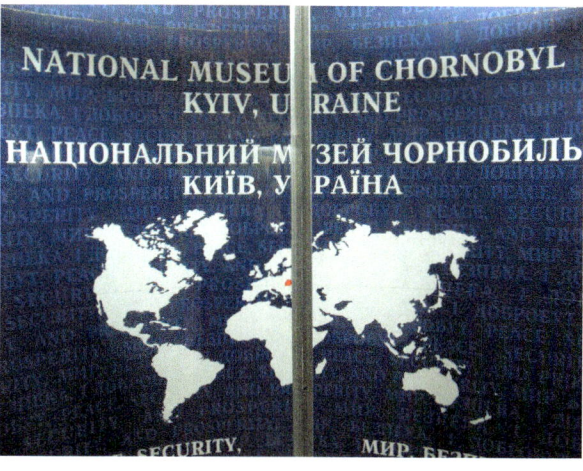

The National Chornobyl Museum

SAINT MICHAEL'S
Cathedral

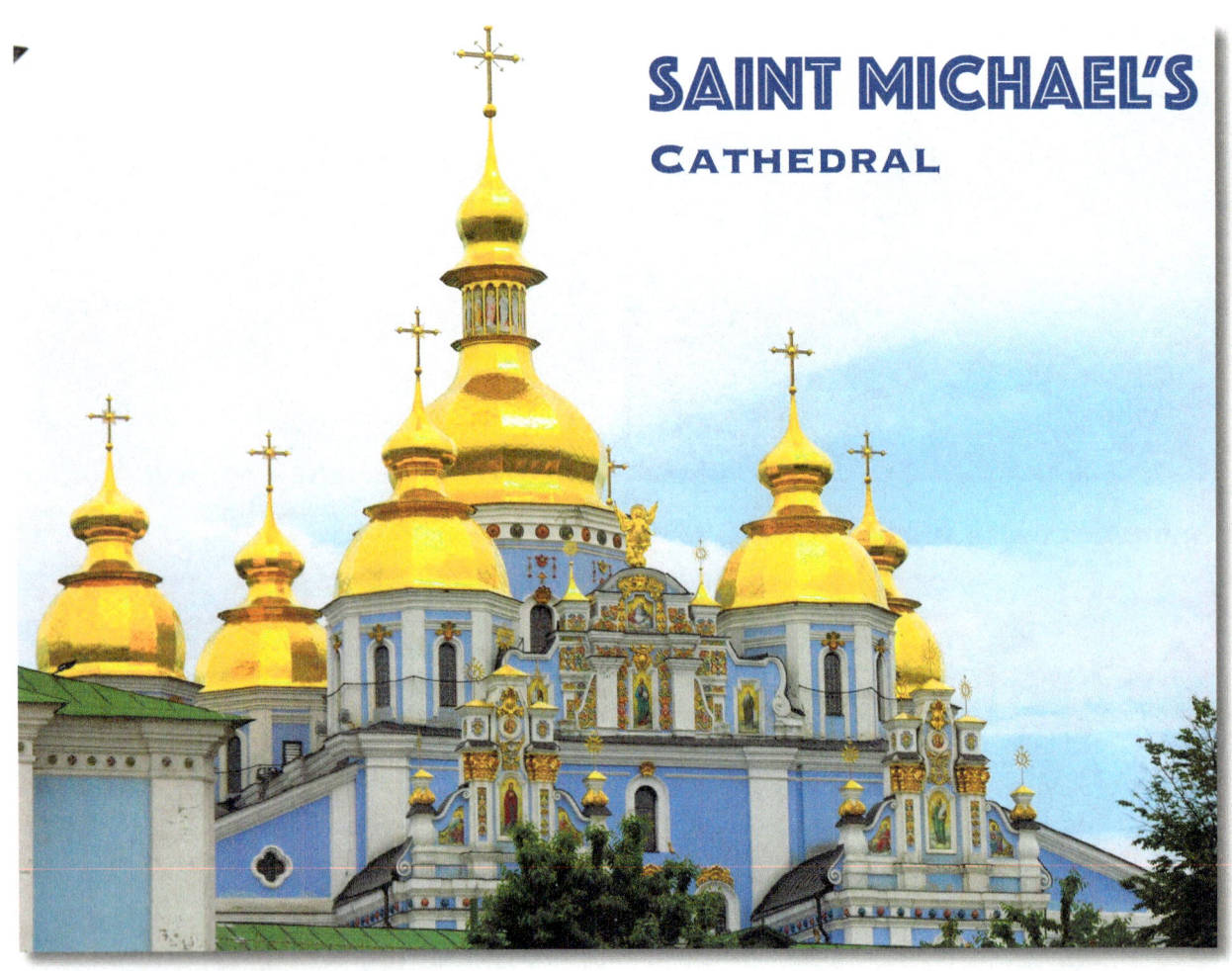

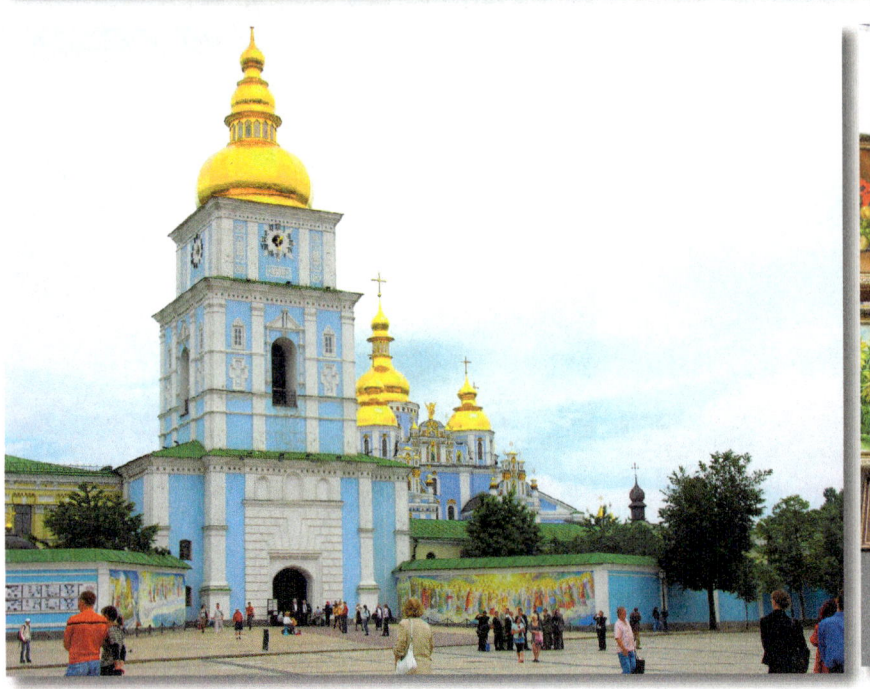

OCEANIA CONTINENT: 14 COUNTRIES

	Australia		Palau
	Fiji		Papua New Guinea
	Kiribati		Samoa
	Marshall Islands		Solomon Island
	Micronesia		Tonga
	Nauru		Tuvalu
	New Zealand		Vanuatu

OCEANIA CONTINENT

Oceania is a continent of breathtaking beauty and unparalleled diversity, unfolds like an enticing adventure, boasting some of the world's most extraordinary natural wonders and vibrant cultures. The very name "Oceania" evokes the majesty of the Pacific Ocean, harkening back to the ancient Greek word "okeanos," which once represented the boundless waters encircling the Earth in Greek cosmology. As the 19th century dawned, "Oceania" became the collective term for a vast region encompassing Australia, New Zealand, Polynesia, Melanesia, and Micronesia. Brace yourself for an electrifying journey through this captivating realm, where each moment promises to fill you with boundless excitement and joy.

Now, let's embark on an enthralling journey through the captivating continent of Oceania, where a realm of enchantment beckons to be explored. Our odyssey takes us to some of the world's most breathtaking destinations, each offering a unique and compelling experience.

Our journey begins at **the Great Barrier Reef**, a natural marvel that beckons travelers to its pristine shores. Stretching over a staggering 1,400 miles along the coast of Queensland, this sprawling coral reef system is a living spectacle of marine life. Delve into its depths on a guided snorkeling or scuba diving tour, and be entranced by the kaleidoscope of colors, from vibrant fish to graceful sea turtles, and the occasional awe-inspiring encounter with sharks.

Transitioning from the underwater beauty of the Great Barrier Reef, we arrive in the vibrant city of **Sydney, Australia**. This city invites us to delve into a myriad of captivating experiences, from the iconic Sydney Opera House to the majestic Sydney Harbor Bridge. The city's vibrant neighborhoods and world-class dining establishments beckon exploration, and a visit to the famous Bondi Beach promises a chance to surf the waves or bask in the golden sands while soaking in the sun and the bustling beach vibes.

Our journey takes us to **Kangaroo Island, Australia**, leaving behind the majestic cliffs of Milford Sound. This island is a sanctuary for native Australian wildlife, offering a seamless transition from New Zealand's rugged fjords to this lush haven. Kangaroos, wallabies, sea lions, and koalas are just a few of the island's residents, and encountering them in their natural habitat is a profound experience. A visit to Seal Bay allows you to seamlessly transition from one breathtaking natural wonder to another, as you observe Australian sea lions basking on the pristine shores. As the sun sets, immerse yourself in the island's pristine wilderness, where the transition from day to night unveils a stunning starlit sky that seems to stretch on forever.

Venturing further, we reach the **Whitsunday Islands**, an archipelago off the coast of Queensland, Australia. Transitioning from Fiji's serene shores to the Whitsundays' breathtaking island scenery is a journey that promises to enchant you. These islands, with their powdery white sands and crystal-clear waters, serve as the gateway to the Great Barrier Reef. Seamlessly transition from beachside relaxation to underwater exploration with snorkeling adventures that reveal the vibrant marine life and corals of the reef. The iconic Whitehaven Beach, with its pristine silica sands, offers a seamless transition into a scenic paradise, culminating in a place in which relaxation and adventure blend effortlessly. If you are a big movie-goer, you will love this part of the world as there are many movie set locations like Australia's Outback and the movie "Mad Max 2 or the entire trilogy of Lord of the Rings was filmed in New Zealand in Waikata's "Hobbit town" where over 20 odd film locations were used for production.

Continuing our odyssey, we find ourselves in the heart of **New Zealand's Fiordland National Park**, gazing in wonder at Milford Sound. This fjord, renowned for its majestic waterfalls and towering cliffs, offers the intrepid traveler a chance to hike the world-famous Milford Track. The journey rewards with panoramic views of the surrounding mountains and valleys, leaving you breathless in the face of nature's grandeur.
Nature enthusiasts will discover their paradise in **Aoraki / Mount Cook National Park, New Zealand**. This pristine wilderness is home to Aoraki / Mount Cook, the country's highest peak, surrounded by awe-inspiring alpine landscapes. The park offers a plethora of adventurous pursuits, from hiking to stargazing, and even glacier exploration, making it an ideal transition from the tranquility of Milford Sound to the thrill of the great outdoors.

From here, we journey to the geothermal wonderland of **Rotorua, New Zealand**. This transition from underwater beauty to the Earth's fiery core is seamless as nature's forces take center stage. Bubbling mud pools, spouting geysers, and vivid mineral springs come to life in a mesmerizing display. Rotorua also offers an immersive cultural experience, allowing a seamless transition from nature to culture through traditional Maori performances and a Hangi feast, immersing you in the ancient rituals and customs of this fascinating indigenous culture.

For those yearning for a tropical paradise, the **Fiji Islands** offer a dream come true. Here, crystal-clear waters lap at white sandy beaches, surrounded by lush greenery. The Yasawa Islands, a group of volcanic gems, beckon with some of Fiji's most exquisite beaches, setting the scene for a romantic escape or a tranquil retreat.

Our voyage then takes us to the blissful haven of **Tahiti in French Polynesia**. This tropical paradise seamlessly marries French and Polynesian cultures amid stunning beaches and turquoise waters. Explore the intriguing black sand beaches, immerse yourself in the crystal-clear waters, and savor the delectable fusion of French-Polynesian cuisine. Don't miss the chance to relish the traditional dish of "poisson cru", made with raw fish and creamy coconut milk.

Our next destination in this odyssey is the renowned **Bora Bora in French Polynesia**, often referred to as the "Pearl of the Pacific." This idyllic island offers the allure of overwater bungalows and mesmerizing coral reefs. Dive beneath the surface to snorkel and explore these underwater wonders, or venture into the lush interior to discover the island's hidden treasures.

As we move from the tropical paradise of Tahiti, let's venture to the remote and mystical **Rapa Nui**, more commonly known as **Easter Island**. This unique and captivating destination is famous for its enigmatic Moai statues. The transition from Tahiti's palm-fringed beaches to Rapa Nui's ancient archaeological wonders is a journey back in time. Explore the ahu platforms where the Moai stand, and you'll seamlessly transition from beachside bliss to archaeological exploration, pondering the mysteries of these colossal stone figures. As you witness the sun setting over the Pacific Ocean, the transition from day to night on Easter Island is a profound experience, casting an ethereal glow over the Moai statues and their intriguing history.

Oceania is a diverse continent with native tribal cultures, pristine beaches, top snorkeling and diving spots and stunning volcanoes. There are also several remote islands that are perfect destinations for a camper trip or bit of solitude to recharge ones' spirit and are excellent places for just simple meditation. These remarkable destinations are just a glimpse of the wonders that Oceania holds. Each place we've visited presents a unique blend of natural beauty, adventure, and cultural richness, ensuring that your journey through this captivating continent will be filled with exhilaration and unforgettable memories. So, pack your bags and prepare to be swept away by the wonders of Oceania, where enchantment awaits at every turn.

THE BEST TIME TO VISIT THE OCEANIA CONTINENT

Oceania, a vast and diverse region encompassing Australia, New Zealand, and the myriad islands of the Pacific Ocean, offers an array of experiences throughout the year. From the rugged landscapes of the Australian Outback to the pristine beaches of Fiji, Oceania's four distinct seasons present travelers with a wide range of possibilities.

Spring (September - November): As winter gives way to spring in the Southern Hemisphere, Australia's diverse landscapes come to life. Sydney, with its iconic landmarks like the Sydney Opera House and Sydney Harbour Bridge, is an inviting destination with pleasant weather. In New Zealand, spring is a great time for exploring the lush forests, fjords, and stunning landscapes of the South Island. Fiji, in the South Pacific, is a tropical paradise where you can enjoy the warm waters, snorkel among colorful coral reefs, and relax on palm-fringed beaches.

Summer (December - February): As summer unfolds, Oceania's coastal regions and islands beckon sun-seekers. Australia's Great Barrier Reef offers world-class snorkeling and diving experiences amidst the vibrant marine life. New Zealand's North Island comes alive with outdoor adventures, from hiking in Tongariro National Park to exploring geothermal wonders in Rotorua. The island nations of the South Pacific, such as Tahiti and Samoa, provide idyllic settings for a tropical escape with warm temperatures and clear waters.

Fall (March - May): As summer wanes, Oceania offers tranquil and temperate experiences. Melbourne, Australia, showcases its cultural charm with events like the Melbourne International Comedy Festival and the Melbourne Food and Wine Festival. It's also an excellent time to explore the Yarra Valley's wineries. New Zealand's Hawke's Bay region comes alive with grape harvest festivals and wine tours during the fall season. In the South Pacific, the Cook Islands offer a serene escape with lush landscapes, inviting lagoons, and a laid-back atmosphere.

Winter (June - August): While some regions in Oceania experience milder winters, others offer unique winter experiences. Queenstown, New Zealand, transforms into a winter wonderland with opportunities for skiing, snowboarding, and breathtaking scenery. The Australian Alps, including destinations like Thredbo and Perisher, provide excellent snow sports conditions during the winter months. In French Polynesia, Bora Bora and Moorea beckon with overwater bungalows, turquoise lagoons, and serene relaxation during the Pacific winter. Oceania's seasons offer an array of experiences, from exploring vibrant cities and outdoor adventures to indulging in tropical paradises and wine regions. Whether you seek thrilling activities, cultural immersion, or tranquil escapes, Oceania invites travelers to explore, savor, and create cherished memories throughout the year.

Prepare to embark on a thrilling and enchanting voyage as I unveil the extraordinary stories and breathtaking photographs that capture the essence of my exhilarating expedition across the captivating continent of Oceania. My journey through Oceania was nothing short of a symphony of extraordinary experiences, each one more magnificent than the last. From the pristine beaches that stretched as far as the eye could see to the lush, untamed wilderness that whispered ancient secrets, every step was a revelation. The beauty of the natural world was matched only by the warmth and hospitality of the diverse and fascinating people I had the privilege of meeting along the way.

The joy and enrichment I garnered from my sojourn in Oceania are beyond words. It's as if this remarkable continent opened its arms wide to embrace me, allowing me to become part of its tapestry of life. I look back on this adventure with profound gratitude, for the opportunity to immerse myself in the magic of Oceania has left an indelible mark on my soul. I am absolutely elated, and my heart brims with boundless gratitude for the treasures it has bestowed upon me.

AUSTRALIA

Australia is a country that never ceases to amaze with its vastness and diversity of experiences. From the bustling cities, unique wildlife, breathtaking beaches, and the world's largest coral reef system, this place has something for everyone. I feel fortunate to have visited Australia multiple times, exploring all six states and two territories, including New South Wales, Queensland, South Australia, Tasmania, Victoria, Western Australia, Northern Territory, and Australian Capital Territory.

One must-see destination in Australia is the city of **Sydney**, home to the iconic Opera House and Harbor Bridge, along with a lively arts and culture scene. Another must-visit city for culture and food enthusiasts is Melbourne, renowned for its trendy cafes, restaurants, and thriving arts scene. But the crown jewel of Australia is the Great Barrier Reef, the world's largest coral reef system located off the coast of Queensland. The Reef is a natural wonder that evokes a sense of wonder and joy in visitors.

I have visited t**he Great Barrier Reef** several times and I have experienced the joy of snorkeling in its crystal-clear waters. The vibrant coral and diverse marine life make this place a feast for the senses, and every turn reveals a new wonder to behold. The playful antics of schools of brightly colored fish and the graceful movements of sea turtles are just a few of the wonders one can experience. As I explored the reef, I encountered a kaleidoscope of colors that are almost impossible to describe. The vibrant corals are a true work of art, with their delicate tendrils reaching out in every direction, while the fish that dart among them seem to have been painted in the brightest colors imaginable. The curious eyes of a giant clam and the playful darting of a school of clownfish make the reef alive with character and charm. The Great Barrier Reef is truly a sight to behold, the reef's beauty and the sensation of floating weightlessly through the water left me awestruck and filled with a sense of wonder and awe. It's important to remember that the Great Barrier Reef is a fragile ecosystem that requires our protection, and we have a responsibility to preserve it for future generations to enjoy.

Another stunning place that I visited was **Whitsunday**, home to the Whitsunday Islands and **Whitehaven Beach**, which left me speechless. The natural landscapes and pristine beaches are beyond compared, and it's no wonder that this destination is considered one of the most beautiful in the world. The Whitsunday Islands are a group of 74 islands located off the coast of Queensland. One of the most popular destinations within the Whitsundays is Whitehaven Beach, renowned for its pristine white sands and crystal-clear waters. The sand is so fine and pure that it squeaks when walked on, and it reflects the sunlight in a way that creates a brilliant, almost ethereal glow.

The waters surrounding Whitehaven Beach are equally as stunning, with shades of turquoise and deep blue that change with the light and tides. The Hill Inlet, a swirling pattern of sand and water created by the tides, is one of the most breathtaking sights on Whitehaven Beach. But it's not just the beauty of the beach and waters that make the Whitsunday Islands so awe-inspiring. The islands are also home to a diverse array of wildlife, including sea turtles, dolphins, and colorful fish.

Visiting **Uluru** was an experience that left me in awe and wonder. The massive sandstone rock formation, also known as Ayers Rock, is located in the heart of the Australian Outback and is one of the most recognizable landmarks in Australia. For the Anangu, the Aboriginal people who have lived in the area for tens of thousands of years, Uluru is more than just a physical landmark. It is a deeply spiritual place that is imbued with the power of their ancestors and the Dreamtime.

The Anangu have many Dreamtime stories about Uluru that describe the creation of the rock and its significance to their culture. According to these stories, Uluru was created by ancestral beings during the Dreamtime, a period of creation and spiritual significance in Aboriginal culture. The ancestors carved the rock out of the earth and imbued it with their power, leaving behind many sacred sites and important landmarks. For the Anangu, Uluru is a living entity that is inhabited by the spirits of their ancestors. They believe that the rock has the power to heal and protect and that it is a source of spiritual guidance and wisdom. It is a physical manifestation of their culture and heritage, and a symbol of their connection to the land and the Dreamtime. The spiritual significance of Uluru is deeply ingrained in the culture and traditions of the Anangu people, and they have a deep respect for the rock and its power. In 2019, the Australian government announced that it would ban climbing Uluru, a move that was welcomed by the Anangu and many others who support the protection of the rock and its spiritual significance.

Overall, Australia is a stunning country with warm and friendly people, beautiful cities, and stunning beaches. The Whitsunday Islands and Whitehaven Beach are truly some of the most stunning destinations in the world, and exploring the Great Barrier Reef was an adventure of a lifetime. The reef is a true treasure of our natural world, and it is our duty to protect and preserve it for future generations. Visiting Uluru was a humbling experience, and it reminded me of the power and significance of cultural landmarks. It was a joy to learn about the Anangu culture and their connection to the land, and to witness their deep respect and reverence for Uluru. It is clear that this magnificent rock formation holds a special place in the hearts of the Anangu people and is a testament to the spiritual richness and depth of their culture.

Bondi Icebergs Pool

Twelve Apostle in Melbourne

The Great Barrier Reef

New Year' Eve in Sydney

Young Surfers at Bondi Beach

Koala and baby

Hot air balloon ride in Cairns

Uluru Rock

The Devils Marbles in Australia

White Haven Beach

Swagging in the outback

Whitsunday, Queensland, Australia

NEW ZEALAND

New Zealand is one of my favorite places to visit. Experience rugged coastlines, sublime mountains, world class cuisine and some of the warmest and welcoming hospitality in the world. New Zealand, a land of captivating beauty and diversity, is a paradise for those who appreciate the wonders of nature. With its stunning landscapes, exotic wildlife, and vibrant culture, this country has captured my heart and left me in awe. It is a world-renowned destination that attracts tourists from all over the globe, and for good reason. With two main islands, each with its own distinct character and attractions, a visit to both the North Islands and South Islands is highly recommended to experience the full range of what New Zealand has to offer. The best time to visit is during the summer months of December to March as you can enjoy outdoor activities such as hiking and mountain climbing.

Starting with the **North Island**, **Rotorua** is undoubtedly one of the most popular destinations. This region is famous for its geothermal wonders and Maori culture, making it a unique and fascinating destination. I visited Rotorua and witnessed numerous geysers, hot springs, and mud pools, including the iconic Pohutu geyser, which erupts up to 20 times a day. But what makes Rotorua truly special is the opportunity to connect with the Maori people, the indigenous people of Aotearoa New Zealand. **The Maori culture** and tradition are deeply rooted in their connection to the land, nature, and their ancestors. Their culture is not just a set of practices and beliefs, but an integral part of their identity and way of life. Imagine traveling the entire depth of the Pacific Ocean in a narrow canoe only guided by the southern cross and the migration of the whales. This what the Maori did centuries ago from their south pacific islands to tame the wild New Zealand countryside.

One of the best places to learn about Maori culture is **the Whakarewarewa Maori Village**, home to the Tuhourangi Ngati Wahiao people. This village is famous for its geothermal activity, including bubbling mud pools, hot springs, and geysers, which the people of Whakarewarewa use in their everyday lives. They use the natural steam and heat to cook their food, warm their homes, and even provide healing therapies. I had the incredible experience of savoring a meal that was cooked using the heat from a hot spring and natural steam oven. The unique cooking method added a special touch to the flavors and textures of the food, making it a meal that I will never forget. A highly distinctive aspect of Maori culture is their tattoos, known as tā moko. Tā moko is a highly sacred and spiritual practice that involves the carving or incision of designs into the skin, reflecting a person's ancestry, social status, and achievements. Maori music is also an important part of their culture, with songs and dances often performed at important events and gatherings. The haka, a traditional Maori war dance, is perhaps the most famous Maori dance and is often performed by the New Zealand national rugby team, the All Blacks, before matches.

Moving on to the **South Island**, **Marlborough**, located on the northeastern tip, is the most famous wine region in New Zealand. The region is renowned for producing some of **the best Sauvignon Blanc wines in the world**, making it a popular destination for wine lovers and tourists alike. With over 150 wineries and vineyards, Marlborough is the largest wine region in New Zealand, thanks to its unique climate and soil conditions that are ideal for growing grapes, especially Sauvignon Blanc. The region's cool climate and long, sunny days provide the perfect conditions for growing grapes that are high in acidity and bursting with flavor. I had the opportunity to enjoy sampling some of the region's finest wines while taking in the breathtaking scenery.

One of the South Island's must-visit destinations is Milford Sound and Doubtful Sound. **Milford Sound** is a place of unparalleled beauty located in the heart of the Fiordland National Park on the southwestern coast of the South Island. As the boat approaches Milford Sound, I was greeted with a dramatic landscape, towering mountains rising up from the water with peaks shrouded in mist, while waterfalls cascade down their sides. The still waters of the sound reflect the beauty around it, creating a mirror-like effect that adds to the sense of awe. The area is home to unique wildlife, and I spotted seals and dolphins while exploring the area. The sheer scale of the scenery is humbling, and it reminds me of just how small we are in comparison to the natural world. It's a place that makes me appreciate the beauty and power of nature, and it's a must-visit for anyone traveling to New Zealand.

My journey to **Doubtful Sound** in the Fiordland National Park of New Zealand's South Island was an experience that filled me with joy and excitement. This remote and pristine wilderness is one of the largest fiords in New Zealand and is often referred to as the 'Sound of Silence.' As I journeyed across Lake Manapouri, one of New Zealand's most picturesque lakes, before entering the fiord itself, I was filled with anticipation.

As we entered Doubtful Sound, I was greeted by towering mountains and cascading waterfalls, and the sheer scale of the landscape left me in awe. The tranquility and serenity of the area were remarkable, and nature reigns supreme in this untouched wilderness. The boat ride itself was an adventure, and every moment was filled with breathtaking views that left me speechless.

Hiking on **Fox Glacier** was another unforgettable adventure that filled me with joy and excitement. The helicopter ride over the rugged mountains and forests of the West Coast region was breathtaking, and the view of the massive, glittering ice kingdom before me was simply stunning. As the helicopter landed on the glacier and we disembarked, the crisp, cold air filled my lungs, and the crunch of the ice underfoot echoed through the valley.

Equipped with crampons, we followed our guide through the maze of ice formations, navigating deep crevasses and climbing steep ice walls. The constantly changing landscape revealed the deep blue hue of the ice, and the layers that had accumulated over centuries were fascinating to witness. Our guide's insights into the glacier's formation and the impact of climate change added depth and meaning to the experience. As we reached the terminal face of the glacier, the thunderous sound of the ice breaking off and crashing into the valley below left me breathless. The power of the glacier was on full display, and I couldn't help but feel small and insignificant in the face of such majesty.

Overall, a trip to New Zealand is a once-in-a-lifetime opportunity to witness some of the world's most breathtaking scenery and unique culture. Exploring the geothermal wonders of Rotorua, cruising through the majestic fjords of Milford and Doubtful Sound, hiking on Fox Glacier, or tasting the finest wine are all experiences that left me with unforgettable memories. The raw beauty of the natural wonders and the rich culture and traditions of the Maori people reflect their deep connection to the land, nature, and their ancestors, making New Zealand a truly remarkable destination.

CHAMPAGNE POOL
ROTORUA, NEW ZEALAND

Auckland, New Zealand

Christchurch before the earthquake

the Whakarewarewa Maori Village

Afternoon tea at the Maori Village

The Maori dancers

Lupins at Lake Tekapo

Hiking on Fox Glacier

Hiking on Fox Glacier

Fox Glacier

New Zealand Ferns

Waterfall in Milford Sound

Kayaking in Milford Sound

PAPUA NEW GUINEA

Visiting Papua New Guinea is an extraordinary journey filled with boundless excitement and joy, as this diverse and vibrant nation offers a unique blend of natural wonders, cultural diversity, and warm hospitality. From the moment you arrive in this remote Pacific paradise, the anticipation of incredible experiences begins to build.

Papua New Guinea is a land of breathtaking landscapes and pristine wilderness, where excitement thrives. The country's rugged terrain includes lush rainforests, towering mountain ranges, and idyllic beaches. The thrill of exploring remote, untouched areas, such as the Highlands or the Sepik River, is boundless. Hiking through lush forests and crossing roaring rivers, you'll encounter diverse flora and fauna, adding to the excitement of your adventure.

The cultural tapestry of Papua New Guinea is equally captivating. With over 800 different languages and a rich heritage of traditions and rituals, every interaction with the diverse indigenous groups is a source of joy. Engaging with local communities, participating in traditional ceremonies, and discovering ancient customs and artistry will fill your heart with appreciation for the country's cultural wealth.

The lively and colorful festivals, such as the Goroka Show or the Mount Hagen Show, are exhilarating experiences. I had the opportunity to attend the Goroka Show. **The Goroka Show**, also known as the Goroka Cultural Festival, is a dazzling celebration of Papua New Guinea's cultural diversity. Held annually in the town of Goroka, this multi-day event in September showcases the traditions of over 100 different tribes from the highlands and surrounding regions. As the sun rises over the Eastern Highlands Province, the town comes alive with vibrant colors and the rhythmic beat of traditional drumming. Each tribe is easily distinguishable by their distinctive body paint, intricate costumes made from natural materials, and elaborate headdresses adorned with feathers and shells. The sing-sing performances take center stage, telling the stories of the tribes through exuberant dance, chanting, and rhythmic drumming. It's a visual and auditory feast that leaves visitors in awe.

The festival also features a competitive spirit, with judges assessing the performances and awarding recognition to the best. This friendly competition adds an extra layer of excitement to the event, as tribes put their heart and soul into their presentations. The exchange of traditions is a key element of the Goroka Show. Participants and visitors have the chance to interact with indigenous communities, learn about their customs. The Goroka Festival is a captivating and joyous celebration that immerses you in the heart of Papua New Guinea's cultural identity, where excitement, tradition, and cultural exchange come together in a vibrant and unforgettable experience.

Papua New Guinea's underwater world is a source of awe and joy. With some of the most pristine coral reefs and marine biodiversity in the world, diving or snorkeling in its warm, crystal-clear waters is an adventure like no other. The excitement of swimming among vibrant coral formations and encountering exotic marine life, including colorful fish and graceful manta rays, is an experience that will leave you beaming.

The cuisine in Papua New Guinea offers a delightful blend of fresh seafood, tropical fruits, and indigenous flavors. Savoring traditional dishes like mumu or kokoda is a culinary adventure that fills your taste buds with pure delight.

The warmth and hospitality of the locals create an atmosphere of joy. Their welcoming smiles and willingness to share their stories, art, and traditions make you feel like a part of their community.

Whether you're trekking through the dense jungles, immersing yourself in the fascinating cultures, or snorkeling in the vibrant waters, Papua New Guinea is a destination where excitement and joy are intertwined with every moment of your journey. It's a place where adventure and cultural immersion come together to create memories that you'll treasure forever. Papua New Guinea is a land of diverse and boundless joy, waiting to be discovered.

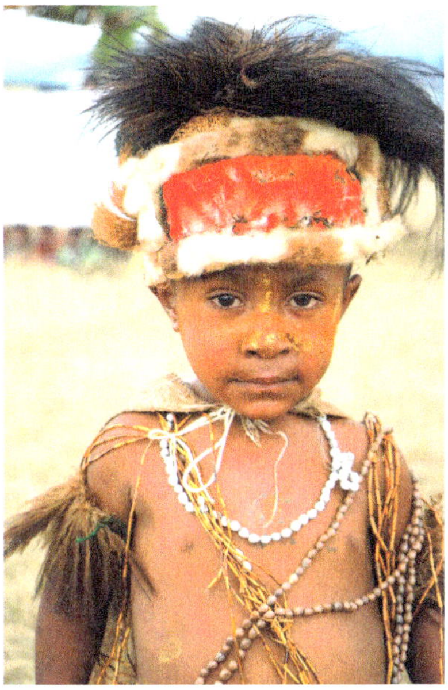
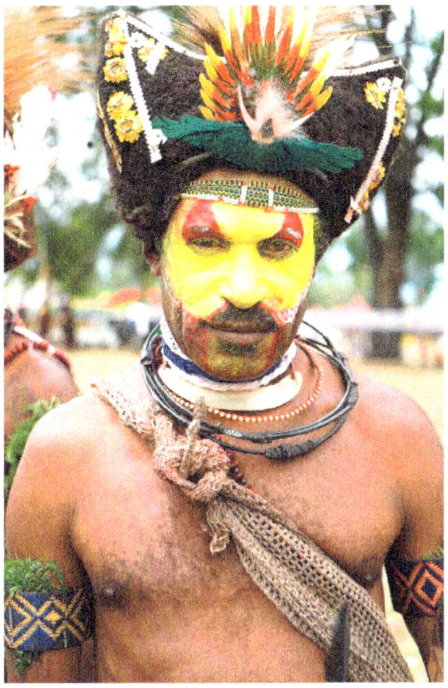
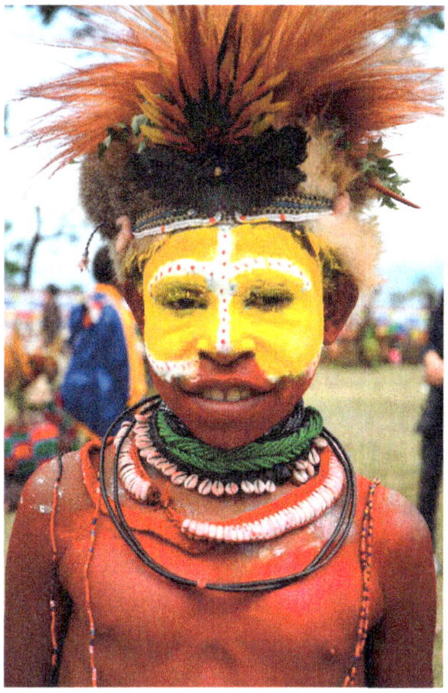
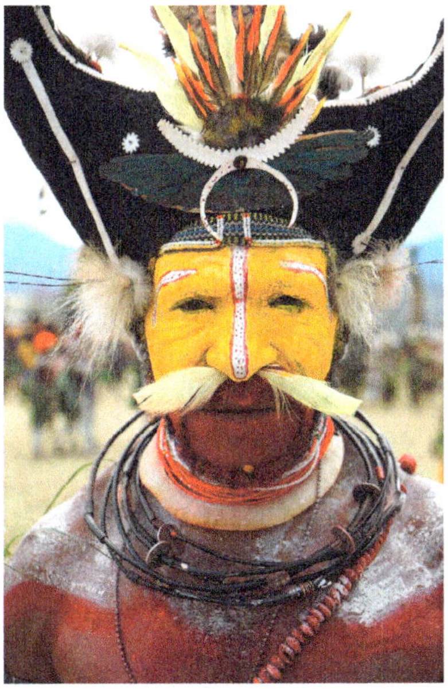
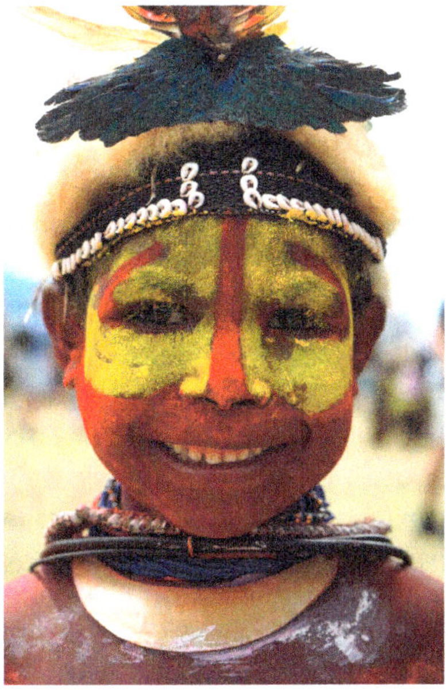
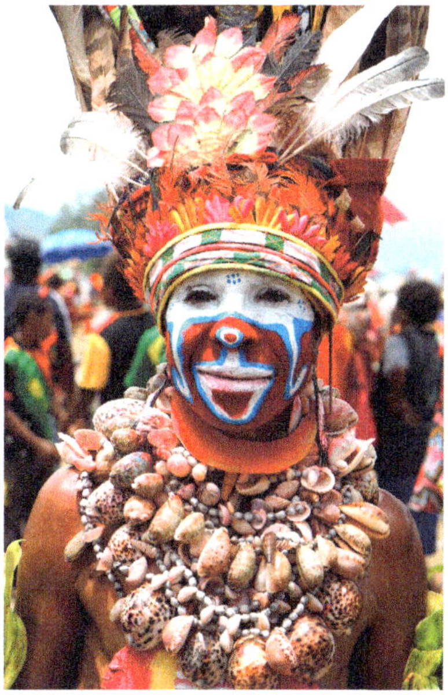
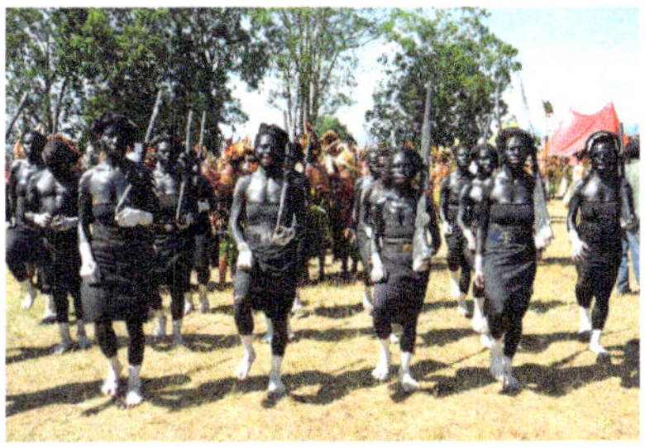
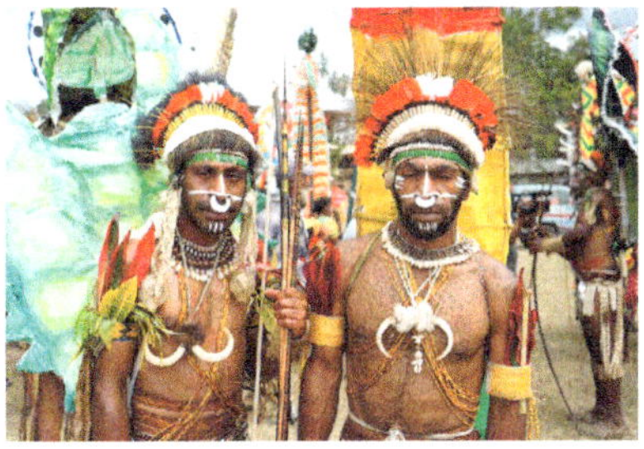
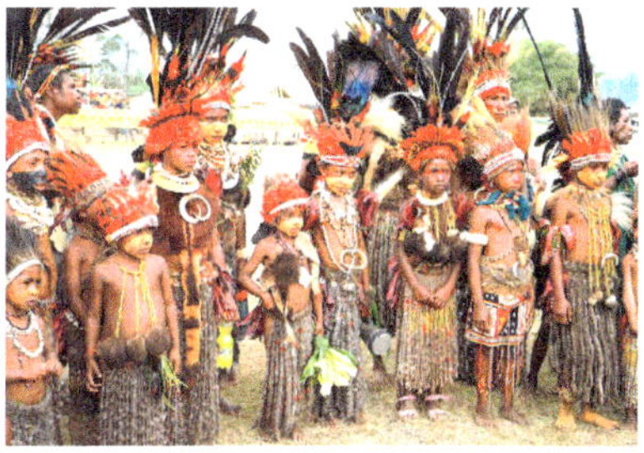

TONGA

Tonga, an exquisite island nation situated in the South Pacific, is renowned for its breathtaking beaches, pristine waters, and extraordinary marine life. Among my many captivating experiences in Tonga, one that stood out for me was the exhilarating opportunity to swim with humpback whales during their annual migration. Every year, these majestic creatures embark on an incredible journey from the icy Antarctic waters to the warm tropical embrace of Tonga. Taking place between July and October, this migration ranks among the longest and most impressive in the animal kingdom.

The epic voyage undertaken by humpback whales from the frigid Antarctic to the inviting tropical waters of Tonga spans thousands of miles, lasting several months. Throughout this arduous expedition, these remarkable animals navigate treacherous seas and endure extreme weather conditions, showcasing an extraordinary display of endurance and unwavering determination. I felt incredibly fortunate to have been given the opportunity to swim alongside these magnificent beings in Tonga. The experience of swimming with humpback whales was nothing short of magical, etching indelible memories that will undoubtedly accompany me throughout my life. It presented a unique chance to forge a profound connection with nature, an experience that was both humbling and exhilarating.

The migration of humpback whales to Tonga was not solely a testament to their physical fortitude; it also played a pivotal role in their life cycle. The waters surrounding Tonga provided an ideal breeding ground for these whales, offering shallow and protected waters that served as a sanctuary for newborn calves. Additionally, the warm waters of Tonga provided respite from the frigid Antarctic waters, where the whales predominantly fed during the summer months. Upon their arrival in Tonga, the whales engaged in a variety of behaviors associated with courtship and mating. The male humpback whales captivated with their elaborate and acrobatic displays, featuring breaching, tail slapping, and their renowned haunting songs. These melodious tunes, believed to facilitate communication and courtship among the whales, were one of the species' most distinctive characteristics.

During this incredible adventure, licensed guides accompanied us, ensuring the whales were not harassed or disturbed while offering valuable insights into their behavior and biology. Swimming alongside these majestic humpback whales proved to be an exciting and unforgettable experience, granting a rare glimpse into the lives of these awe-inspiring creatures. It was a captivating encounter that left me both exhilarated and humbled. Witnessing the sheer size and power of these animals up close was truly awe-inspiring, while their graceful and elegant movements through the water were nothing short of breathtaking. This experience served as a reminder of the astounding diversity and intricacy of life on our planet, reinforcing the importance of preserving and protecting these magnificent beings.

As I boarded the boat in the early morning light, an overwhelming sense of excitement and anticipation engulfed me. I was about to embark on an adventure that I had cherished for years: **swimming with humpback whales** in the warm waters off the coast of Tonga. Venturing into the calm, turquoise waters, we navigated our way towards the area where the whales congregated. Approaching our destination, our guide instructed us on the proper protocol for swimming with these gentle giants. We were to enter the water calmly and quietly, allowing the whales to approach us on their own terms. Finally, in the distance, we spotted a mother humpback whale accompanied by her calf. As our boat slowed down, we prepared ourselves to enter the water. Filled with excitement and nervousness, I secured my snorkel and fins, feeling my heart race. The moment arrived, and I immersed myself in the crystal-clear water. Instantly, I was captivated by the beauty and tranquility of the underwater realm. Schools of vibrant fish darted around me, and the coral formations resembled masterpieces. Suddenly, I caught sight of a dark shadow gliding towards me beneath the water's surface. My heart skipped a beat as I realized it was the mother humpback whale, an immense creature nearly 40 feet in length. However, she moved with a grace and elegance that defied her size.

She swam right past me, almost within arm's reach, and I could discern the curiosity in her eyes. The calf, even more spirited, playfully circled around us, treating us to a few breathtaking breaches above the water's surface. The echoes of their vocalizations—the renowned haunting songs of humpback whales—resonated through the water, adding to the already profound experience.

Throughout the day, we were fortunate enough to have multiple encounters with humpback whales, each one leaving us spellbound. One particular moment stood out vividly in my memory: a group of three juvenile whales approached us, their curiosity mirroring our own. They gracefully swam around us, their enormous, intelligent eyes fixated on us. Every now and then, they would blow bubbles or spyhop, raising their heads above the water's surface to get a better look at us. At one point, one of the juveniles even approached me directly, stopping just a few feet away. I was awestruck by the intricate details of its skin—the rough, barnacle-covered surface that felt like sandpaper when I touched it. A profound sense of respect and awe washed over me, fully aware of the creature's immense size and power compared to my own.

Another highlight of the day unfolded when we witnessed a mother whale patiently teaching her calf how to breach. While we had observed breaches from a distance earlier, this was our first up-close encounter with the breathtaking display. The mother whale would launch her massive body out of the water, crashing back down with a resounding splash. The calf watched intently, attempting to mimic its mother's graceful movements, sometimes successfully, and other times falling short. It was a mesmerizing showcase of the bond between mother and child, illustrating the whales' remarkable intelligence and social behavior.

For the following hour, we continued to swim alongside these magnificent creatures, marveling at their playful interactions and the juxtaposition of their peaceful yet powerful movements. It was an extraordinary experience that has been etched into my memory forever. To be in the presence of these gentle giants of the sea, observing them up close and witnessing their natural behaviors, was undeniably awe-inspiring. Swimming with these majestic creatures was an unparalleled encounter, like no other.

One of the most incredible aspects of swimming with humpback whales was the remarkable sounds they produced. These vocalizations, known as "whale songs," served as a form of communication among the whales. As we swam alongside them, their hauntingly beautiful songs reverberated through the water. The complex melodies and patterns of humpback whale songs continued to captivate scientists, who have yet to fully understand their purpose. While these songs facilitated communication within the whale community, they also hold cultural significance for the people of Tonga. In Tongan culture, humpback whale songs symbolized good luck and prosperity, and they were often incorporated into traditional ceremonies and rituals.

As the day drew to a close and we made our way back to the shore, a profound sense of gratitude enveloped me. Swimming with humpback whales in Tonga had always been a cherished dream, and the reality surpassed all expectations. Being in the presence of these magnificent creatures, witnessing their beauty and power firsthand, left an indelible mark on my soul. However, beyond the thrill and adventure of the day, the experience also instilled in me a sense of profound responsibility. Humpback whales were still recovering from the impacts of commercial whaling, and their populations remained vulnerable to threats such as climate change and ocean pollution. Swimming with them served as a poignant reminder of the urgent need to protect our oceans and safeguard the incredible animals that inhabit our oceans.

In recent years, concerns about the humpback whale population and the influence of human activities have grown significantly. These whales faced numerous threats, including entanglement in fishing gear, contamination from ocean pollution, and disruptions caused by climate change-induced shifts in their food sources. Consequently, the conservation and preservation of these majestic creatures and the ecosystems they rely on have become more crucial than ever.

Overall, the migration of humpback whales to Tonga was a natural wonder that evoked both awe and humility. The arduous journey undertaken by these animals was a testament to their exceptional endurance and unwavering determination. The behaviors and songs they displayed in the warm waters surrounding Tonga showcased their remarkable abilities. The experience of swimming with humpback whales in Tonga was an unforgettable, once-in-a-lifetime opportunity to witness these magnificent creatures in their natural habitat and to fully appreciate the wonder and beauty of the ocean. Moreover, it served as a poignant reminder of our responsibility to protect and preserve our oceans and the incredible creatures that call them home.

SWIMMING WITH HUMPBACK WHALES

"LIFE IS NOT MEASURED BY THE BREATHS WE TAKE, BUT BY THE MOMENTS THAT TAKE OUR BREATH AWAY."

—Maya Angelou

HUMPBACK WHALE BREACHING

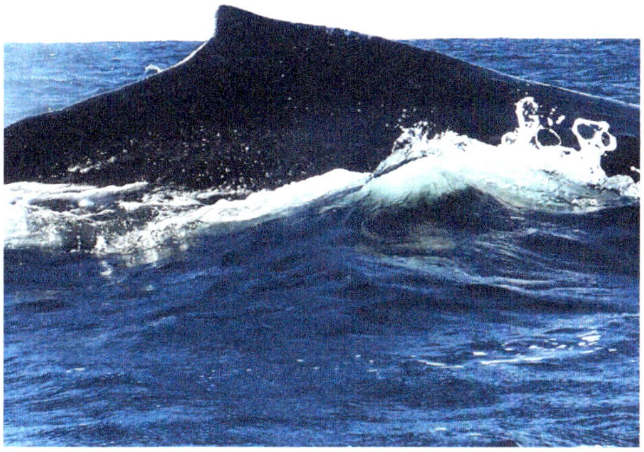

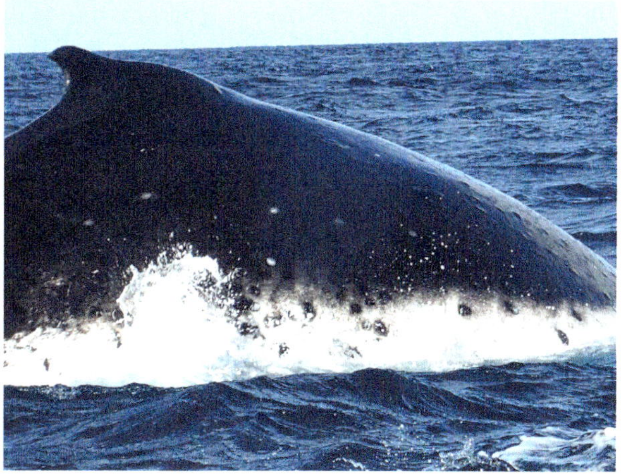

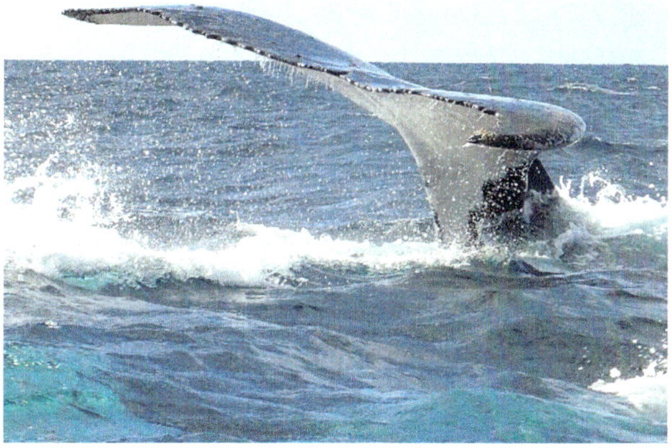

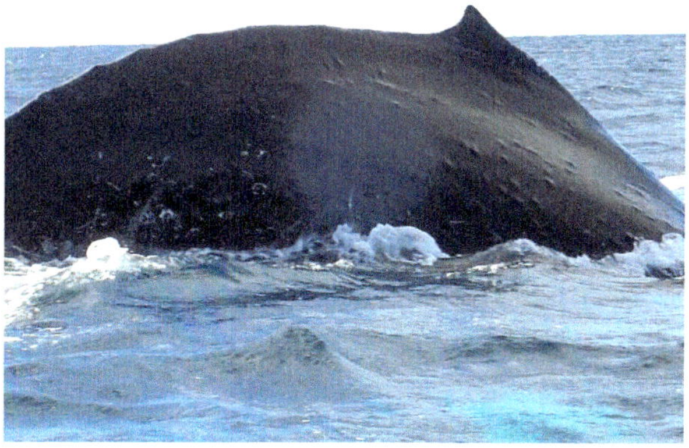

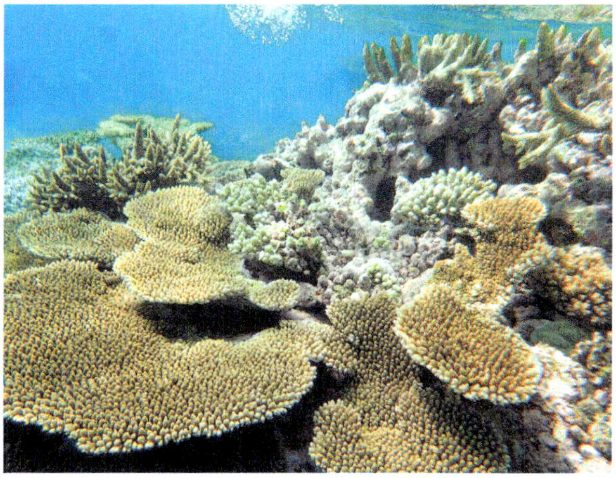

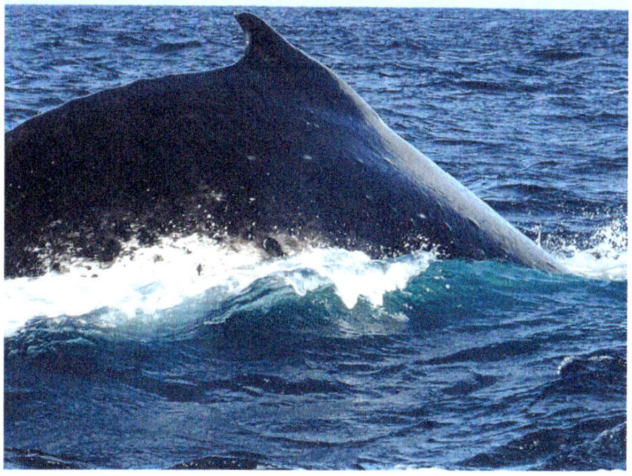

MY OLYMPIC JOURNEY

The Olympics, a breathtaking global spectacle seamlessly blending sports and international camaraderie, undeniably stands out as one of the most thrilling experiences. As a fervent sports enthusiast and avid globetrotter, attending this monumental event is a privilege for which I am immensely grateful.

Having had the extraordinary opportunity to **partake in eleven Olympic Games**, spanning both the exhilarating summer and winter editions, I can confidently assert that being present at the Olympics is an awe-inspiring journey. It's a heart-pounding fusion of unparalleled athletic prowess, a jubilant celebration of human excellence, and the euphoric ambiance of a worldwide carnival. Every Olympic event I've witnessed has left me utterly astounded, serving as a dazzling testament to the remarkable capabilities of humanity.

From the moment I set foot in the host city, the palpable electricity in the air was invigorating. The streets adorned with vibrant banners, flags dancing in the breeze, and the iconic Olympic rings gleaming in every corner—it was a visual feast that set my heart racing. As athletes, coaches, officials, and fans from every corner of the planet descended upon the city, a vibrant tapestry of cultures and languages unfolded before my eyes, unique to the Olympic Games alone. It was a true melting pot, a glorious amalgamation of humanity, united by a shared passion for sport and the relentless pursuit of excellence.

The Olympics is a celebration of unity and camaraderie on a global scale. The infectious festive spirit permeates every nook and cranny, forging an unbreakable bond among spectators, transcending boundaries of nationality and language. It's a time when differences fade into the background, leaving only a profound devotion to sport and the universal pursuit of excellence. The sheer thrill of witnessing the world's greatest athletes in action is nearly impossible to put into words. Every sprint, every jump, every dive, and every routine is executed with such precision and grace that it's nothing short of a sensory symphony—a spectacular display of human capability and the boundless heights we can reach.

Perhaps one of the most memorable aspects of attending the Olympics, for me, is the radiant joy emanating from the spectators themselves. The cheers, the applause, and the tidal wave of enthusiasm create an electrifying atmosphere that must be experienced to be believed. The passion and pride radiated by fans for their respective nations are positively contagious, and the roar of the crowd amplifies the emotions of both athletes and spectators alike. The festive atmosphere envelops you, weaving you into a tapestry of nations and cultures. Strangers morph into friends, bonded by their love for sport and the shared moments they're experiencing. The cheers and applause spread like wildfire through the stadiums and arenas, echoing a symphony of emotions, a mosaic of colors, and an outpouring of unadulterated joy.

I consider myself incredibly fortunate to have attended a grand total of eleven Olympic Games since 1992, including:
1. 1992 Summer Olympics in Albertville, France
2. 1996 Summer Olympics in Atlanta, USA
3. 2000 Summer Olympics in Sydney, Australia
4. 2002 Winter Olympics in Salt Lake City, USA
5. 2004 Summer Olympics in Athens, Greece
6. 2008 Summer Olympics in Beijing, China
7. 2010 Winter Olympics in Vancouver, Canada
8. 2012 Summer Olympics in London, U.K.
9. 2014 Winter Olympics in Sochi, Russia
10. 2016 Summer Olympics in Rio de Janeiro, Brazil
11. 2018 Winter Olympics in PyeongChang, South Korea

Furthermore, I had the immense honor of attending the Paralympics in Atlanta and Rio—an awe-inspiring celebration of courage, determination, and the indomitable human spirit. The 1996 Paralympic Games in Atlanta marked a historic milestone, showcasing the astounding talents, resilience, and determination of athletes with disabilities from around the globe. Atlanta embraced the Paralympics with open arms, fostering a welcoming and inclusive environment for these extraordinary athletes. These Games spotlighted the profound power of sport to shatter barriers and challenge societal notions of disability. The Para athletes shattered stereotypes and became a global source of inspiration, proving that disability is not a limitation but an opportunity to showcase extraordinary abilities.

The 2016 Paralympic Games in Rio presented an extraordinary showcase of athletic prowess and resilience across a wide range of sports. From the electrifying track events at the Olympic Stadium to the breathtaking swimming competitions at the Aquatics Centre, each event exemplified the incredible abilities and unwavering dedication of Para athletes. The cheers and applause of the spectators resonated through the venues, inspiring the athletes to push themselves to new heights and defying preconceived notions of what's achievable.

The Paralympic Games is an emotional rollercoaster that fills your heart with excitement, joy, and an overwhelming sense of celebration. It's a remarkable experience that reveals the awe-inspiring capabilities of the human spirit and leaves an indelible mark on your soul. Watching the Paralympic athletes in action is a testament to the triumph of the human spirit. Each movement is infused with courage, resilience, and an unwavering determination to defy limitations. Whether it's a sprinter propelling themselves at incredible speeds in a racing wheelchair, a swimmer gliding through the water with grace and strength, or a visually impaired athlete flawlessly navigating a course, every moment is a testament to the indomitable power of the human will.

Looking forward, I am filled with eager anticipation for the upcoming Paris Olympics in July 2024. These forthcoming Games in the heart of Paris, France, are poised to be nothing short of a historic spectacle, captivating the entire world and leaving an indelible imprint on those fortunate enough to be in attendance. The city of Paris, with its iconic landmarks and timeless charm, will serve as a mesmerizing backdrop for the Games. The Eiffel Tower, standing tall and bathed in the glow of Olympic spirit, will serve as a symbol of unity and celebration for the global sporting community. From the historic Louvre Museum to the serene Seine River, the city will come alive with a pulsating energy, ready to embrace athletes and spectators from every corner of the globe.

Reflecting on my journey as an Olympic spectator fills my heart with profound gratitude for the opportunity to bear witness to history, to draw inspiration from the world's greatest athletes, and to be part of a global celebration that transcends borders and unites people in unprecedented ways. The Olympics, with their infectious festive spirit, the extraordinary feats of athletes, and the unbridled joy of spectators, stand as a powerful reminder of sport's ability to transcend boundaries and foster unity. They are a celebration of the human spirit, a testament to our potential when we push ourselves to the limits. The experiences and memories I've gathered from attending these Olympic Games are immeasurable, and I feel incredibly blessed to have been part of this extraordinary journey. The pursuit of excellence, the camaraderie among athletes, and the collective celebration of global achievements serve as an everlasting source of inspiration.

1992 Olympics   Albertville

1996 Olympics   Atlanta

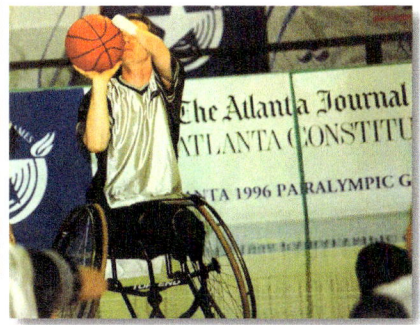

1996 Paralympics Atlanta

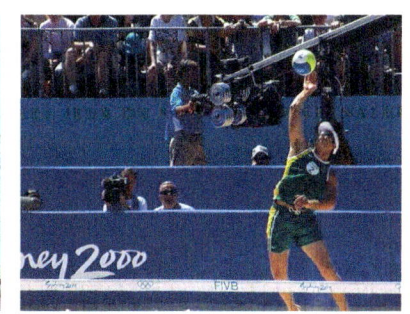

2000 Olympics Sydney

2002 Olympics Salt Lake City

2004 Olympics Athens

2008 Olympics Beijing

2010 Olympics Vancouver

2012 Olympics London

2014 Olympics Sochi

2016 Olympics Rio

2016 Paralympics Rio

2018 Olympics PyeongChang

MY STRATEGY FOR VISITING EVERY COUNTRY IN THE WORLD

Embarking on the awe-inspiring challenge of visiting all 193 countries on our planet is more than a mere task; it signifies a passionate and exhilarating quest teeming with boundless excitement. To undertake this thrilling odyssey, one must dedicate a substantial amount of time, financial resources, and, above all, an unwavering passion for exploration and adventure. Allow me to share the strategies I fervently embraced not only to make this monumental goal attainable but also to infuse every step of the journey with the pure joy of travel.

Primarily, I strategically employed the concept of clustering countries. This innovative approach entails grouping together neighboring or geographically proximate countries that can be experienced in a single, unforgettable expedition. It stands as a testament to the very essence of travel passion. By minimizing the distances between destinations, it not only economizes precious time and financial resources but also immerses the intrepid traveler in an exquisite tapestry of diverse cultures, traditions, and captivating landscapes.

However, it is essential to acknowledge that not all countries neatly fit into these clusters. Here, the heart of the passionate traveler beats strongly for the round-the-world (RTW) journey. The RTW voyage becomes a symphony of exploration, an orchestrated movement through countries that defy easy clustering. It's a chance to savor the thrill of visiting nations scattered across different continents, embracing the world's contrasts and harmonies with fervor.

Beyond these core strategies lie a myriad of tactics, each contributing to the realization of the goal. Meticulous planning and budgeting become the architects of a diverse range of cultural encounters and breathtaking landscapes. These tactics transform the abstract dream of visiting every country into a concrete plan, ensuring that each step of the journey becomes a brushstroke on the canvas of a global masterpiece.

1. The Art of Clustering: The strategic employment of the clustering concept forms the bedrock of my journey encompassing all 193 countries. This approach involves the artful grouping of neighboring or geographically proximate countries, transforming a mere travel itinerary into an unforgettable expedition. Picture the thrill of experiencing a mosaic of nations, seamlessly connected by shared borders, where every step unfolds a new chapter in the story of global exploration. For example:

   a) **Southeast Asia**: Countries like Thailand, Cambodia, Vietnam, Laos, and Myanmar are located close to each other and often have similar visa requirements. By exploring these countries in one trip, you can immerse yourself in the rich cultural heritage, visit ancient temples, indulge in local cuisine, and explore stunning

landscapes like Angkor Wat in Cambodia or Ha Long Bay in Vietnam.
b) **Scandinavian Countries**: Denmark, Sweden, Norway, Finland, and Iceland form a cluster of countries in northern Europe. These countries offer a unique blend of natural beauty, vibrant cities, and cultural experiences. By visiting them together, you can witness the awe-inspiring Northern Lights, explore the fjords of Norway, and stroll through the charming streets of Copenhagen.
c) **Central America**: Explore the countries of Central America in one trip. Visit countries like Costa Rica, Panama, Nicaragua, Honduras, and Guatemala, which are in close proximity to each other. Experience the lush rainforests, ancient Mayan ruins, pristine beaches, and vibrant local cultures within this region.
d) **Balkan Peninsula**: Journey through the Balkan Peninsula in Southeast Europe. Discover countries like Croatia, Slovenia, Montenegro, Bosnia and Herzegovina, and Serbia. These countries share a common history and stunning landscapes, making it convenient to explore their rich cultural heritage, beautiful coastlines, and historical sites in one go.
e) **West African Tour**: Embark on a West African adventure by visiting countries like Ghana, Senegal, Ivory Coast, Burkina Faso, and Nigeria. These countries offer a blend of cultural diversity, historical landmarks, vibrant markets, and captivating music and dance traditions. By exploring them together, you can gain a comprehensive understanding of the region.
f) **Arabian Peninsula**: Discover the countries of the Arabian Peninsula, including the United Arab Emirates, Oman, Qatar, Bahrain, and Saudi Arabia. These countries boast architectural wonders, ancient historical sites, stunning desert landscapes, and vibrant souks. By visiting them together, you can immerse yourself in the Arabian culture and experience the hospitality of the region.
g) **Caribbean Islands**: Explore the diverse and picturesque islands of the Caribbean. Plan a trip that includes countries like Jamaica, Cuba, the Dominican Republic, Barbados. Enjoy the white sandy beaches, crystal-clear waters, vibrant music, and flavorful cuisine as you hop from one island to another.

2. Round-the-World Trips: The round-the-world (RTW) voyage is an invitation to savor the thrill of visiting nations scattered across different continents, a journey that embraces the contrasts and harmonies of the world with fervor. It's a narrative unfolding not linearly but in a grand, interconnected tapestry. Here are some examples:
a) **Around the World**: Start in North America, where you can explore the United States and Canada. Then head to South

America and visit countries like Brazil, Argentina, and Peru. From there, fly to Oceania and explore Australia and New Zealand. Continue your journey to Asia, visiting countries such as Japan, Thailand, and India. Finally, head to Europe and experience the diverse cultures of countries like France, Spain, and Greece.

b) **The Great Expedition**: Start your journey in North America, exploring cities like New York and San Francisco in the United States, and then head to Canada to visit Toronto and Vancouver. From there, travel to Asia and explore Japan, China, and Thailand. Next, venture to Australia and New Zealand in Oceania, followed by a visit to South America, where you can explore countries like Brazil, Argentina, and Peru. Finally, end your trip in Europe, visiting iconic destinations such as Paris, Rome, and London.

c) **Cultural Capitals**: Focus on visiting major cultural capitals around the world. Start in New York City and explore its vibrant art scene and iconic landmarks. From there, head to Europe and visit cultural hubs like Paris, Berlin, Barcelona, and Florence. Next, travel to Asia and experience the cultural richness of cities like Tokyo, Seoul, and Beijing. Continue to Africa and explore the cultural heritage of cities like Marrakech, Cape Town, and Cairo. Finally, end your journey in South America, visiting cultural centers such as Buenos Aires, Rio de Janeiro, and Lima.

d) **Natural Wonders**: Design your trip around the world's most breathtaking natural wonders. Begin by visiting the Grand Canyon in the United States, then head to the Iguazu Falls in Brazil and Argentina. Next, explore the stunning landscapes of New Zealand, including Milford Sound and the Tongariro Alpine Crossing. From there, travel to Africa and witness the majestic Victoria Falls in Zambia and Zimbabwe. Finally, end your trip by visiting the Amazon Rainforest in Brazil and the Great Barrier Reef in Australia.

3. Regional Tours: Organized tours and cruises offer a unique approach, covering multiple countries in a specific region. This tactic is not merely a convenience but a time-efficient way to weave through diverse cultures, landscapes, and historical narratives in one seamless journey. It's an exploration of regions bound by shared histories and interconnected destinies, where each stop unfolds a new chapter, building a comprehensive understanding of the tapestry of humanity. Examples include:

a) **Mediterranean Cruise**: Embark on a Mediterranean cruise, visiting countries like Italy, Greece, Croatia, Turkey, and Spain. Enjoy the ease of travel as your accommodation, transportation, and sightseeing activities are taken care of while you explore the stunning coastal cities, ancient ruins, and picturesque islands.

b) **Southeast Asia Highlights**: Embark on a regional tour of Southeast Asia to explore the diverse cultures, stunning landscapes, and vibrant cities of the region. Start in Thailand and visit Bangkok's bustling markets and ancient temples. Continue to Cambodia to witness the awe-inspiring Angkor Wat complex. Then, head to Vietnam to experience the bustling streets of Hanoi and the picturesque beauty of Halong Bay. End your tour in Indonesia, exploring the iconic temples of Bali and relaxing on the beautiful beaches of the Gili Islands.

c) **Central American Adventure**: Embark on a thrilling tour through the countries of Central America, exploring their rich history, vibrant cultures, and stunning natural landscapes. Start in Costa Rica and discover its rainforests, volcanoes, and abundant wildlife. Continue to Nicaragua to explore its colonial cities and pristine beaches. Then, visit Guatemala to experience the ancient Mayan ruins of Tikal and the colorful markets of Antigua. Conclude your tour in Belize, where you can snorkel in the Belize Barrier Reef and explore ancient Maya sites.

4. Travel Hacking and Reward Programs: The art of travel hacking and leveraging loyalty reward programs transforms the financial aspect of this global odyssey. Saving money on flights, accommodations, and other travel expenses isn't just a pragmatic approach; it's a strategic move that allows for a more extended and enriching exploration. It's a testament to the savvy traveler's ability to navigate the complex world of rewards, ensuring that every dollar saved becomes an investment in yet another adventure. Examples include:

a) **Credit Card Rewards**: Utilize credit card rewards programs to earn points or miles that can be redeemed for travel-related expenses. Research credit cards that offer attractive sign-up bonuses, travel rewards, and flexible redemption options.

b) **Airline Alliances and Frequent Flyer Programs**: Join frequent flyer programs offered by airlines and take advantage of airline alliances. Accumulate miles by flying with partner airlines within the alliance, allowing you to earn and redeem miles across multiple carriers.

c) **Hotel Loyalty Programs**: Sign up for hotel loyalty programs to earn points or receive exclusive benefits during your stays.

d) **Travel Hacking Communities and Websites**: Join travel hacking communities and follow websites dedicated to maximizing travel rewards and finding the best deals. Platforms like FlyerTalk, The Points Guy, and AwardWallet provide valuable information on credit card rewards, loyalty programs, and travel strategies. Engage in discussions, read guides, and stay updated on the latest tips and tricks shared by experienced travel hackers.

5. Connect with Travel Communities: Engaging with travel communities and forums adds a social dimension to this solitary pursuit. It's not just about traversing physical landscapes but about connecting with a community of like-minded individuals. The insights and guidance shared by experienced travelers become invaluable companions on this journey. It's a way to transcend the limits of individual experiences, creating a shared narrative of exploration that extends beyond borders, reflecting the collective wisdom of those who have treaded similar paths. Examples include:

a) **Travel Meetups and Events**: Join travel meetups and events in your local area or in destinations you plan to visit. These gatherings bring together like-minded travelers who share a passion for exploring the world. Attend meetups organized by travel groups, online communities, or travel agencies.

b) **Online Travel Communities**: Engage with online travel communities to connect with fellow travelers from around the world. Join forums, social media groups, and platforms dedicated to travel discussions. Examples include the Lonely Planet's Thorn Tree forum, TripAdvisor's travel forums, and Facebook groups centered around specific travel interests or destinations.

c) **Attend Travel Conferences and Expos**: Attend travel conferences and expos to network with industry professionals and fellow travelers. These events bring together travel enthusiasts, travel companies, and tourism boards. Examples include the World Travel Market, TravelCon, and ITB Berlin. Participate in panel discussions, workshops, and networking sessions. Connect with industry experts, fellow travelers, and potential travel partners to gain valuable insights and build connections within the travel community.

d) **Volunteer with Travel Organizations**: Consider volunteering with travel organizations that promote sustainable and responsible travel. Organizations like Workaway, WWOOF, and HelpX connect travelers with hosts who offer accommodation and meals in exchange for volunteer work. Engaging in volunteer opportunities allows you to connect with locals, learn about their culture, and contribute to meaningful projects. It also provides an opportunity to meet other like-minded travelers who are passionate about making a positive impact through travel.

By incorporating these strategies into your travel plans and adapting them to suit your preferences and circumstances, you can craft a meticulously planned and highly efficient itinerary. This journey becomes a personalized odyssey, where every decision aligns with your unique interests. Whether you're a history buff, a nature enthusiast, a culinary connoisseur, or an adventurer seeking thrilling experiences, customization ensures that each moment resonates with personal fulfillment and meaning. It transforms a global pursuit into a deeply personal exploration of the world's wonders.

As you embark on this ambitious quest, remember the importance of prioritizing safety. Keep abreast of travel advisories, research the local laws and customs of the places you plan to visit, and take necessary precautions to ensure your well-being throughout your travels. Respect for local cultures and traditions is paramount, fostering positive interactions that leave a lasting impression of goodwill. This, in turn, enriches your travel experiences, allowing you to forge connections with people from diverse backgrounds.

Embrace the transformative power of this global adventure. Every country you visit has something unique to offer, and these experiences have the potential to broaden your horizons, challenge your preconceptions, and inspire personal growth. It's not just a collection of passport stamps; it's a kaleidoscope of moments that shape your worldview, contributing to a deeper understanding of the human experience.

So, as you embark on your journey to visit every country in the world, let these strategies be your guide. Adapt them to your needs, stay safe, respect the cultures you encounter, and savor every moment of this extraordinary adventure. It's not just a travel goal; it's a life-changing odyssey that will leave you with memories and experiences to treasure for a lifetime.

SVETI STEFAN
Montenegro

PERSONAL REFLECTIONS ON WORLD TRAVEL

As I reflect on my travels, I am filled with an overwhelming sense of joy and gratitude. The experiences I have had, the people I have met, and the places I have visited have left an indelible mark on my soul. Each adventure has been unique and special in its own way, and I feel truly blessed to have been able to explore so much of our incredible world.

Someone once asked me, "Where does the man who's been everywhere go?" This question gave me a moment of real pause, as I have visited every United Nations country in the world, all 50 U.S. states, and 7 continents. I had to stop and ask myself, where would I like to go next? The more I travel, the more I realize that real travel is about so much more than just checking off a list of destinations. It's about connecting with people, experiencing new cultures, music, traditions, and tasting new cuisines, sharing other peoples' hopes and dreams, in a meaningful way that leaves a positive impact on both the people and the environment.

In my journeys, I seek inspiring and endearing experiences that energize my five senses and allow me to see a destination through the lens of a local. I enjoy feeling like I am part of something new and exciting. Returning to places like Venice, New Zealand, Spain, Argentina, Patagonia, and Thailand feels like starting over again, with a fresh perspective and a renewed sense of wonder. However, I am increasingly aware of the impact that tourism has on our planet. That's why I have become passionate about sustainable and responsible travel.

As travelers, we have a responsibility to protect our earth and the environment. We can make a positive difference by reducing our carbon footprint, choosing eco-friendly transportation, and supporting local businesses that prioritize sustainability, which helps to ensure that our travels leave a positive impact on the places that we visit. We can also make a difference by being mindful of our waste and making an effort to minimize it.

The thrill of exploration in a new city or country, where everything is unfamiliar and unknown, is what truly gets my heart racing. It's in these moments that I feel truly alive, and I create memories that will last a lifetime. But it's not just about the adrenaline rush of adventure travel. What I love most about travel is the way that it expands my cultural horizon, knowledge of others, experience, and opens a whole new world of taste and exploration. Every new destination that I visit exposes me to different cultures, customs, and ways of life. I get to try new cuisines, learn new languages, and discover new perspectives. The world is an incredibly diverse and fascinating place, and I feel so grateful to have been able to experience it in all its diversity and beauty.

The most profound aspect of travel is the hope it brings for a better world. Travel breaks down barriers, fosters understanding and compassion, and reminds us that we are all more similar than different. As we travel, we have an opportunity to make a positive impact through purposeful travel. By seeking out meaningful experiences that support local communities and it helps us learn from other's unique perspectives, together we can create a brighter future for ourselves and for generations to come.

As someone who has had the privilege of traveling to many parts of the world, I can attest to the transformative power of travel. It has expanded my worldview, challenged my assumptions, and deepened my understanding of the incredible diversity of the human experience. It has also taught me the importance of being a responsible and mindful traveler, and the impact that our travel choices can have on the environment and the communities that we visit. Finally, it has reinforced in me the need to see others, with a clear transparent perception, devoid of cultural bias and perceptions.

So I urge you to embrace the power of travel to transform yourself and the world around you. Seek out new experiences, challenge yourself, and immerse yourself in the local culture. But also be mindful of the impact that your travels have on the environment and the communities that you visit. By doing so, we can create a brighter and more beautiful future for ourselves and for the world.
Happy and safe travel!

Michael

THE MEANING OF LIFE IS TO FIND YOUR GIFT.

THE PURPOSE OF LIFE IS TO GIVE IT AWAY.

-Pablo Picasso